Raising Chickens, Goats & Backyard Beekeeping For Beginners

3-in-1 Compilation

Step-By-Step Guide to Raising Happy Backyard Chickens, Goats & Your First Bee Colonies in as Little as 30 Days

Small Footprint Press

Table of Contents

Raising Chickens for Beginners

Raising Goats For Beginners

Backyard Beekeeping for Beginners

Raising Chickens for Beginners

A Step-by-Step Guide to Raising Happy Backyard
Chickens in as Little as 30 Days

Small Footprint Press

Introduction

As children, many of us had a fascination with dinosaurs. You may not be aware that chickens are closely related to dinosaurs! According to Sataksig (2018), when 68-million-year-old DNA from a *Tyrannosaurus ex* was compared to the DNA of 21 modern animal species, the closest match was that of the chicken! It may seem surprising that chickens are closely related to dinosaurs, but think of them as a T-Rex third cousin separated by more than 100 million years.

Casting the compelling dinosaur connection aside, chickens have evolved into the hottest backyard hobby or business for the last decade. Every year, thousands of people are entering into the ownership and care of our fine feathered friends. Keeping chickens in your backyard is not a new concept, and at one time in our history, it was quite common. During the Great Depression, it was encouraged to keep backyard chickens because food was hard to come by. When a family kept backyard chickens, they had access to fresh eggs and could raise their own meat birds.

Going forward from this era, small corner mom and pop grocery stores began popping up and supplying clean, white eggs and fresh roasted chicken, eliminating the need for individuals to keep their own chickens.

The rebirth of the backyard chicken movement can be attributed to the new generation of people interested in the green movement and the ability to control how their animals are fed, cared for, and the satisfaction of raising your own animals.

If you've never had the privilege of sharing time with chickens, then you have been missing out. Chickens have distinct personalities, and once people realize how individualized they are, their chickens become beloved pets and are often bestowed with loving names that embrace their behaviors and personalities.

No matter how your interest began, chickens have a charming way of working their way into the lives of people who had never given them a second thought. Even if you have no bird interest or experience, you will likely at one point find yourself wondering how you ever got along without them!

The first time anyone sees a chicken up close, they are immediately taken by their plumage, and that is quickly followed by the variations between breeds, the size differences, and their soft clucks. People have the misconception that chickens are noisy, which is not true. Outside of some clucks, the only time you will hear hens are when they are laying eggs, being attacked by a predator, or something interesting has been introduced to the flock like a slice of watermelon to attack or even a mouse in the hen house. Yes, it's true, chickens do eat mice, and they are omnivores. Roosters, on the other hand, are extremely noisy and not just in the wee hours of dawn's first light, but all the livelong day.

Before the backyard resurgence of chicken owners, there never seemed to be much information on how to get started in chicken ownership, keep them safe, make sure they were fed well, or how to pick the best chickens for beginner flock owners. Now, with the chicken business booming, there are books, blogs, seminars, and chicken experts that work for feed companies where you can pose any question you might have and get an answer quickly. The bottom line is hens must be cared for if you want them to thrive and produce.

It doesn't matter if you just want a few hens to supply you with eggs or you want to start your own little egg empire. Everyone must start somewhere. Depending on your local competition, you will find that you have more buyers than eggs since the appeal of farm-fresh eggs has captured the attention of buyers. Many of them want the product of healthy, free-range hens that truly get to go out and run around on the grass as they were meant to.

Backyard poultry for eggs and meat has become very appealing, and we can understand why consumers like to know where their dinner comes from. Since the United States began to allow our chickens to get shipped to China for processing, we have been very particular about what brands we choose to bring home for the dinner table, and there is a definite advantage knowing that your meats have come from just a few miles away. It brings a smile to your face to pick up a dozen eggs and see the hens frolicking outside.

There have been many animal husbandry fads over the years, but many of those quickly fade from the limelight. However, chickens are different; they are not a fad. Chickens are less than just the allure of having your own little egg stand and more about having a closer relationship with nature, knowing where your food comes from, and appreciating all the little tidbits of information that you will learn through your exposure to chickens. The more you learn about chickens, the better understanding you will have regarding these quirky birds and nature.

As a company, Small Footprint Press is focused and determined on providing the best help possible. We want to make it easy for people to return to the land and live more sustainably for the long term.

We do this by doing in-depth research for all our books, with topics ranging from survival training to various self-sufficiency methods and prepping for disasters (natural or human-caused). We work our hardest to teach you how to care for the planet Earth and its inhabitants in the most holistic and mutually beneficial manners possible. Our team is made of dedicated and enthusiastic nature lovers, who altogether have over three decades of combined knowledge of outdoorsmanship and conservation. We can't wait to pass it all along to you.

Our goal is to help empower you to achieve the sustainable lifestyle that you want. Like you, we feel that giving back to our planet is crucial for our continued survival as a species. We whole-heartedly believe that being outdoors (in a sustainable manner) makes us humans happy, and we want to share that happiness with you as well.

Chicken Choices

There are so many stories about how people got initiated into the world of chickens. The tales run the gambit from adopting chicks from school science projects to dyed Easter chicks that end up in the animal shelter after the cuteness factor has worn off, but the best way is to do a little homework before you dive right in. If you are lucky, there may be a local breeder nearby. The first decision you will need to make is what your ultimate goal is. There are four main functions for chickens, and you will need to figure out which niche interests you the most. These functions are eggs, meat, show or breeding, or fun. There are no wrong choices, just what interests you the most.

Egg Chickens

We all are familiar with egg and their plain white eggs, but some chickens lay brown, deep pink, blue, green, and a couple of other shades of brown eggs specific to a chicken's breed. A hen will never change the color of the eggs she lays during her lifetime but check out some fun egg color facts below.

- White eggs will be white all the way through.

- Brown eggs will be white on the inside.

- Blue eggs will be blue on the inside.

- Green eggs will be green on the outside, but blue on the inside.

Meat Chickens

Meat chickens, commonly called broilers, are a chicken bred to be a quick grower, and the number one choice for meat birds is a White Rock and Cornish Cross hybrid chicken. There is a big difference between a stewing hen, a broiler, or a roaster, and you should decide which you choose to raise.

Showing and Breeding Chickens

Show and breeding chickens are often fancier breeds. If you are serious about showing your chickens in competition, there are a lot of details that you will need to learn. Often the size of the comb or the angle of a tail can be important. To expand your knowledge, you should become familiar with the American Poultry Association's *American Standard of Perfections* that pertains to your specialized breed. Go to some poultry shows so that you know what a good animal looks like. Showing requires knowledge of genetics, good management, and excellent nutrition to breed champion bloodlines.

Urban Chickens

The backyard or urban chicken is less likely to end up in a stew pot and more likely to receive a proper burial like any beloved pet. Most of these chickens, even well after they stop laying, will be kept as cherished members of the family.

Everyone has their own story on how they became interested in and started raising chickens. But even if you tried it and the first time wasn't a positive experience, take heart, because armed with our knowledge, you will excel at the coop life and be one of those folks that tell others all about your chickens even if you weren't asked. Remember that all the cool people raise tiny dinosaurs!

Chapter 1:
Everyone Should Raise Chickens

You know you own chickens when...you watch them play in the yard more than you watch TV.

–Unknown

Ever host Olympic donut jumping with your flock? No, seriously! String about three donuts on a cord and lower and raise it slightly just to test your hen's jumping ability. Just make sure they win the prize and don't tease them by making the goal unattainable.

According to Jerome Belanger (2010), there are about a billion chickens in the world at any given time. That's three and a half chickens for every single human on Earth.

Is everyone suited to raise chickens? Without a certain commitment to the welfare of your animals, we would say no. You need dedication to provide for any animal, and it doesn't matter if it is a chicken, a dog, or a goldfish. They all need freshwater, food, shelter, cleanliness, love, and devotion. Sharing your life with any animal is a 365 day responsibility. While there are plenty of super dedicated owners out there, you should always have a willing helper to cover your precious flock when you are unavailable.

Chickens do require daily attention because they still need to be fed and watered every day. You should at least give the girls a cursory glance to ensure that they are all still feeling and acting their best. You will always want to clean and sanitize your flock's feeders and waterers once a week, possibly more in warmer weather. You should also plan on cleaning their coop at least once a week, but if you take a few minutes each day, their coop will be easy to maintain. Utilizing this method, you might only have to perform a strip once a year.

Raising Your Own Flock Is Easier Than You Think!

Looking back over your family history, we are sure that someone in your family tree raised chickens. The only difference is that they probably were born into a farming family and already possessed experience without ever picking up a book.

How much do you need to know to raise chickens? Truthfully, it depends. Some breeds are easier to raise than others. Often, folks just get lucky and choose the heartiest and best egg producers without even realizing what they are doing. Just diving in is how many people get started, but some crave every bit of knowledge before delving into the ownership of their own little flock. People should know what's involved if chickens are right for them.

Be honest about your goals. Some get into chickens to make money, but if you are an urbanite with three or four hens, obviously, making money is not first and foremost in your mind. Your backyard chickens are going to lay the best eggs you have ever tasted.

You may just want a small flock to provide eggs and meat for your family. As a backyard operation, you will certainly be able to provide more than enough eggs for your immediate family. Keep in mind that the majority of chicken owners don't raise them for meat since butchering is seldom allowed within the city or suburban limits. If your dream is to raise and slaughter meat birds, you had best check all the rules and regulations governing your area before you get your heart set on a new venture.

Why Chickens?

Many people want a greener lifestyle and buy a large portion of their food locally, but what could be more local than your own backyard? Perhaps you already planted a substantial garden full of fabulous vegetables, and you may even keep bees, so why not add chickens and their eggs to your little slice of heaven?

Even though the push to be green may have initiated the growth of urban backyard poultry owners, urbanites have kept their chickens for a multitude of reasons. There is no stereotypical person that will choose to keep chickens, and most of them will have nothing in common with other chicken owners except for their flocks. Whether you keep chickens for pets, eggs, insect control, education, meat, composting, or fertilizer production, you are, without a doubt, a crazy chicken lady or man (that is a compliment, by the way).

We have already mentioned that chickens are entertaining, and there is nothing better than pulling up a chair and watching your girls catch bugs or take part in a dust bath. With too many stresses that take over our lives, it can be satisfying to relax and watch nature at its finest.

Reasons to Raise Chickens

As if people need reasons to keep chickens! But if you insist…

Some chickens have silky feathers, frizzled tops, feathers growing on their feet, or they might even sport a spiked look that would make the best punk-rockers jealous. The point is that there is a chicken for everyone, so whether you pine for bantams or clamor for more traditional breeds, choosing your first chicken can be a difficult decision. The great thing is that you do not have to decide on just one breed since most flocks are mixed.

If you like eggs, this is a no-brainer, but some people raise certain chickens for meat, shows, or just plain old entertainment and companionship. If you only have a few birds, you probably fall into the entertainment category.

Eggs, Eggs, and More Eggs!

Once you have tasted fresh eggs from your chickens that have been enhanced by free-ranging and feeding decisions that you have made, you will have a tough time forcing yourself to buy eggs at the store. Their taste will be richer than their store-bought competition, and they will taste better simply because you and your girls have made this happen. How many people can brag that they collected eggs this morning in the PJs? People that use fresh eggs swear that their baked goods turn out lighter and fluffier, but it is up to you to do that comparison testing. Remember, you can't make a cake without breaking a few eggs!

According to Deborah Niemann (2013), research has proven that eggs produced by free-range chickens test lower in cholesterol and higher in vitamins and minerals than their mass-produced sister eggs. She went on to compare the eggs produced by pastured hens, finding that they will have four to six times more vitamin D, seven times more beta-carotene, three times more vitamin E, and twice the amount of Omega-3 fatty acids than their grocery store competition.

Fewer Bugs

Chickens do a remarkable job eating ticks, fleas, mosquitoes, flies, or any other bug dumb enough to cross into a chicken's territory. Chickens not only eat the bugs but their larvae as well, so there will be fewer bugs being born on your property.

Preserve Important Chicken Breeds

Yes, you heard that right. Just like GMO-raised crops, the large factory farms utilize a breed of hybrid chicken that is designed to eat less, produce more and larger eggs, and do it all from a small crate-like box. Without the backyard hobbyist, certain breeds of chickens could become extinct.

Local Food Production

It can be refreshing to enjoy something that you only had to travel to the backyard to retrieve instead of a product that may have traveled up to 1,500 miles just to get to your local grocery store.

Pet Chickens!

Perhaps you aren't a dog, cat, or small rodent fan, but your kids really want a pet. The good news is chickens can double as a pet! Chickens are intelligent, trainable, and most breeds, when handled daily after hatching, will be friendly. If you do have other pets, rest assured your chickens will clean up all those nasty ticks, and your dog or cat won't suffer from that either. Your children can work on their mathematical abilities by counting eggs or working out how long a 50-pound bag of feed will last for your flock. Chickens can become very attached and will come running if they hear their names and know that you have treats for them.

Anti-GMO

If you are anti-GMO, then you are probably aware that caged hens are fed a diet consisting of GMO crops like corn, soy, and cottonseed meals. When you have control over what feeds your girls consume, then you can rest easy.

Chickens Provide You With Free Fertilizer

Imagine going to your local farm or garden center to *buy* chicken poop! If you have a garden, your chicken's manure will be a great addition to the soil.

Chicken TV

Free entertainment can be had by watching your chicken's antics. Besides watching your first egg being laid, it can be pretty entertaining to watch your girls corner a mouse. You can also give them plenty of fruits and veggies that may be past their prime for you to eat. Hens make pretty short work of cantaloupes and stale popcorn as well.

Cruelty-Free

You know for a fact that your girls are well cared for and happy. You may believe that you are currently buying cruelty-free eggs already, but you should be aware that what those egg cartons say and what it really means can be two different things. For example, when you see a carton that is stamped "free-range," there is no actual defined description of what that is. It may conjure scenes of hens frolicking in meadows, but less than one percent of chickens in the United States are considered to be free-range. Some wording to be aware of is found below.

- "All-natural." Sure, it sounds appealing, but it promises you nothing other than it's a real egg from a real hen.

- "Cage-free" doesn't mean cruelty-free. Simply put, these hens are given the freedom to be out of restrictive cages; that much is true. However, what these hens have been given is access to roam a facility, but that doesn't mean that they are enjoying the great outdoors.

- "Free-range" adds a step to cage-free by allowing hens to live in or are able to get access to outdoors.

- "Farm fresh." Yep, sorry, that is also a marketing ploy. What it really means is that you are buying an egg from a hen that is kept on a commercial farm.

- "Organic" eggs come only from free-range hens. To be certified organic, these hens must be fed only organic feed, and nothing labeled poultry by-products, antibiotics, any animal drugs, or manure.

- "No hormones" isn't ground-breaking since no egg-laying hens found in the US are allowed to receive hormones.

- An "Omega-3" label doesn't instantly mean that those eggs contain proven levels of this important fatty acid. Hens that lay Omega-3 branded eggs can only eat feed that contains flaxseed.

- "Vegetarian diet." Nope. Remember when you read our introduction and found out that the chicken is related to the T-rex through DNA? Well, Tyrannosaurus Rex surely wasn't vegan, and neither are chickens. That's right, chickens are omnivores and enjoy the occasional small animal, like frogs and mice, in addition to their plants, bugs, and spiders. They will even eat cooked chicken! When chickens are forced to follow a vegetarian diet, they can fall ill and even start pecking at each other. Depriving your hens of the needed amino acid, methionine, will cause them to become sickly.

- "Pasture-raised" hens mean that those hens have spent their lives or parts of them at least with access to a pasture. This also means that they have been allowed to forage naturally supplementing facility-provided foods. Unfortunately, there are no standards for the pasture or what the facility believes constitutes a pasture. No inspections for pasture-raised are presently required. These terms can be a real eye-opener, can't they?

Educational Lessons for You and Your Children to Share

Were you aware that chickens have a great memory? Hens are a tight-knit community that enjoy playing. They dream, feel pain, distress, mourn for each other, and they also make excellent mothers. Hens talk to their chicks while still in the confines of the egg, and they will turn their eggs about 50 times each day. Your hens will follow a social structure based on a determined hierarchy, or if you prefer, "pecking order." By keeping chickens, your children can learn about nature, math, agriculture, and the responsibility of caring for living creatures.

Chickens Eat Food Scraps

Want to cut down on food scraps that you send to the local landfill? Your chickens can eat most kitchen scraps, including fruit and vegetable peelings, bread, cooked beans, cooked rice, pasta, oatmeal, and more.

Weed Control

While they can be good at weed control, they will also pick your flower bed and garden clean, so cleaning up the weeds might be best when left for after the growing season. At that point, you can turn the girls loose, and they can eat all the leftover veggies you declined to eat and drop some fertilizer in there for the next growing year.

Chickens for Therapy?

Chickens are being viewed as therapeutic for the elderly and children suffering from autism. Because chickens are always on the move and socializing within the flock, they have been found to calm patients suffering from dementia and other psychiatric disorders.

Owning Chickens can Open Social Doors

Want to share your newfound passion with others? Look no further than a quick internet search to find similar-minded chicken owners full of their newfound passion and ready to share their tips and helpful suggestions.

It's a Fun Hobby

Some people may not be able to understand your chicken passion, but then again, personally, we find coin collecting tedious. To each his own!

It's Relatively Inexpensive

Yes, there are startup costs, but once you have built your dream coop that keeps your flock safe, you will only need food, bedding, and a few pieces of equipment.

Chicks, Pullets, or Full-Grown Chickens?

Even if you have settled on one choice, you may be limited by what's available at the time. Traditionally, chicks are hatched in the spring, so there is a small window of opportunity to make your livestock purchase. Most young hens, or pullets, are mostly available in summer and fall. There was a time when chickens of this age weren't even an option to purchase, but there have been some visionaries that started raising their chicks to sell as pullets, but these sellers might be hard to find. Your best bet is to plan on starting with chicks in spring or early summer.

You can go online and contact some of the hatcheries for their catalogs. This is an excellent way of learning more about the different breeds. The majority of people get their first chickens via mail-order.

So, What's a Bantam?

A bantam is just a small chicken or a smaller version of a bigger chicken. These fun little birds usually weigh no more than two pounds and are about one-fourth the size of an average chicken. Because of their size, they don't eat much, make great pets, and they tolerate confinement well. They will almost always have a personality that is bigger than life.

Almost every chicken breed has a bantam counterpart, but there are some breeds that are only available in the bantam size. These birds are popular to show because they are easy to handle.

Chapter 2:
What Makes Your Chickens Happy?

The oldest chicken to have ever lived was a Red Quill Muffed American Gamebird named Muffy. Well cared for chickens typically live 7 to 8 years, but miracle Muffy lived until she was 22 years old. She must have been happy indeed!

— Unknown

All living creatures yearn to belong socially, feel love, and enjoy freedom; your chickens are no different. There is nothing wrong with showing your chickens that they are special and a part of the family. They have the same intelligence as your family dog or cat, so why not extend your sentiments to your family chickens? Your flock wants to be loved and cared for, and here are some pointers to make them feel special.

- **Never keep a solitary chicken.** Probably *the* most important thing to remember is that chickens are not solitary souls. They like to socialize with others of their own kind and need to in order to be happy and healthy. We recommend no less than three chickens as a bare minimum. If you only get two, but one is killed by a predator, then you are going to have one lonely, depressed chicken!

- **Call to your flock.** By announcing your arrival, especially at dinner time, your chickens will recognize that food is *en route*, and you are the bringer of the said feast. When they hear you call out to them, they will come running because they have learned to associate you with food and treats. Who doesn't enjoy those? You can make their favorite treat something you provide at bedtime as an encouragement to return to the coop for the night. For example, cracked corn can be used to entice them in for the night or out in another area while you clean up their coop.

- **Spoil them with live or freeze-dried mealworms.** Nothing will bring your hens running and cackling quicker than a tasty mealworm.

Sit back and watch them enjoy pecking apart a squash, pumpkin, or watermelon.

- **Spend some time with your flock.** Just as you would pay attention to your dog or cat, simply sit and visit with them. Plop down in a lawn chair in their pasture or sit in their coop, so they become acclimated to your presence. Take care to not sit in too tall of a chair so that you seem to tower over them. It doesn't matter if you watch them, read a book, or watch a movie on your phone. Just being around them without trying to catch them will calm any flighty hens you might have. You can even toss some treats out around your chair. We can guarantee you that if you appear uninterested in them, they will pester you for your attention. The more you can do this, the quicker your hens will bond with you.

- **Always move slowly.** Birds are easily frightened by quick movements. Resist any urges to run, jump, or move quickly around them. If you hold a chicken too tightly, they will start to panic, so take care to hold them in a supportive but unrestricted way. Take care, especially with a rooster if you have one; they have been known to attack the eyes of their human handlers when too close to a human face.

- **Know your rooster well.** If you are breeding, you want to use only the cuddly roosters. Aggression has no place in a flock of chickens.

- **Approach chicks carefully.** Baby chicks experience a whole new level of nervousness because, let's face it, they are tiny and afraid of everything. When you stand over them, they see you as a predator until you can build their trust level. The best way is to try and keep yourself at their level as much as possible.

- **Chickens will respond to gentle handling.** If you have smaller children that handle the birds, you should teach them proper ways to handle chickens, especially young chicks. When your chicks are content, they will spread out in the brooder and move around practicing their scratching, eating, drinking, and cuddling under the light to sleep. You will hear them emit happy, quiet chirps when content.

- **Toys!** Believe it or not, your flock loves to play with stuff. Chickens need physical and mental stimulation that will keep them entertained. If you don't believe me, just add a chicken swing or a chicken ladder and watch the antics that this causes. There are pre-made swings, but also tutorials on making one if you feel that you are a handy person. Your flock will also find loads of entertainment playing with old tree stumps or hollowed-out stumps, unbreakable mirrors, old balls, or even a low-hanging cabbage.

Chickens Like Their Space

Chickens need room to roam. It is very important to make sure that you have given your chickens enough space, if you will forgive the expression, to spread their wings. This is a vital piece needed to keep your flock happy and content.

How much room you need to allow for your new hobby is going to hinge on how many chickens you plan on adding to the family. You would never want to have less than three or four chickens, so let's plan on using the average of six to get started. You should take into account that your chickens will be kept in a coop at nighttime and given free rein to roam during the daylight hours. A coop for six chickens would need a bare minimum of 18 square feet with a run of around 90 square feet. When you combine these, you should have right around 110 square feet to keep six chickens.

We can almost hear the wheels turning in your head. You're thinking that bigger is better, and your six chickens are going to be given the Taj Mahal of coops with tons of room to roost and nest. If you live in a warm climate, you can probably get away with that, but if you are living in a colder climate, your six chickens are going to have difficulty generating enough heat to keep their coop warm.

Allowing your chickens to roam is one of the easiest ways to provide your chickens with sun-filled afternoons spent chasing bugs in the pasture. They can forage for themselves and claim healthy greens, bugs, and the occasional small rodent or two. Depending upon where you live, your chickens may even score a few scorpions or tarantulas (funny story on tarantulas later)! If you don't want them running free all day, you can easily schedule them for an hour in the morning and evening, allowing you the ability to watch them. Whatever routine you set for them, you will find that they can get into the groove of a routine fairly quickly.

Besides providing your flock with their very own coop, you will need to add nesting boxes, so the girls will have a place to hang out and lay their eggs. You can purchase individual plastic nesting boxes online or from specialty stores. You can also build a sectioned nesting box. Another option, and one some of our friends have chosen, is to use an old piece of vintage furniture that has some sections already in place and tear off the backer while placing this in a cut-out area of your coop with the doors facing out. This will allow your chickens to nest, and you can just open the doors from the other side to collect the eggs. The first time we saw this, we thought it was brilliant. If you are in a hurry to quickly collect eggs mid-afternoon, then you don't even have to enter the coop part. No matter how you choose to set up your nesting boxes, they should be about a square foot per chicken (they may need to be larger if you have chosen a larger breed).

Outside for a breath of fresh air and sunshine, your basic six chickens will need about 90 square feet (6 x 15). This isn't a large piece of land when you think about it, and an area of grass that is roughly 10 x 10 is adequate, but if you want happy hens, the more room you can give them, the better. Where you allow your chickens to roam is completely up to you. Whether you choose a portable run, create a permanent run, or just allow them free roaming rights, this is all a very personal choice, and each has its advantages and disadvantages. The bigger the space, the more exciting their days will be.

Your free-range chickens are going to be given more space than their commercial counterparts. Remember that the US Department of Agriculture states that a free-range chicken should have access to the outside, but there are no rules governing how much space they are allowed or for how long they need to remain outside to qualify for this description.

Keep it Clean!

Keep their coop clean. This may seem a bit daunting at first since chickens poop *everywhere*, but that doesn't mean that they enjoy being dirty or living in filth.

An advantage to frequent cleaning, besides happy, healthy hens, is your familiarity with the condition of the coop. Coops will need repairs from time to time, so in order to keep your flock safe, you should pay close attention to any areas that might need fixing.

A clean coop will keep your flock healthy by preventing diseases. Should you have nearby neighbors, they too will thank you for keeping the smell at a minimum.

To have a tidy coop, we recommend you clean every day (during the winter twice a day, if they are kept inside). By keeping on top of the mess, especially in the winter, you can quickly flip droppings into a dustpan with a paint scraper and then empty the dustpan into an empty feed bag. You can then either compost it outside or, if you have too much compost, just dispose of it. We still love the deep bedding method, and you can also strip and rebed twice a year. We'd love for your coop to sparkle!

The middle-of-the-road approach is to clean the coop once a week and do spot cleaning every other day. If you have hens that like to sleep in the nesting boxes, then there will be a lot of poop in those nests, and they will need to be cleaned out daily. If you stay ahead of the mess, it will save you time when you do a complete cleanout, and you only need to allow 15 minutes or so each time you clean.

Many people like the deep litter method, which is simply adding materials to the coop floor, allowing the waste to compost inside the coop. Then a few times a year, they will strip and rebed the entire coop, scooping all the waste into the garden.

No matter what method you decide to use, you should always level out the bedding, so there are no bare spaces. If you think the levels seem a bit low, you can always add more bedding to the floor of the coop.

When setting up your food and water areas, you should take care to keep them far away from any roosting bars or nesting boxes. We like to use a hanging feed and water container so that they cannot poop in it. You should also be taking these down and cleaning them out regularly to wash away any dirt and prevent anything disgusting from growing inside.

If you don't keep your nesting boxes clean and tidy, your hens may stop laying. If you keep on top of it, the process won't take long. Regularly remove all the bedding and simply replace it with fresh nesting materials. There are several different materials that you can use for nesting, including shredded paper, hay, pine or cedar shavings, straw, or some people even use mulch.

Chickens like to roost. It's hardwired into their instinct, and they prefer to choose elevated roosts to avoid predators. A roost can be an elevated branch or plank on which your chickens can perch to sleep. Your provided roosting perch will be a place where your birds will stay all night, keeping the balance of their flock all around them. As an added value in the winter, they will be able to keep warmer. Ideally, your roosting perch should be around 1.5 to three feet high. When you are planning your roosts, you may want to consider a small, lower perch just for those older arthritic hens. Heavier birds, like an Orpington or a Jersey Giant, might benefit from lower perches as well because larger birds are more prone to get leg injuries. When you choose your breeds, you may want to configure your roosts to take their individual needs in mind.

Your roosting bars will need to be kept clean because chickens will still poop on them. Our personal favorite tool to clean perches is a garden hoe. If you run this garden tool over the bars, you can knock off all the poop, and if necessary, the bar can be sprayed down with a water hose to remove any lingering poop. You can provide some sanitizing to the bar by soaking a sponge in white vinegar and running this over the bars.

Never Underestimate the Power of a Good Dust Bath!

After a long, hard day of working outside, we love nothing better than hopping in the shower to wash away our daily dose of dirt. We need to understand that chickens don't bathe as we do, and it may seem counterintuitive, but chickens get clean by getting dirty. Yes, we are sure that you have reread that last sentence a couple of times, and you are probably shaking your head thinking that it doesn't make any sense, but hear us out.

All chickens need dust baths, and it is a natural behavior. They will dig a shallow pit by choosing the finest, most irritating dust that they can find. We bet that you are dying to know why they roll around in it until they have covered every possible area of skin and feather. It's because it keeps the parasites away. Yep, mites and lice find all this dust to be irritating, so oddly enough, all that fine silty sand, dust, or ashes are appropriate materials to supply for your chicken's dust bath.

Your girls will probably make this a social event that will involve everyone in the flock, and you may witness a community event. These dust baths aren't just for chickens alone. Should you have a mixed flock with some added turkeys or quail, they will also enjoy the benefits of the dust bath.

Will your chickens use a dust bath in the winter? Yes, but not as often, since lice and mites are less of a problem during colder months. Your chickens should have something to use year-round.

The area for a dust bath needs to be big enough for a hen, but if they have a dust bath party, it should be big enough for several hens to flop around comfortably. If you are trying to design your own area, you should take the number of birds you have into consideration. The dust bath for the average size chickens should be around eight inches deep and only six inches if you are raising bantams. The rule of thumb is that they should be deep enough to fit a chicken.

Your chickens will probably decide on the perfect place for a dust bath, but the area should be a dry, covered area that your chickens will have easy access to. If you don't provide one, they will most likely make one in your favorite flowerpot! Even if you believe you have created the best dust bath area, your hens may just pick out a spot and plop down. We guess as long as they are happy, that's all that matters.

So, what are some materials that you can provide for your chicken's bath *du jour*? The bulk of it can be just clean, dry, sand, but here are some other alternatives you can add.

- Charred wood or fire ash from a wood fire. Some chickens will even pick charcoal out from the ash you provide and consume it. It is believed that this helps to absorb any toxins residing in their gut.

- Diatomaceous earth, commonly known as DE. A little goes a long way, but a super fine grade of DE will kill lice, mites, and other parasites just by contact. There is some debate on the use of DE. See below in supplements.

- They will not appreciate a bubble bath, but you can provide them with some nice, dried herbs in their dustbowls, and many of these also provide protection from pests. Try some lavender, lemon balm, mint, rosemary, or sage. If you are growing your own herb garden, you will have these readily available.

- Sawdust can be used, but make sure that they are not camphor or heavily fragrant.

- Topsoil. Chickens love to toss loose dirt over themselves, and even if you buy a bag of topsoil at your home improvement store, it doesn't cost much to make your hens happy.

Avoid adding any of these to the dust bath area.

- Straw. The hollow nature of straw is an excellent hiding place for lice, mites, and mold. These are the very things your hens are trying to avoid.

- Coal ash can contain mercury, sulfur, and heavy metals.

- Kitty litter is often manufactured to include fragrances and deodorizers.

- Fire log ash is a product of commercially compressed logs or pellets. In the industry, they grind up many things like wood, adhesives, varnishes, stains, and added glue. They may even use old pallets that housed who knows what. It would be risky to expose your birds to potentially harmful chemicals.

A Fed Chicken Is a Happy Chicken

Well, every animal enjoys eating, but giving them a good quality feed will keep their insides healthy, which in turn will keep them happy. If you remember that you are eating their eggs, it isn't too difficult to rationalize that the better the food, the better the egg. So, keeping their tummies happy in turn keeps ours happy as well.

Freshwater is a given for every living creature, but sometimes it can be a challenge with chickens. If you provide a dish on the floor, you can expect to not only see them stand in it but poop in it as well. Our personal favorite is a bucket that has nipples and a lid that you can hang from a support system. Not only will this keep your chickens from soiling the water, but it will keep pests out of it too. Just remember to freshen the water at least once each day.

Keep their environment safe. We all feel happier knowing that we are safe and secure. Your coop should be free from pests and predators, which can include the family cat or dog. If you have other family pets that enjoy chasing your chickens, this will stress out your girls, and they may either stop laying eggs or hide them.

Supplements & Herbs

Supplements are fed in addition to your feed. Some of our personal favorites are garlic, apple cider vinegar, and diatomaceous earth. If your flock indulges in a lot of free-range time, they shouldn't need any supplements.

Garlic

Garlic is a natural antibiotic and can strengthen your chicken's immune system while also boosting its respiratory system. Garlic is a natural deterrent for lice and mites and is an active ingredient in natural dewormers. You might be wondering how to give your chickens garlic, and there are a few methods. We prefer to crush bulbs and mince them, then offer it as a treat by itself or mixed with other treats. There are some that prefer to add powdered garlic to their feed, but there have been some arguments that this method is not as powerful as giving fresh, raw garlic. This is not something you need to provide for your flock daily, once or twice a month is perfectly adequate. Overfeeding could cause your birds to be unable to balance the bacteria in their digestive system. Of course, only feed organic garlic!

Organic Apple Cider Vinegar

Organic apple cider vinegar (ACV), for example, Braggs, which is known for its quality and benefit of "the mother," can help your chickens with their immunity, improve their overall health, help optimize digestive health, and help a chick get over the sour crop (see chapter 4). The best way to dispense ACV to your chickens is to add a single tablespoon to every gallon of freshwater. **Note that ACV should not be administered in any metal water dispenser!** This should be offered to your flock 1 to 2 times a week.

Diatomaceous Earth (DE)

Diatomaceous earth is debated by chicken owners; some feel that it is safe, while others believe it to be a health hazard. All we can tell you is that there are benefits and risks. The ultimate decision is yours. DE is a natural substance made from fossils of microscopic aquatic algae, called diatoms. This mined substance is ground into a fine powder, but these fossilized diatoms are made up of almost pure amorphous silicon. The reason this is important to know is that this is a crystalline form of silica, which can cause silicosis (a form of lung cancer). In the US, a product that is less than 2% crystalline silica is considered safe. However, when you compare that to other countries' standards, that is considered to be high. While this is effective against external parasites, such as red mites, northern fowl mites, fleas, and lice, there are other, more safe alternatives to use. The main concern of this product revolves around the risk of breathing in the dust. Diatomaceous earth is a dusty powder that, even if you handle it with care, can fly everywhere.

You can grow an herb garden for your flock! Some herbs help with your chicken's health and well-being below. We have listed some of the more popular herbs and how they help:

- **Chamomile** can be a wonderful addition to your chicken's supplements. It can be used in your flock's fight against lice, mites, and fleas. Chamomile is also well known for its calming properties, and chickens are no exception.

- **Chives** provide an excellent source of iron for your flock and, in addition, can help with digestion.

- **Cilantro** is believed to help build strong bones, aid in vision, and act as a fungicide.

- **Dandelion** is good for the overall health of your chickens, and if you are an urban farmer that is dedicated to improving the Earth, you probably have an abundance of these. People actually used to plant dandelions! For a greener earth, we need to embrace these gifts from nature.

- **Dill** helps with your flocks' digestion, respiratory health, and appetite. It also serves as an antioxidant.

- **Lavender** not only smells great but can help your chickens reduce their stress. And if placed in the nests, lavender can help repel insects.

- **Lemon Balm** helps reduce stress, is antibacterial, and can help reduce pests.

- **Marigold** can help keep bugs away, aids your hens to produce more orange yolks, and promotes healthy beaks and feet.

- **Mint** is always a favorite staple of any herb garden because of its ability to keep mice away and bugs too. Mint has been said to increase your hen's egg production and overall eggshell quality.

- **Nasturtium** is a nice little flower, but while it isn't an herb, it can do some very impressive things besides repelling bugs! Nasturtiums work as a natural chicken dewormer and act as an antibiotic. It is also believed to aid in egg production.

- **Oregano** is a powerful antibiotic and a staple of any herb garden. Oregano can fight coccidia, salmonella, E. coli, avian flu, and helps to strengthen the chickens' immune systems.

- **Parsley** is always a highly undervalued herb but contains high levels of vitamins A, B, and C, along with high calcium and iron levels.

- **Rosemary** is another herb that bugs tend to hate, but it can also be used as a pain reliever and help out with respiratory health.

- **Sage** is great for the overall health of your birds and is believed to aid in fighting salmonella.

- **Thyme** can help our chickens fight parasites, stimulate laying, and promote healthy respiratory systems.

Chicken Behavior

Chickens are social creatures that establish their own "pecking order" and have developed their own language. Taking the time to understand your chicken's behavior can make your experience more interesting, rewarding, and infinitely more fun.

Let's delve into the social life of chickens to gain a better understanding of our feathered friends.

The Pecking Order

Almost everyone that has heard the term knows that it is closely associated with chickens. The term "pecking order" was first used to describe chickens in 1921, and it just sort of stuck. In the world of chickens, the inclusion in the pecking order begins at six to eight weeks of age. At this age, chickens will display signs of dominance, submissiveness, escape, avoidance, and attack. According to Jerome Belanger (2010), researchers have discovered that an individual chicken can recognize and remember more than a hundred other chickens!

Once a pecking order has been established within your flock, it is accepted as chicken law by all members, and there is peace throughout the chicken kingdom. In this hierarchy, every chicken will know its place. Chickens live in flocks similar to human communes. They share a communal approach when it comes to the raising of their young or the incubation of the flock's eggs.

While watching some of your lower-ranking chickens, you may notice that they will keep their heads lower than their more dominant flockmates. These lower-ranking chickens are monitored by their higher-ups, and if they slip and forget their place, they will be quickly reminded where they stand.

If your flock does have roosters, they will develop their own ranking and should demonstrate a passive dominance over the hens. After all, they are the protectors of the flock. Your hens will form their own order outside of the roosters, and interestingly, larger combs may award a hen with a higher rank.

When a new bird is introduced to your flock, it can cause chaos, and the hierarchy will have to be established all over again. A good rule of thumb is that if you must introduce new birds, you should not make it a frequent habit. Frequent changes can stress out your birds, which can lower their immunity and cause some of them to develop an illness or stop laying altogether.

Great care should be taken when introducing new members to your flock. It can be hard to believe that your contented flock can turn into a bunch of bullies when you try to add a new hen to the group, but it is possible. If you want happy chickens, you will need to be careful and considerate of your existing flock when you add new birds.

If you need to introduce a new chicken into your flock, it should take place gradually and, for some reason, more toward dusk. Your new chicken can be kept in a cage or crate where they can all meet and greet each other without any physical altercations. The acceptance of newcomers can vary from flock to flock because some chickens or breeds of chickens can be more socially acceptable than others.

We have a friend who swears by sneaking the new chicken in the coop while all the other chickens are sleeping and placing her on a roost. In her experience, the flock will wake up and not even care about the new addition. She says that it's like they wake up and think the new chicken has always been there. We have to admit, we haven't tried it.

You should also be aware that if you remove hens or roosters from the group, this will also add disruption to the flock, and a new pecking order will have to be put in place.

Want to Make a Difference?

You can adopt a former battery hen. Until recently, we weren't even aware of this ourselves, but you can help a once caged chicken to enjoy the creature comforts of your backyard's free-range offerings. A battery hen has never stepped foot outside of her cage, scratched through the dirt to find some delectable bug, nor even enjoyed a dust bath. These hens have never experienced freedom, and it can be a difficult transition for them while trying to adjust.

You will find that these hens have experienced years of trauma, and unfortunately, that isn't going to go away by spending an afternoon in your backyard chicken retreat. These girls have no idea how to perch or rest in a nesting box, so you have to give them time to adjust to a whole new world.

Having never enjoyed a moment of freedom, former battery hens may find themselves overwhelmed and even frightened by their new surroundings. As their new owner, you need to stay patient and keep calm because it is going to take them as long as it takes them to be at ease in a new world.

They are going to have a lot to learn since they have never had to worry about pecking orders, farm dogs, or exposure to alien noises. You will need to introduce them slowly to the flock, and above all, keep an eye on their health. Battery hens will have below-average resistance to diseases, and you should make it a top priority to have them given any necessary vaccinations they might need, treat them for worms, parasites, and coccidiosis, in addition to any other diseases you or your vet deem relevant.

As they begin to feel safe and are fed a healthy diet, they will start to grow back any feathers they may have lost due to their prior lifestyle. They may not have any eggs left at this point, but they can still make gentle pets if you just give them a chance. Please take great care when introducing these lost souls into a new life.

Foraging

You can blame their wild counterparts for all the walking, scratching, and pecking to continually forage for food even though you provide your flock with plenty of good feed and treats. When hens are kept from foraging as their instinct drives them to do, this can create stress and invite behaviors like feather picking. Chickens were not meant to be kept in a cage.

Nesting

Before your hen lays an egg, she will search for an appropriate nesting site. They prefer a darkened space that feels out-of-the-way, but some younger hens have no such protocols and will simply squat in the middle of the hen house to lay their egg on the floor.

When straw or other nesting materials are provided, a hen will spend time arranging her nest to her satisfaction. Your urban hens are lucky that they get to experience the comfort of their nesting boxes. A caged, egg-laying hen has no such luxury, and they must spend their lifetimes being frustrated since they are never able to fluff a nest.

Some hens become close and will often share a nest and even be in it at the same time. If the eggs are fertilized, they may hatch their eggs together and raise their chicks together. Some hens can be unpredictable and may see strange chicks and decide to attack and even kill them.

Broodiness will occur when a hen stops laying and will instead focus on the incubation of eggs already laid. The term most chicken keepers use is to "go broody." This broody hen will sit on a nest and protect it, rarely leaving even to indulge in food or water. A broody hen will task herself with maintaining a constant temperature of the eggs in the nest as well as turning them regularly as part of incubation. An owner may stimulate broodiness in their hens by placing artificial eggs in the nest. If they want to discourage the behavior, they may place the hen in an elevated cage with only an open wire floor. Some breeds have more of an inclination to be broody, and these are the Cochin, Cornish, and the Silkie. They make excellent mothers for chicken eggs but also care for other species like quail, pheasants, geese, or turkeys. Owners have told us that their chicken eggs can also be hatched by using a broody duck, but don't expect them to swim!

Preening

Chickens have a gland near their tail that produces an oil that they use while practicing preening. While preening, a chicken will spread that oil over its feathers, keeping them water-resistant and supple. During a molt (when chickens lose their feathers in favor of new fresh plumage), preening may be an indication of feather follicles that are irritated.

Chicken Chat

If you have never been exposed to chickens and the way they communicate, then you probably weren't aware that they make 30 different sounds with 30 different meanings. As a first-time chicken owner, you may not be able to distinguish a cluck from a chirp, but once you begin to pay attention, you will start to understand chicken speak.

Chick Chat

Did you know that chicks start communicating before they hatch? If the momma hen is around, there will be a conversation between them. After they are born, you may hear some of these sounds.

- Chicks will give off a pleasure thrill that can often be heard when they are settling down for a nap.

- Distress peeps are usually handed out when the youngster is miserable. For example, they may be hot, cold, or hungry.

- A panic peep will be a loud and insistent peep to draw attention to the chick and may be interpreted as a cry for help.

- A fear trill is a loud, sharp, and repeated sound that, above all, relays the message to not harm the frightened chick.

- The startled peep is a sharp chirp.

Momma Says

Hens typically are not very vocal, so when they say something, it's pretty darn important.

- A short cluck that is low-pitched and gets repeated is telling her chicks to stay close.

- The food trumpet is high-pitched and has a staccato sound that sounds like tuck-tuck-tuck. A hen will tell her chicks to get a move on because she just found some food.

- If your hen gives her chicks a hush sound that resembles a vibrating *errrr*, she is telling them to stay put because there is danger.

Hen Speak

While hens aren't very vocal, the girls do tend to announce when they have laid an egg or feel broody.

- The laying cackle announces that your hen has just laid an egg, and she is darn proud of it too.

- A broody hiss may make you believe that you are raising snakes instead of chickens. Your hen will probably fluff their feathers and deliver a dirty look to boot. Broody hens usually do not want you to touch their eggs, and they will probably give you a peck or two as well. You can usually use something to create a barrier between them and you, so that you don't end up with a bunch of holes in your hand.

- On the other hand, a broody growl is much more intimidating than the hiss. This is a warning to leave your hen and her eggs alone, or she will end you.

- Have you ever heard a chicken sing? Well, they don't really sing, but what they do is use rapidly repeated notes randomly. You can compare it to someone blindly humming nothing in particular.

- A contented call can be made by either a hen or a rooster, and it sounds a lot like a low-pitched repetitive sound.

- When a hen is in search of a nest, she will use a nesting call when she chooses one.

- The roosting call is a loud and low-pitched sound that is repeated while the hens settle in for the night.

Rooster Rap

Roosters rule the roost, and they serve their hens by protecting them.

- Crowing. We are all aware that this means that they are in charge.

- The announcement for the arrival of food resembles an excited *tuck-tuck-tuck* sound.

- When a rooster makes a low rumbly sound, this is considered a courtship croon for one of his hens.

- A flying object alert is announced by a chirping sound while your rooster looks toward the sky.

- Roosters can be startled, and they will give a short, intense, and loud squawk.

- Quick repetitive calls tell the flock that there is something dangerous in the vicinity.

- When a rooster or dominant hen sounds an alarm cackle, it sounds like a *kuh-kuh-kuh-kuh-kack*. It is the chicken version of "danger, Will Robinson!"

- A rooster will make a loud warning sound letting his hens know that there is a raptor in the sky.

- The startled squawk can be expressed by a chicken just pecked by another, or it could be that they are slightly injured.

- Distress squawks are loud and repetitive cries by a chicken that has been captured and might be in the process of being carried away. This distress call will garner an attack from the rooster or perhaps another dominant hen.

When you understand how your chickens communicate with one another, you can better understand them and their needs.

Chapter 3:
Know Your Chickens Inside and Out

It's time for the science portion of your lessons on chickens, so don your white lab coat and get ready for some science-fun facts. For instance, the scientific name for a hen is *Gallus gallus domesticus*, and the next time you talk to your friends, you can boast that chickens were first domesticated over 10,000 years ago! Did you know that the top speed of a chicken is six miles per hour? How about their proficiency regarding their flight abilities? Even though chickens have wings, they are known to mostly *fly* only when threatened.

How many breeds of chickens are there? Funny, you should ask. No one knows for sure! According to the American Poultry Association (APA, 2019), they recognize 53 large chicken breeds, which do not include any bantam chicken breeds. If you are into bantam chickens, they have their very own organization, the American Bantam Association, and they maintain their own list of recognized breeds. There are chicken breeds from all over the world that are not part of the APA, so if you are eyeing a breed from Indonesia or Switzerland, they may not be breeds that you can show at exhibitions. Some breeds have been dropped from the APA. For example, a breed called the Russian Orloff was originally recognized by the APA in the year 1875 but then dropped 19 years later. A breed of chicken removed from the APA doesn't mean that it is no longer a breed. It just means that they are no longer considered common.

Chickens were first kept for entertainment in the forms of cockfighting and special ceremonies, depending upon the culture in question. It's an interesting tidbit that chickens were not kept for food until the Hellenistic period (4th-2nd centuries BCE). It is hard to imagine that people before that time didn't realize the true gift that chickens offered to us, especially their yummy eggs! Over the centuries, the chicken's role has changed, and they are now primarily kept for their eggs, meat, and serving as beloved pets.

Chickens in Greek Mythology

In Greek mythology, Alectryon was a young soldier who was ordered to stand guard outside the door of Ares (the god of war) while he was engaged in a love affair with the goddess, Aphrodite.

Poor Alectryon fell asleep while on duty, and the lovers were discovered and reported to Aphrodite's husband. Ares was understandably furious and punished Alectryon by turning him into a rooster. From that time on, Alectryon was never allowed to forget the arrival of the sun each morning and impelled to crow, becoming the god of chickens and roosters for eternity.

Understanding How the Inside of Your Chicken Works

When you understand how the inside of your chicken works, it helps you produce the best eggs, meat, and bloodlines. So here's the scoop from the inside of the coop.

Biology

Fun fact: chickens were the first birds to have their DNA sequenced; this took place in 2004.

Roosters can be easily identified by their long, flowing tail feathers, brighter plumage, comb, or the development of spurs on the males' legs. You may have noticed that males are always the more colorful ones when it comes to separating the male from the female.

Adult chickens will sport a fleshy crest on their heads, which are called combs or cockscomb, and under their beaks are hanging flaps of skin which are referred to as wattles. Both male and female chickens will have wattles and combs, but overall, they are far more pronounced in the roosters.

Domesticated chickens, while possessing the ability to fly, are not able to do so for long distances. The typical chicken can fly for short distances like over fences or into trees to roost from predators. They may occasionally fly to flee danger.

According to the *Guinness Book of World Records* (2021), the oldest chicken died at the ripe old age of 16 due to heart failure. The average lifespan of a chicken, depending upon the breed, is five to 10 years.

Did you know that chickens dream? According to Andy Schneider (2017), they do, and they even experience REM sleep. So, what do you think your chickens dream about? Raising their chicks? Tasty mealworms? Maybe just enjoying a good swing!

Anatomy

According to Veronica Hirsch (2003), chickens can see in color, possess a small brain, and possess a large hypothalamus, which is responsible for the autonomic nervous system. Their well-developed hypothalamus controls their body temperature, thirst, hunger, sleep, and any emotional activity your chickens may experience.

Overall, chickens have a lightweight skeleton, and some of their pneumatic bones (connected to the respiratory system) are even hollow. Unlike humans, a chicken possesses rather rigid lungs that do not expand or contract in conjunction with the chicken breathing, and they are attached to the chicken's ribs. Therefore, when holding a chicken, you must be careful not to restrict the movement of the breastbone because this must be allowed to move freely, or you may risk suffocating your bird.

Chickens have no teeth and use their beaks to shred their food. Their barbed tongue then moves the food back toward the esophagus. Within the esophagus is a small pouch called a crop, where the chicken's system can store the food for a short time before moving it off to the stomach. After that, the food moves from the stomach into the gizzard. Inside this area, the food will be crushed with the help of any gravel and grit that the bird has swallowed before moving into the intestines. Here is where proteins and enzymes (supplied by the gut, pancreas, and liver) will dissolve the food and remove all the nutrients. After the intestines, the food paste will move into the ceca. It is here that chicken poop comes from.

From eating to pooping, the chicken will take about four hours to process the food, eight hours if they are laying, and 12 hours if the hen is broody. If you guessed that the poop of a broody hen would smell worse, you would be correct.

Hens are born with two ovaries, but usually, only one of them will develop and be functional. Typically, it's the left one. When hens lay eggs, they will pass through the cloaca, a chamber that is also the route her feces take via the rectum. For this reason, the outside of an egg may be contaminated by bacteria, germs, and other potential diseases that may, on occasion, pass through the shell and into the egg itself.

This is why commercial poultry flocks are often held to strict guidelines for disinfection and are often subject to vigorous inspection procedures.

The composition of a chicken's bones is mainly calcium and phosphorus and can be split into two different types.

- Medullary: The bone marrow within the center of these bones makes blood cells and allows the storage of calcium. Bones of this type are found in the legs, shoulder blades, and ribs.

- Pneumatic bones are the hollow ones We mentioned before and are connected via air sacs to the respiratory system. Examples of these bones are the pelvis, collar bones, skull, and humerus (arm bone).

While watching your birds at play, you have probably noticed that the neck and backbone look very flexible. Well, you are correct! Their spine contains 39 bones, and between this and their neck being quite long, this can provide a bird with a large range of motion while looking for food. For example, chickens can turn their heads 180 degrees!

The largest bone found in a chicken's body is the sternum. This bone covers half of your chicken's body cavity, and even their wings are attached to the sternum by strong muscles.

A chicken's legs are similar to human anatomy until you get to the hip bone, which is fused with a chicken's backbone.

Reproduction

First-time chicken owners may not be aware of this, but it is really important to those potential owners in urban areas that do not allow roosters; you do not need a rooster to get eggs! That's right; a hen is born with a predetermined number of eggs. There are only two reasons that you need a rooster. The first one is if you want their protection for your girls, and the second is if you want baby chicks.

Roosters may *dance* in a circle near a hen to begin a courting ritual. He may lower his wing closest to the hen in question. If his dance triggers a hen to respond, the rooster may mount the hen and proceed with mating.

When a rooster and hen mate, the hen can maintain the sperm in her oviducts or expel the sperm. Should the hen keep the sperm, it will be viable for fertilizing her eggs for about 30 days. This kept sperm will fertilize the eggs, and the hen will lay fertilized eggs. If you see her become broody, you will notice her tuck several eggs into a nest, and she will sit on them until they hatch.

Eggs are a wonder of nature because they contain all the nutrition a young chick needs to grow. Eggs are usually laid in a grouping because nature realizes that some will hatch and survive, but some won't. Chicken offspring are better developed at the time of their hatching because they will be able to walk and stand. Other baby birds are sequestered in their nests until they develop enough to fly, hop, or stand.

Health & Wellness

Everyone likes to start with healthy stock and keep them that way, but if one of your flock isn't feeling well, it will not be difficult to ascertain that something is wrong. A healthy bird will be active, vibrant, and perky. Their feathers will be glossy, and their eyes will look bright. Should one of your chickens act uncharacteristically lifeless, there will be some tell-tale signs you might notice. For example, their eyes may look dull, and their feathers could appear dull and ruffled. If something is wrong, you may hear noisy, labored breathing.

People with backyard chickens never want any of their flock members to experience illness because our hens become like any other family pet. Because chickens cost so little to purchase or maintain, it seems unfair that most of their diseases are often difficult to diagnose and costly to treat. Smaller, urban flocks are more unlikely to see chicken diseases, unlike the large commercial operations, but you should be aware of them.

There are four main disease types you should be aware of:

- Behavioral diseases may show up as pecking at other birds, excessively plucking of feathers, or acting aggressively. Birds suffering from stress may revert to cannibalism and begin eating eggs. Because chickens can start this habit, we do not agree with giving them crushed eggshells. Keep your chickens comfortable and make sure they have fantastic nutrition to help curb the development of behavioral disorders.

- Metabolic or nutritional diseases are caused by unhealthy living environments. Your chickens can experience a reduction in eggs, develop soft bones, soft beaks, or even exhibit lameness due to poor nutrition and exercise. Taking proper care of your birds will prevent most of these issues.

- Infectious diseases can be born from bacterial, viral, or fungal issues and will be spread easily from bird to bird. You can protect your flock by isolating any birds exhibiting symptoms that aren't normal.

- Parasitic diseases are often brought about by contact with other infected birds or because of compromised living conditions. Common culprits include ticks, mites, lice, fleas, or roundworms, and they will often be visible but cause your birds to have feather damage, irritation, or parasites in your birds' feces. Keep any chicken housing clean to help prevent parasitic poultry diseases.

Aspergillosis

This respiratory disease is caused by a fungal species known as aspergillus, but many refer to it as brooder's pneumonia or fungal pneumonia. This is common to bird species but is non-contagious. Younger stock will be the most susceptible to this type of infection, although if you have older birds that have been under a lot of stress or have had bouts of poor health, they can also develop chronic aspergillosis.

One of the most common sources of aspergillosis is from contaminated poultry bedding with high levels of ammonia. Still, it can also be present in inhaled spores, or a contaminated hatching machine, or during incubation of infected eggs. This type of respiratory infection can be either acute or chronic. Poor quality of feed can also be a cause of this respiratory disease.

- Acute infections usually target younger chickens with symptoms that develop within the first three to five days after the initial exposure. What you might witness is rapid, open-mouthed breathing caused by gradual air passage obstruction. When the disease progresses, you will notice a lack of appetite, increased thirst, drowsiness, emaciation, eye swelling, blindness, and torticollis, which is a twisting of their neck to one side.

- Chronic aspergillosis will typically affect an older chicken with a compromised immune system. Chronic cases can lead to severe neurological dysfunction, respiratory distress, blindness, and eye discharge.

Unfortunately, there is no known treatment for aspergillosis, so the best prevention is to keep your chicken's habitat clean and ensure that you are feeding them with quality ingredients. Here is your prevention checklist:

- Keep the chicken coop clean and free from bedding contamination.

- Clean and sanitize any equipment used in your hatchery and brooding areas.

- Keep your grain and water feeders clean to avoid any contamination.

- Store your chicken's feed in clean, dry containers. Always throw away any spilled and uneaten food to prevent fungal growth.

- Replace nesting boxes and bedding regularly to impede the growth of fungus. Discard any wet bedding because even if it's only water, it will break down shavings or other beddings to create an environment for fungal growth.

- Keep any eggs that will be hatched away from dusty areas that may have spores.

Coccidiosis

Your bird may be immune to one kind of coccidiosis, but there are still five other species of this parasite. This is probably more commonly experienced by the small flock keeper, and you will notice that your chicken has loose droppings, weight loss, or bloody or watery diarrhea. Coccidiosis is caused by a parasite damaging your chicken's gut wall. The parasites enter your chicken's system by ingesting them, whether found in contaminated water, soil, or even feces from other infected birds.

Coccidiosis most often occurs during spring and summer because this is when the soil is warm and moist, providing ideal conditions for parasites. Your younger stock will be more susceptible than your older flock members. Once a bird has been infected and cured, it should never contract that same strain of coccidiosis. Most affected are chicks, which is why it's a good idea to start them off on a medicated starter feed which is formulated specifically to boost the immune system and protect against parasites.

This can be treated with antibiotics or with sulmet, which is added to their drinking water. There are several medications and treatments, and many of them can be found at your local farm store. And great news, treatments always work quickly! Treatment will usually run for seven days, but your sick chickens may often show improvement in 24 hours.

Egg Bound

The term "egg bound" is used for hens that have difficulties passing an egg. Depending upon the hen, it could just be a single occurrence. However, some hens can develop a chronic problem. Either way, this can be a critical situation for your hen.

When a hen is egg-bound, they tend to stand upright, like a penguin, and their abdomens will feel hot. In the best-case scenario, the egg may pass, however, should the egg get caught in the hen, it can result in her death. If an egg breaks inside of your hen, she will die.

You can help your hen by immersing her vent and backside in a tub of warm water and then gently massaging the area around the egg, but you must be careful not to break the egg. Another option would be to place a small amount of mineral oil on a latex glove and gently massage the oil up the chicken's vent.

You should never breed a chronic egg-bound hen as this can be passed on to the next generation.

Fowl Pox

Fowl pox can show up as either a dry or wet form. If you are experiencing the wet form, the disease will show up as lesions that appear around the mouth, and your bird may show discharge from their eyes. The dry form will look like wart-like lesions that show up in the unfeathered area of your bird. These lesions should heal in about two weeks.

Generally, sick chickens should be quarantined and made as comfortable as possible. There is no specific treatment for fowl pox, but it should go away after a few weeks. Mosquitoes can transmit this disease from flock to flock.

Infectious Bronchitis

Yes, chickens can catch a cold! What's more, is that it is just as contagious as the human equivalent. Should your flock experience a cold outbreak, you will notice a drop in egg production, their appetite will decline, and there may be a discharge from either the birds' eyes or nostrils, perhaps both, and your birds will exhibit labored breathing.

Similar to humans, they pretty much have to ride out their colds. Not much can be done except to give your birds some antibiotics for a few days. At least we can curl up in bed and drink chicken noodle soup.

Though there are some preventative vaccines out there, they come with no guarantee. Your best defense is to practice biosecurity and keep rodents to a minimum.

Marek's Disease

When you order chicks from a hatchery, you are probably going to hear about Marek's Disease, commonly referred to as MD, but also known as fowl paralysis.

MD is considered avian cancer that is very contagious and transmitted via the air found inside a poultry house. This disease affects mostly young birds, and unvaccinated chicks between 10 to 12 weeks old can show up to a 50% mortality rate.

Symptoms include paralysis of the legs or wings, tumors on feather follicles, depression, diarrhea, and a general sense of being weak. You may also see combs that shrivel or blindness that often occurs in only one eye.

Some hatcheries make it a practice to vaccinate all their chicks for MD, while others may charge a fee for vaccinating your chicks. Even though you are unlikely to experience MD within your flock because of high vaccination rates, there is no known cure or treatment for this disease. Since it is a virus, it will be transmitted from bird to bird, and any that experience this disease will be a carrier for life, so you will have to remove it from the rest of your flock as soon as possible and keep it separate.

If you are hatching chicks, they should be vaccinated upon emerging from their shells. You should know that the smallest dose available is for 200 chicks and that any unused portion of the vaccine cannot be saved for later. Anything left over must be discarded.

Newcastle Disease

This is a respiratory disease that affects your chicken's ability to breathe and creates nasal discharge, murky-looking eyes, and as with most diseases, a reduction in egg production. Sometimes, though not as common, birds can experience a twisting in their neck and paralysis that takes over their legs and wings. There are varying strains that may appear to be more lethal than others.

While your adult chickens should recover from Newcastle disease and will not be carriers, your chicks will most likely not survive. You can give your affected birds antibiotics for a few days to avoid any additional infections while your chicken is recovering.

This disease is typically carried by wild birds, so keeping your chickens vaccinated is key, along with practicing good sanitation in and around your chicken's living quarters. You should also know that you can infect your birds if the disease is carried on your clothing or shoes.

Pullorum

This is a nonrespiratory bacterial disease. In most states within the US, this is a reportable disease. What this means is if one chicken has pullorum, then the entire flock must be destroyed, whether they are ill or not. While this disease is not a threat to humans, it could wipe out the poultry industry if allowed to get out of hand. Fortunately, it is extremely rare in North America.

The usual way this is spread is from hen to chick, through the egg, although there is also a danger of it being transmitted by contaminated incubators, houses, or equipment. When present in chicks, it may start with excessive huddling, droopiness, gasping, a pasted vent, and excretions that appear to be chalk-white stained with green bile. This is a serious illness that, if suspected, should be verified by your veterinarian. Any outbreak is handled by your local state or federal regulatory agency.

Wry Neck

Other common names for this condition include stargazing, twisted neck, or crookneck, and this usually affects newborn chicks, and on occasion, full-grown chickens. Tell-tale signs of this condition include difficulty to stand, and your chicken's neck will twist often, looking like it is stuck looking upward toward the stars.

Wry neck is usually the result of a genetic disorder, a head injury, a vitamin deficiency, or by the ingestion of certain toxins. Chickens can live with this condition; however, they may be highly stressed because eating and drinking will be frustrating and difficult. In addition, they will be unable to move very well and may get picked on by the rest of the flock.

Separating affected birds is the kindest thing you can do for them because this will keep their stress levels down. While separated, you can raise the affected bird's vitamin intake by targeting the addition of vitamin E and selenium. These should be given to your affected bird two or three times each day until you see any improvement in your chicken's condition. Natural sources of vitamin E include spinach, broccoli, dandelion greens, and asparagus.

You will have to be patient because wry neck does not go away quickly. It can take upwards of a month before the condition resolves itself, and you would be wise to continue the extra vitamin intake for at least two weeks after that, making sure that your chicken is back to its old self.

The best prevention is to feed a high-quality diet to your flock. And there certainly isn't anything wrong with adding in some goodies that provide vitamin E as a bonus treat!

Poultry Pests

Let's face it; nobody likes pests. However, if you allow wet litter to remain in your coop, you will have your fair share of the little creepy-crawlies. This is one of the main reasons we are so finicky about cleanliness. We just hate bugs!

The House Fly

Poultry poop is the preferred place for these pests to breed, and since flies are known to carry several diseases, you are going to want to keep your chicken manure pile far from your coop.

Blow Flies

These pests love to breed in broken eggs and wet garbage. Daily cleanup is essential to prevent a build-up of these pests.

Lice

On the bright side, poultry lice are host-specific, so their lice will not transfer to you or the family dog. Chickens will contract lice from wild birds or other chickens. As we mentioned previously, your chicken's dust baths will help out with parasites.

Mites

While several different mites can affect poultry, the two most popular are the scaly leg mites and depluming mites.

Scaly leg mites are described as being round, tiny, and flat. These mites will burrow under the scales of your chicken's feet and lower legs, raising those scales and giving your chicken the appearance of having deformed feet. You can either rub in petroleum jelly or dip their legs in linseed oil and then wipe the legs clean. Whatever treatment you choose, you should apply it for several weeks at the rate of once or twice a week.

Depluming mites can be found on your chicken's skin at the base of their feather shafts. Depluming mites are so named because your chicken will peck at the mites and will even pull out their own feathers, leading to bacterial skin infections and even cannibalism. Permethrin spray and dust treatments are the most commonly used for these mites.

It seems that most chicken maladies can be easily curbed by limiting exposure to wild birds, keeping your coop clean, and feeding a good quality diet. Let your chickens be happy, keep them stress-free, allow them to enjoy their dust baths and should any of your chickens not seem to be themselves, keep them isolated.

Keep a Wellness Checklist

Routine health checks can head off any minor problems before they progress. If you have a flock of fewer than ten birds, you may not feel the need to keep a written record, but it can be a handy thing to refer to. If you are breeding and hatching chicks, this may be a more important step.

You can set up a basic health chart in any application like Excel. Just remember to check all vital areas and leave room to make some notes. You can perform this monthly unless you have some chickens that seem under the weather, in which case you may want to adjust your chart for daily observations during their illness. This is our basic chart, but you can change it in any way that suits you.

Name/ Breed	Comb /Wats	Beak	Eyes	Feathers	Crop	Legs & Feet	Vent	Active	Remarks
Hera/BO	✓	✓	✓	✓	✓	✓	✓	✓	molting
Bertha/	✓	✓	✓	✓	✓	✓	✓	✓	dusted 4 mites

BR									
Rosie/ RIR	✓	✓	✓	✓	✓	✓	✓	✓	broody

1. The first column is for your chicken's name, breed, or even tag number.

2. The second column is only for the comb and wattles and how they look. If your hen has been molting or brooding, this may influence how the comb looks. If you see any indication of an injury, it may need to be addressed. If you are in a colder climate, you may want to check these areas for frostbite.

3. The third column covers the appearance of your chicken's beak. You should check how they are aligning or if, by some odd occurrence, it may be fractured. If you suspect that it is overgrown at the tip and your chicken is experiencing problems eating and drinking, you can file the tip with a Dremel tool. But whatever you do, don't get carried away because their beaks are sensitive.

4. The fourth column is all about your chicken's eyes and whether they appear to be bright and alert. Make notations about any drainage or discharge you might see. If you have concerns, a veterinarian can take a swab of the discharge and have it tested. *Tip: Should you have a sight-challenged bird, always keep your feeders and waterers in the same place.*

5. The fifth column is all about feathers and their appearance. Your chicken's feathers should appear to be glossy and tight unless you have a specialty breed like a Frizzle or a Frizzle-cross. *Tip: Within your flock, the best layers are the quickest to molt and regrow their feathers. This is a perfect time to put a star by their names, so you have identified your egg superstars!*

6. The sixth column is where your chicken will store their food while it is waiting to be digested. The rule of thumb is that it should be empty in the morning and full at bedtime. Crops should never feel rock-hard, only mushy. If your hen's crop feels hard, it could mean that she has

an impaction. If so, you will need to get her to the vet ASAP. Signs of a sour crop include breath that smells like rancid milk, an unwillingness to eat, or acting lethargic.

7. The seventh column is for observations about the chicken's legs and feet. Scales on the feet should be smooth and uniform and should never appear to be raised or uneven. If you have a chicken with feathers on its toes, you will need to check this carefully since it can be very easy to overlook something due to the heavy feathering.

8. The eighth column covers the vent, and any chicken that is laying will have a pink, moist appearance. Should a chicken be past its prime in laying, its vent will appear to be pale and dry even if they are laying the occasional egg here and there. If you have a hen that has a prolapsed vent, she must be isolated from her flockmates for her safety as the others may peck at it. During this time of inspection, you should trim off any poop-filled feathers.

9. The ninth column is very simply covering if your chicken is displaying normal activity.

10. At the end of your line is a final column for any general remarks you may wish to make. This can cover anything from molting to the removal of bumblefoot.

Choosing the Best Chicken Breed for You

Almost any chicken will make a fantastic addition to your family, but some breeds are more friendly, easier to handle, and are generally calmer than other breeds. Of course, how you raise and treat your chickens has a lot to do with how friendly they are and how they interact with others. There are far too many breeds of chickens to list them all, but We have pulled out our favorites when it comes to new chicken owners. When chicks are tiny balls of fluff, it is hard to be objective about their breeds because all chicks are adorable, but if you consider one from our list below, you won't be disappointed.

Araucanas

This breed of chicken will lay beautiful blue or green eggs and weather the cold well. The hens are friendly, but the roosters can be more aggressive. There are a couple of characteristics that separate the Araucanas from other chickens. They possess tufts, which are found around their ear lobes or neck area, and they have no tail! Yes, that's right, they have no tail nor tail bone. They also have no wattles, a pea comb, and have facial feathers. Araucanas do well in areas of confinement, but they do enjoy fresh grass. This breed makes a great mother, though they do tend to be a broody chicken and just a little bit on the flighty side, and as far as their ranking within the pecking order, they tend to be in the middle of the flock. It is always fun to have colorful eggs to collect, and the Araucana is known to produce three to four medium-sized eggs each week. This breed lives around seven to eight years and is a relatively healthy breed. The roosters for this breed are known to be cranky but not aggressive. It should be noted that this breed can struggle when it comes to hot environments and humid weather.

Australorp

They will give you big, brown-colored eggs and are surprisingly consistent egg layers. This breed of chicken was originally developed from Orpington stock, and they tend to thrive in colder climates. Their feathers feel soft, and their large size is a delight to see in your backyard flock (although there is also a bantam-sized version of this chicken). The Australorp is considered to be one of the best multipurpose chickens that you can add to your flock, and their friendliness makes them a perfect pet. While the hens are very friendly, it should be noted that the roosters can be aggressive toward children or in general.

Barred Plymouth Rock

The Barred Rock chicken is the standard hen that everyone pictures when you start to talk about chickens. Besides being a classic breed, these hens are calm as well as productive. The Barred Rock is a favorite of backyard flock owners for over 100 years because they are hardy, docile, and productive. This breed is known for its barred black and white feathers, and once they get to know you, they will prove how friendly they are by begging for treats. This breed will also make excellent therapy birds because they enjoy being picked up and cuddled! These hens settle well into the backyard coop and love to forage for food. She will lay light brown medium to large eggs to the tune of around four each week, which averages out to be about 200 a year. Hens are not overly broody birds but make good mothers. This breed has no major health concerns and tolerates confinement, but they love to free-range. Although the roosters are protective of their girls, they have been known to sit on the eggs so the hen can have a break, and although they tend to be more laid back than many other breeds of roosters, they should still not be left alone with small children.

Buff Orpington

If a plump hen comes to mind when you picture a chicken, then you are probably dreaming of a Buff Orpington. Considering how popular these chickens are with backyard chicken enthusiasts, it is hard to imagine that these chickens were considered endangered until 2016, according to the Happy Chicken Coop (2021). Orpingtons are available in both large and bantam sizes, with the large hen weighing in at about eight pounds. Generally, all the Orpingtons are described as being docile, but the buff tends to be calm, friendly, and addicted to being cuddled. As long as they are kept dry, they will tolerate cold well, but in warmer climates, they will need and seek out shade to hide in during the heat of the day. Hens can be broody and also be great mothers, often accepting and hatching other eggs placed under them. Even though the hens are thought to be great for families with children, you should know that they have strong beaks that can peck pretty hard! Because they are friendly and docile birds, they are often an excellent choice for a 4-H animal. Their ability to tolerate a lot of handling, strange environments, and confinement, makes them a great show bird as well because it seems that it is tough to ruffle their feathers. They are good egg producers and lay about 200 to 280 large brown eggs each year. Since this is such a docile chicken, you should avoid putting them in a flock with more aggressive breeds such as Rhode Island Reds or Welsummers because they will get picked on, and they are most likely at the bottom of any flock's pecking order. Due to their dense feathering, you should check them frequently for any signs of lice and mites.

Healthwise, one thing you should monitor is their weight since they tend to be lazy and obese. A Buff Orpington hen will, without a doubt, be one of your favorite hens.

Cochin Bantams

These are also a great choice if you have children, and the cochins do have a full-sized equivalent. These bantam-sized chickens tend to work well when dealing with autistic children because of their friendly temperament and the fact that they love to be held or even sit next to a child on a swing. While the full-sized roosters rarely become aggressive, the bantam size roosters are not as mellow and can be fairly aggressive. Described as head-to-toe feathers, once you see one of these, they will stick in your mind, especially since you cannot see most of their toes, only the feathers that cover them. Cochins are slow to mature and can take up to two years to be fully grown. This particular breed tolerates small spaces, so if you don't have a lot of room, this particular breed might be an excellent alternative. It should also be noted that Cochins are prone to become obese, and they do not forage for much, preferring instead to park in front of your feeders. For these larger and often overweight birds, you should provide some roosts near the ground so that they do not injure themselves by jumping down. Because they are *puffy*, you will need to check them regularly for lice and mites. If you choose to keep the cochin, either large or small, you should be aware that you will need to keep them in a safe space since they are easily picked off by predators. They get along well with other chickens and sport cool feathers on their feet. Both roosters and hens tend to love people and, like the Mille Fleurs, have winning personalities. These chickens are not the best layers, but they make up for it with their tolerance and love for children.

Easter Egger

Even though this is not considered a pure breed, they are great with children and also offer a bantam-sized chicken. You should think of them as the lovable mutts of the chicken world. There is nothing wrong with Easter Eggers, but you should know the difference, and since they are a hybrid of either the Ameraucana or the Araucana, they may end up with the muffs or beards known to be a characteristic of these breeds. There are no strict breed

51

standards, but Easter Eggers will often lay a wide variety of egg colors, and they possess outstanding personalities. These chickens have become a backyard favorite because they are friendly, low-maintenance, and deliver some show-stopping egg colors. Make sure that you give serious consideration to adding one or more of these curious and gentle birds to your flock.

Frizzles

Will always bring a smile to your children's faces (and probably yours too)! These birds look just like their name implies because they lack conventional feathers and instead sport ones that turn up instead of lying flat. This lends them a messy-looking appearance that is endearing. You can also get variances within chicken breeds, so you could even see frizzled Cochins, frizzled Orpingtons, and yes, sometimes even frizzled Silkies. Between their fun, wind-blown look and the fact that they don't mind the activity levels of children, the Frizzles make great chickens for your children. Oddly enough, how you breed a Frizzle is to cross a Frizzled parent with a traditionally feathered chicken. If you try to breed a Frizzle rooster and hen, there is a 25 percent chance that they will have brittle feathers (which could prove to be life-threatening). These are very patient chickens, but this can also make them a target for hens with a bullying nature. As with your bantams on this list, you should have plenty of feeding stations, so your favorite chickens never miss a meal.

Jersey Giant

Aptly named, the Jersey Giant is the largest purebred chicken in the US and likely the world! The size of this bird is impressive, and luckily, they are gentle giants! This breed of chicken was created around 1917 in New Jersey, and by 2001 the breed was listed as being critically endangered. There is still some work to do in order to keep this breed safe because, in 2017, this chicken was still listed on the watch list, but backyard breeders are embracing this breed and helping it make a comeback. Roosters can weigh as much as 13 to 15 pounds, with the hens weighing around 11 pounds. Both hens and roosters are friendly, docile, and mellow birds, and despite their size, they are generally good with children, although their stature might be found to be intimidating. The hens will not go broody much, and unfortunately, because of their weight, they are prone to breaking their eggs. In these cases, it may be worth it to set these eggs under a broody but smaller hen.

Overall, the Jersey Giant is a great choice for the backyard flock owner since they get along well with other breeds, and most of the other chickens give them a wide berth simply because of their size. This breed is easier to handle than some breeds and never flighty. Since they are larger birds, hawks also tend to give them a pass. This chicken is one of those instances where you would want to increase your coop size based upon your chickens' needs. While not a top egg producer, they still lay 150 to 200 eggs or an average of two to four eggs each week. It's no surprise that their eggs are on the larger side and range from light to medium brown. Because of their size, they are slow to mature, and considering their size and weight; this is another breed that you would want to provide perches lower to the ground to avoid leg injuries. If you have a smaller free-range area, this may not be enough space to host these giants. These are easy birds to raise, but their feed intake will be more costly because of their slower rate of growth.

Black Copper Marans

While described as a docile bird, the Maran is not at all cuddly. Right now, the hens from this breed are making a comeback in the backyard coop, especially because of the dark, chocolate-colored eggs that it lays. Overall, this breed is described as quiet and gentle, but the roosters have been known to be more aggressive with other roosters. However, they have proven to be hardy in the winter months if given adequate shelter in their coop environment. The average hen production is between 150 to 200 eggs each year or about three per week. This breed is a bit more costly than most, and if you live in a colder climate, their overly large comb may make them more likely for frostbite, which can cause their comb to die off. Overall, hatchery chicks are most likely your best avenue for purchase unless you are looking for a show chicken, in which case, you may want to investigate some reputable breeders.

Mille Fleurs

This Belgian chicken is kid-friendly, and even though they are on the smaller side, their personalities are *huge*. Mille Fleur bantams were originally developed to be show birds, and they normally weigh about two pounds. These birds tend to love to be in the company of humans and would also make a fantastic therapy chicken! This breed of chicken is usually the first at the coop door every morning waiting for their human to arrive. The roosters are known to be as patient as the hens and typically don't show any territorial actions. The only problem you as an owner will have with this gentle-natured bird is that between their size and demeanor, they will always be on the bottom of the flock's pecking order. To make sure that they get their fair share of the chow, you should have plenty of feeding areas so that they don't get pushed out.

Plymouth Rock

Known as one of the oldest breeds in America, the Plymouth Rock breed was at one time the nation's primary source of chicken eggs and meat. This breed is known for its black and white bar plumage. These hens average about four eggs each week, which equals around 200 eggs each year. In the first couple of years, the hens lay well, but by the third year, most owners will see a decline in the number of eggs they receive. However, this seems to balance out since these hens are known to lay into their tenth year. These hens usually make good sitters and even better moms. The Barred Rocks are generally mellow birds that are known for good attitudes and getting along well with all their coop companions. Even the roosters in this breed are described as docile, calm, and sweet. They are often described as curious birds that love to follow their owners around just in case they are hiding some treats. Even though they tolerate confinement, they relish their free space. This breed has considerable longevity and can live from 10 to 12 years. They are a good choice for first-time chicken owners, and if you like to make a fuss over your chickens, this breed is a fantastic choice, and should your children be involved in 4-H, this would be an excellent breed for them to exhibit. This is a versatile breed that can fill any direction you wish to take.

Rhode Island Reds

This is an appropriate choice for someone who has never had chickens before. They are friendly, easy-going, and easy to care for. Someone new to chickens will be pleased with their egg production (250 to 300 light brown eggs a year). This popular breed is found in every corner of the globe, and they are personable as well as hardy. Since they are active foragers, they are entertaining to observe and usually end up somewhere in the middle of the pack in the pecking order. While the Reds tolerate confinement, they do enjoy getting out and stretching their legs and certainly aren't opposed to the occasional mouse that crosses its path! The hens are laid back for adults and children, but the roosters can be aggressive. If you are hemming and hawing about what chickens to add to your flock, choose some red hens because you just cannot go wrong with this choice. The only problem you might find with the Rhode Island Reds is that you may not find all their eggs because they are predator savvy and like to hide them.

Silkies

Silkies are great with children, and as their name implies, they will feel, well, silky! A Silky's feathers are different because they lack barbicels, which is what gives other feathers their stiff appearance. Silkies are known to be quiet and tolerant as well as good mothers. They are known for becoming broody and will even hatch other breeds of chickens.

Sussex

This breed has been around for a couple of centuries, and with good reason, the Sussex is a dual-purpose hen that provides steady egg production as well as being a good meat bird. The gentle disposition of this bird makes them a favorite because they are easy to handle. The Sussex is considered a year-round bird that is hardy in the winter and will tolerate the hot rays of summer as long as there are shady places and cool water. Both the hens and roosters are described as being mellow, and since they are not an aggressive breed, they should never be put in with breeds that demonstrate any signs of violent behavior. The Sussex will always be at the bottom of the flock's pecking order and may even be subjected to flock bullying. This breed is an excellent choice for first-time chicken owners since they are low maintenance, fast to mature, and docile. Their eggs are brown and tend to run largely with about four to five eggs each week, translating to 208 to 260 eggs each year. One interesting thing about this breed is that they will continue to lay during the winter months when other breeds are on strike. They tend to be broody and make great mothers. Except for leaning toward obesity, this breed of chicken has no health issues that stand out. If you want their egg production to remain steady, you will have to make sure they stay slim and trim. Children love this breed since these birds enjoy the company of humans and like being held and stroked. If you talk to them, you may just receive some chicken conversation when they decide to chime in. Besides being an excellent breed for beginner owners, they also make great birds for 4-H projects.

White Leghorn

While white is the color most closely associated with the Leghorn, they do come in other colors. Leghorns are intelligent, active, and resourceful birds that are also a bit on the aloof and flighty side. They can also be described as noisy birds, so they are not for people that have nearby neighbors who can get easily annoyed. The Leghorn hens are popular because they will lay 280 to 320 eggs each year or four or more eggs per week. An odd fact about this breed of hen is that her eggs start off as large and are actually transformed into extra-large by the end of her laying cycle. They have been purposely bred to resist being broody, and they are considered to be pretty poor mothers, so if you want to raise chicks, you will either have to get a surrogate Silkie to sit on her eggs or place them in an incubator. If they are in colder climates, you may have to watch for frostbitten combs and wattles, treating them with Vaseline. Leghorns are not noted to be overly friendly or cuddly, and if you cannot locate them, you may find them roosting in a nearby tree. They can still provide you with hours of chicken entertainment, so pull up a chair and watch for a while.

And Now for Something Completely Different… Guineas!

While not quite a chicken, Guinea hens are an occasional layer, but their best job is as a pest control agent. They can be a bit difficult to allow free range without barriers as Guineas tend to go *walkabout* to borrow an Australian phrase. Visitors will definitely give these birds a second glance because they just cannot figure out where to place them. Is it a turkey? A chicken? While they are chicken-like birds, this family of fowl will scour your gardens, pastures, and yards for beetles, locusts, spiders, ticks, cockroaches, wasps, flies, termites, grubs, snails, and even scorpions!

Guineas are native to Africa but arrived in North America with early settlers. They are a rather unique-looking bird with its white featherless face, gray polka-dot feathers, and bright red wattles. Because these birds prefer weeds, seeds, and insects (along with the occasional mouse or scorpion), they are often put to work clearing rows between crops and hunting the pests that reside in the fields.

Free-ranging guineas will spend almost all of their day foraging, and if you have several, they work in tandem and snap up anything they startle, for example, a small snake. They are a bit noisier than chickens because when they find some prey, the pack of them will all emit whistles, clicks, and chirps of excitement and commentary on their subject. If you have less than forgiving neighbors, guineas may not be a good fit for your flock because they are noisy. Be forewarned that they can easily destroy blossoming plants in a heartbeat. However, they can provide some great protection for the rest of your flock.

Guineas do not take confinement very well, so they may also not be a good fit if you have limited space. While guineas are not overly friendly, dislike snow, and are difficult to catch, they are considered low-maintenance poultry that will lay about 100 eggs each year. Guineas that are raised with chickens are tamer than guineas that are the sole species of bird. While you may find that a guinea will mate with a chicken, the sterile offspring tend to look a little like a vulture.

Since guineas are not known to be the best mothers, many keetlings are hatched using an incubator. A keet or keetling is what a baby guinea is called, and if you want to raise a few guineas and plan to free-range, we suggest that you start with keets as opposed to purchasing full-grown birds. While still babies, the keets become accustomed to their new home and will be less likely to split the first chance they get, unlike adult guineas.

Because keets are extra small and extremely delicate, they are fragile and can be trampled during their first few weeks of life. Until they reach the three weeks of age mark, keets should be kept off to themselves and before being moved into larger coop areas. You will not see any feathers develop on them until they are about a month old, and these will be a camouflage-brown color.

They are not ready to care for themselves until their gray feathers have grown in.

To feed keets, you should try a 21 to 23 percent protein feed, like a commercial turkey starter or even mashed-up hard-boiled eggs mixed with a little cornmeal, oatmeal, or cottage cheese. When they reach four weeks of age, you can switch them to an 18% grower ration.

Now for the tarantula story that we promised you earlier! Once upon a time, we were visiting some friends out in Arizona who kept a substantial amount of guinea fowl. Suddenly, there was quite a ruckus from the yard, and our friend encouraged us to watch a tarantula migration that had drifted right through the guinea pen area. It was a massacre! Guineas were snapping up those spiders faster than you could blink, and for years afterward, during other tarantula migrations, the herd traveled out and around the guinea enclosure! We are positive that the hens were very disappointed.

Chapter 4:
Know What You Are Getting Into

Raising your own chickens can be a great experience, that is, as long as you have taken the time to prepare for ownership and reviewed all the essential needs that you and your chickens will need in order for you to both be happy.

The last thing that anyone wants to do is jump into a hobby farm without knowing what to expect. This can lead to becoming overwhelmed and frustrated, making chicken ownership a less than fantastic experience.

First and foremost, you need to check any restrictions regarding the keeping of chickens on your property. There are usually rules that prevent you from owning a rooster. Still, they may stipulate how many chickens you are allowed, how far your chicken coop and run must be from a neighboring property line, or even if there is a fine involved in chicken ownership. One of our good friends was disturbed to find out that her city would fine her fifty dollars per bird each day for the breaking of any city rules governing the ownership of chickens.

Can You Do Chicken Math?

If you have space, always plan for more chickens eventually. However, there is this freak of nature called *chicken math*. How this works is that you have plans for one to three chickens, but it quickly turns into three to five, and suddenly you have about ten hens.

The point is that chickens are super addictive, and when you see some cute chicks, then you will want to add more to your flock. Chickens are as addictive as potato chips, and the bottom line is you're going to need a bigger coop!

Be Prepared

Chickens, like any other pet or farm animal, are a daily commitment. It's not that they are complicated because once you have their care down to a routine, you will find that caring for your flock is very easy. Even novice owners will be able to break down which chores are daily, weekly, monthly, or even yearly. It goes without saying that you will need to supply your flock with daily fresh food and water.

Daily, you should always glance at your chickens to make sure that they all look and act healthy. Novices may be surprised at how quickly your favorite hen can spiral downhill. If you notice one chicken that is not quite right, there is no shame in separating her from the rest of the flock while you put in a call to your veterinarian.

There seems to be some debate on what you should do after collecting your hen's eggs, but you never need to wash them until you are ready to use them (unless they are, well, poopy). This is because when eggs are laid, their shells possess a nearly invisible natural coating referred to as *bloom*, and this coating will keep air and bacteria out of the egg. This is nature's way of keeping the egg fresher for a longer period of time. This may seem like a difficult thing to grasp, but as long as you don't wash your eggs, there is no need to refrigerate them. Did you know that the United States is one of the only countries where eggs are refrigerated?

One day out on the counter at room temperature will be equal to a week in the refrigerator. The rule of thumb is that an egg will last longer if you refrigerate them, so if you have more eggs than you can consume within a week, you will want to refrigerate them. However, if you practice washing your eggs as soon as you collect them, then you should refrigerate them immediately. Store your eggs pointy side down to keep them fresher longer. If you have a backlog of eggs, you may find it helpful to mark your eggs lightly with a pencil to keep track of the dates they were collected.

This rule of thumb, however, only applies to your backyard eggs and not the store-bought variety. Through processing, the bloom has already been removed from these eggs, so they will always need to be refrigerated. The same rule will apply to any eggs that have already been refrigerated—once in the fridge, they should stay in the fridge!

If you want to leave your eggs out, you can leave them in a bowl on the counter and rinse them off with some warm water prior to being used. If at any time you feel unsure about one of your eggs, you can always perform the float test.

The Egg Float Test

Let's face it; if you have a sizable flock, you may find that sometimes the eggs will take on a life of their own, and you will be left with a sizable amount of them. You may even miss one tucked in the corner of your favorite hen's nesting box, and you wonder how long that's been there. Perhaps you own a sneaky hen who has hidden some eggs under one of your bushes, and the time frame of when they were laid may be unknown. Yard eggs are perfectly acceptable as long as they aren't cracked.

If you are worried about an egg's freshness, or lack thereof, you can perform the egg float test. To do this, fill a tall glass with warm water. If you use cold water and there is any bacteria present, the chill could cause it to be drawn into the egg. Gently drop your egg into the glass and pay attention to what your egg does next.

- If fresh, an egg will lie flat on the bottom of the glass.

- An egg that is one to two weeks old will start to rise off the bottom of the glass.

- If your egg in question is two months old or thereabouts, you will notice that the egg will be standing straight up, and the pointy end will be touching the bottom of the glass.

- Any egg that is older than three months or floats to the top of the glass is considered bad and should be thrown out.

The reason an egg rises is because air has seeped in through the pores of the eggshell, causing the air sac inside the egg to enlarge and dry out the egg. This will cause one end of the egg to rise. You should note too, that an egg will start losing nutrients as it ages, but it will still be perfectly good to consume. Once you have put your eggs in water, you have removed the natural bloom, and if you are keeping it, you should refrigerate it or use it immediately. Older eggs often peel better if you hard-boil them (and add a dash of salt). Keep to the old adage; when in doubt, throw it out.

Can you test an egg without placing it in water? Some say that you can shake an egg, and should you hear sloshing inside, the egg has probably gone bad. If you are worried about a certain egg, always break it separately in a bowl instead of directly into the dish you are preparing. If it smells bad, looks discolored, or cloudy, you should throw it away.

Tips for Collecting Clean Backyard Eggs

While you may or may not choose to store your eggs on the counter, no one wants to look at messy or dirty eggs, so here are a few tips we can share with you to keep it clean!

- When possible, do not allow your hens to sleep in the nesting boxes. It's true; chickens will poop even when they are asleep. With chickens instinctively looking for the highest place to sleep, you should always place your roosts higher than your nesting boxes. If you have a stubborn hen who insists on sleeping in her box, lift her out and place her on a roost after dark in an attempt to condition them to roost. Should she persist, you may need to block off the boxes during the late afternoon once your hens have laid their eggs.

- Every morning, change the bedding in your nesting boxes. By making it part of your morning routine, it will be simple to fluff your hen's bedding and keep it clean.

- Keep your nesting boxes on the wall that is opposite the coop door. By making your hens walk all the way across the coop, they might hopefully shed any mud or excess dirt they have on their feet.

- Persuade your broody hens to stop sitting on non-fertile eggs. If you don't have a rooster, then your eggs will not be fertilized, and your broody hens don't need to be sitting on them. By hogging a nest, your broody hen may have other hens start picking on her, which can result in the broody hen being injured, broken eggs, or egg eating. Some methods to discourage a broody hen are

- To collect any eggs from her as soon as possible, even if you need to collect a few times a day.

- Gently, remove your broody hen from her chosen nest and carry her to the far end of your chicken habitat, where you have scattered some of her favorite treats.

- Remove her from the nest and place her on a roosting bar after dark.

- Place a frozen water bottle in the nest she covets.

- Block her chosen nest.

- You should collect your eggs regularly to help protect them from predators.

Daily Needs

In addition to providing fresh food and clean water, you should lock your chickens up every night in order to keep them safe from any predators in the area. Keep an eye on your flock's pecking order since an ill chicken may cause a change in her status within the group.

When your hens are laying, they may need to add an additional level of calcium to help make strong eggshells. To aid your hens, you should provide a separate dish with cracked oyster shells. This will serve as a natural supplement to your feed. Serving this free choice allows your chickens to only take what they need instead of putting it in with your feed.

If you are new to chickens, you will probably be overwhelmed at how much and how often your bird poops. There is no denying it; chickens require a lot of cleanup effort. When you multiply that by the number of birds you own, you will need a plan in place on how you plan to deal with all the poop.

Frequent Needs

Even chickens need to be groomed. We already explained the importance of dust baths, but you will have to also keep an eye on their nails and their feet. Watch for ulcers on their footpads as these can lead to other problems, like lameness or infection.

Keep your chickens separated during transport. These can be cat carriers or cages and have holes for proper ventilation. Your chickens should be able to sit comfortably, and you can cushion the box with some soft bedding. You should also take along some food and water so that you can make a few stops during the trip to eat and drink.

Monthly Coop Care

For the best results in cleanliness, you should change the bedding in the chicken coop monthly. Failure to clean your coop monthly could result in an ammonia build-up, which can cause respiratory illness. Some people have used a hack consisting of placing dropping boards under the roosting poles to speed clean up the morning. By doing this, you can lift out the trays, hose them off and place them back inside for the next night.

Twice a Year

It's a great idea to completely clean your chicken coop from top to bottom every six months. What this means is that you not only will remove all the bedding, nests, and feed containers, but you will scrub them down with the preferred solution of one part bleach, one part dish soap, and ten parts water. After washing down everything, rinse them, and then allow them to dry thoroughly before rebedding or replacing food and water containers.

Want to keep the chemicals out of your coop? You can mix up this all-natural coop cleaner!

Ingredients

- 6 grapefruit or 8 oranges or 12 limes or lemons
- Apple cider vinegar
- Glass jar
- Refillable spray bottle

Directions

1. Clean out the juice and insides of the fruits you have chosen to use. Hopefully, you have something in mind to use these for since this recipe utilizes only the skins of the fruit.

2. Place the fruit skins into a large jar (with an air-tight lid) and add apple cider vinegar until the skins are completely submerged.

3. Find an out-of-the-way place for this to sit and ferment for the length of two weeks.

4. Once those two weeks are up, grab a strainer and empty the contents of the jar through it. You will keep the liquid and discard the skins.

5. Use equal parts of water and solution in your sprayer, and the best part is that you can use it as a cleaner in your home as well!

Seasonal Chicken Care

You have done the research and selected the correct breeds based upon your geographical location, but there are a couple of things that you may have to do for seasonal care.

Chickens are usually able to adapt to cold weather changes, but you may need to rub petroleum jelly on their wattles and combs to protect your flock from frostbite. You should have a plan in place to make sure that your chicken's water supply doesn't freeze. If you live in a colder climate, you should have electricity in your coop so that you can use a water heater. Even though it's cold, make sure that there are no drafts present. The presence of a draft can result in illness in even the healthiest of chickens. You may want to shield them with some plastic sheeting surrounding their coop or even their yard.

Overheating is also a danger to your flock, and that is why you need to provide them with shade and ventilation. Times of extreme heat can be a stressor to your birds, so don't be surprised when their egg production drops until temperatures regulate.

Here Come the Rodents

One big thing that people aren't always prepared for is rodent control. There are always mice, rats, chipmunks, and squirrels around, but they can become a huge problem quickly. One way to try and deter them is to use an invasive plant such as mint. It's a quick-growing plant that replicates quickly, and rodents just hate the smell.

Chicken Predators Are Relentless

You have your coop and yard all planned out, and you feel that you have crossed every T and dotted every I until a predator strikes. Every potential predator will notice that you have a new addition, and they will be not only checking out your flock, but they will also be studying how to attack them. The persistence of these predators will frustrate and surprise you with how intelligent they can be.

It's heartbreaking to open your coop door and find out that your flock has been wiped out, so to keep your chickens safe, you will need to predator-proof your coop. You may think that traps or your trusty shotgun might be the best solution, but it can be illegal to seek this kind of revenge. Plus, if you have a coop on a small acreage, trust me, your neighbors will not take kindly to the use of a gun.

Your best defense against chicken predators is to keep a sturdy and tight coop that will make entry impossible. Were you aware that a mink can squeeze through a one-inch diameter hole? Did you also know that weasels can fit through something even smaller? Here are a few ways to predator-proof your coop at night.

- Just before dusk, close and latch all coop doors.

- Use a strong mesh wire to cover all your windows. Do not employ chicken wire because a raccoon can tear through that wire like a hot knife through butter. A one-half-inch square hardware wire will keep out the raccoons and the minks too.

- Use concrete, calking, wire, or expanding foam to fill in any holes or large cracks that form around doors, windows, or in walls.

- Walk around the perimeter of your yard and coop and look for any indication that something has been trying to dig under the coop walls or yard enclosures. You can bury mesh at least one foot deep around the sides of your chicken coop and yard, which will deter predators from digging.

- Do you have piles of firewood, brush piles, or other things on your property in which predators can successfully hide? You are going to want to eliminate any of those potential havens for chicken enemies.

- Install motion detector lights that can startle potential predators as they approach.

- Never leave uneaten food lying around to attract predators. You should always clean up the excess and store any chicken food in air-tight, odor-free containers.

You will have an entirely new set of challenges for the daytime predators who also would love nothing more than to snatch a quick bite to eat. Surprisingly, neighborhood dogs are large chicken killers, but you also have to worry about the predators from above, like hawks, owls, and eagles. There are weasels, minks, and foxes that are out hunting during the day, but it is rare to see a raccoon, opossum, or skunk unless it is at least dusk. Some measures that you can take during the day are found below.

- A sturdy fence will keep your chickens in and thwart the neighborhood dogs and foxes, but not coyotes. A decent height would be about four feet tall. This will keep in your heavier chicken breeds, but if you have some chickens that are smaller in stature, you will want a six or eight-foot fence in place.

- Electric poultry fencing can be a good option against ground predators.

- Provide your flock with some overhead protection. If you want to keep the raptors from diving out of the sky to snatch up your precious flock members, then you will want to cover your runs with wire mesh. If an overhead mesh is not practical for you, then make sure that you give your chickens somewhere to hide not only from predators but the hot sun. Plant a few shrubs or give them something like a picnic table for cover.

Chicken owners can be lulled into a false sense of security when no attempts by predators are made for months, but then suddenly, your whole flock is gone. You would be amazed at how quickly a lot of birds can be wiped out. Prevention is the only way to keep them safe. If you have taken all these measures and are still plagued by wildlife predators, you may need a licensed wildlife trapping service.

You can bet if there is a puzzle, even a complicated one, neighborhood raccoons will figure it out. And if they can't, they are known to pull a chicken's head through the wire mesh in place and leave the body behind. You are not the only one around that loves a good chicken dinner! You will have to outwit many of these following predators.

- Foxes
- Coyotes
- Raccoons
- Bobcats
- Opossums
- Skunks
- Weasels
- Squirrels
- Bears
- Neighborhood dogs
- Neighborhood or feral cats
- Minks
- Owls
- Hawks
- Eagles

- Cats

- Snakes

- Rats

How to Introduce Your Own Dogs to Your Flock

Above, we talked about neighborhood dogs, but what about your own dogs and how they will react to your newest additions? The key is to start with short introductions, and hopefully, you have a well-trained dog that will listen to the sit and stay commands. While your chickens are protected inside the confines of their coop, this is a perfect time to make that first introduction to Fido. Take your dog near the bird enclosure, so each of the species has time to see and smell each other. Continue these short-timed introductions until they seem to accept each other and remain calm.

Once this step proves successful, you can try holding a chicken while your dog is secured and see what kind of reaction you receive. If both remain calm, your next step is to try letting your birds free-range in an area and bring your dog out on a leash. Watch their responses to each other. Each animal has a different response time so give your dog and chickens a chance to be comfortable while having the other around. If you see that things are progressing and there are no negative responses, then you can try a supervised mixer between species.

It is important to take your time because this is a huge adjustment for your dog, and you should know that some dogs will never mix well with chickens. Let your dog know if they are not behaving properly, just like you would if they were refusing to sit or stay. There are some breeds of dogs that have a prey drive and are bred specifically to hunt, and you should realize that this may never be overcome. Your dog should never be allowed to ingest any of the chicken's food or water because they, too, are susceptible to salmonella, and this could make them very ill. If you are using a medicated feed for your chickens, you should be aware that this can also make your dog sick.

Both dogs and chickens can live in harmony. Just take things slow, and should your dog not want to be friends with your chickens, don't be upset with your dog. Sometimes you just can't undo generations of characteristics.

Plan for a Place to Keep Ill Birds

You think that you will never have a sick bird, but then you observe Pricilla, and she looks a bit off. Now, you wish you had planned on an isolation area or sickbay.

It's a common theme when chicken owners reflect on their humble beginnings, that they had all wished they had taken time to plan better and calculated expenses better when they first started. Building a coop and run is not something you want to do twice! Take into account the costs and all the wonderful new inventions that you can equip your coop with, but you may want to skip the widescreen television and the satellite dish.

- Automatic chicken doors
- Chicken swings
- Water base heater
- Goodnature rat and mouse trap
- Electric poultry netting
- Chicken clothing
- Roll out nesting boxes
- Incubator
- Brooder

Chickens Love to Dig

If your goal is to free-range your chickens, you need to know that your property will suffer from the march of the chickens. You may think that it's cool to watch your chickens dig, scratch, and peck at the soil in search of a tasty insect or grubworm, but you should be prepared to watch your vegetables, fruits, and expensive landscape plants fall victim to your chickens' path of discovery. They love nothing more than the challenge of unpotting your potted plants and consuming all your new sprouts of grass you are attempting to grow after last year's march of the chickens.

Besides hunting in the soil, chickens will consume a large number of inedible objects too, so if your yard has pieces of Styrofoam, wood, plastic, glass, nails, or other foreign objects, you might find that they will eat these right alongside your cherry tomatoes.

Zoonosis

If you are unfamiliar with this term, this is what a disease that can be transferred from animal to human is called. While the risk from chickens is rated low, very low, or extremely low, you should still be aware that they exist. Usually, both campylobacter and salmonella are caused by not cooking chicken or their eggs properly. However, all live fowl carry salmonella germs in their guts. Your poultry can have the salmonella germs present in their droppings, which can transmit to their feathers, feet, and even their beaks. As your chickens walk around their coop, they can contaminate their coops, cages, bedding, feed, and water dishes. This is why keeping everything clean is so very important. We encourage you to wear gloves and wash your hands immediately after handling chickens and their surroundings.

The categories with the most risk are children younger than the age of five, adults over the age of 65, or people that have weakened immune systems. Below are some basic rules to follow when handling any kind of poultry.

- Poultry should be kept outdoors. While it might be tempting to allow your favorite chicken to roam around your home, they can spread salmonella germs to your home surfaces.

- Always wash your hands thoroughly with soap and water after handling your chickens, their eggs, or anything within their domain, like feeders or waterers. If you don't have a place readily accessible to soap and water, use some hand sanitizer.

- Do not snuggle, kiss, or hold your live poultry near your face (besides salmonella exposure, they could peck you, and that hurts). You should also avoid eating or drinking in the chicken enclosure.

- Cook your eggs thoroughly until both the white and the yolk are firm.

- Only clean your poultry equipment outside of the home. All cages, feed, or water containers should be cleaned outside of the home. One of the best things that you can do is to dedicate a single pair of shoes to wear while performing your poultry chores, and you would be wise to keep them outside of the home.

- Children under five years of age, adults over 65, or people with weakened immune systems should avoid handling live poultry. Younger children are most at risk because their immune systems are still in development, and they are far more likely to stick their fingers in their mouths. Anyone with a severe immune disease is especially at risk for salmonella.

Avian flu or bird flu is monitored closely by the Department of Agriculture, and to date, there has never been a single case of avian flu in the United States. It is thought that, should there ever be an outbreak, it will most likely come from a large commercial flock and not from a smaller-scale, backyard operation. Most of the cases reported in the world are usually based in Asia or the Middle East and involve children handling sick or diseased chickens.

We never even considered this, but just in case it comes up during some dinner party conversation when you cannot stop talking about chickens, chickenpox has absolutely nothing to do with chickens. The original reason that this disease was so named was that the blisters were thought to look like chickpeas.

Children & Chickens

Young children may not realize how fragile a newly hatched chick is and should not be allowed to hold them for both their sakes. Raising chickens can be a marvelous educational tool, but you need to know that your children are educated before handling any of the chicks or chickens, and you would follow the same rules that you would for them handling a newborn puppy or kitten.

Raising children together with chickens can enrich their lives, bringing them an understanding of food production and responsibility. Given time, children will experience some unforgettable life lessons and may even develop an interest in showing chickens through their local 4-H group.

There are some common-sense avenues to follow while your children share their lives with chickens.

- Pick out some child-friendly breeds. In Chapter 3, we gave you a list of some great starter breeds for your new venture and made comments to those breeds considered child friendly.

- If possible, you should pick out your chicks together, but since many come via mail order that may not always be possible.

- Teach your children the correct way to hold chicks and make sure that they understand how fragile they are.

- Pick out names for your new chicks.

- Build a chicken coop and discuss all the options for keeping your chickens safe and happy.

- Watch your chickens grow through that gawky teenage stage.

- Have a celebration when your new chicks grow old enough to lay their first egg.

- Practice safe chicken handling and practice biosecurity rules.

- **Wash hands!**

What's the Tab?

So, how much does it cost to raise some chickens? Prices change from year to year, so we have included a blank chart to follow, but you are going to want to figure out a five-year cost, add that up, and then divide it by 60 months to get an average cost per month. Of course, this cannot include any medical costs because there is no way to know how much that may or may not be.

Item	Approximate 5 Year Cost
A Hand-Made Chicken Coop for # of Chickens	$

Fencing Costs	$
Chicken Feed	$
Bedding	$
Cost of # of Chickens	$
Coop Supplies: Feeders, Waterers, etc.	$

Add your costs together, then divide by 60 months, and you should come out with a cost per month on your chicken venture. *Tip: Calculate on the high side to be safe. This way, if it ends up averaging a bit less, you will be happy. Adding more chickens and keeping them longer can drive your per month cost down.*

Despite all these concerns, most chicken owners would not only do it all again; they would have done it sooner. Why? Because chickens are cool!

Chapter 5:
If You Build it, They Will Come

Your chickens will need a coop, and this is going to be the biggest and most important item you will struggle with. Designs are extremely personal, and you want to make sure that you have done everything just right, so you won't experience any regrets. How large you should make it is going to depend on how well you do chicken math.

There is an old saying that ingenuity is the mother of invention, and you only have to browse the internet a bit to find some truly innovative ways to set up a coop while not taxing your budget. Even if you are on a strict budget, the chicken coop will be the most important investment when it comes to safely raising your chickens. Truthfully, if you are lacking in carpentry skills, there are still some impressive, prefabricated buildings out there for you to purchase.

Tips for First-Time Builders

We would be remiss if we didn't tell you about some big mistakes that first-time coop builders make, so before we get into construction, you should probably consider some of the following points.

Plan Out Everything

The devil is in the details, so plan out everything before you build. After choosing a suitable plan, make sure that you select materials that are readily available and easy to work with. Doors should open inward, and you will want to take into consideration that your chickens will need lots of fresh air since they still spend a considerable amount of time in the coop, even if they are free-range. Sliding windows will help provide them with some cool summer breezes.

Keeping your floors clean is very important, and you will need to cover them with materials to keep your chickens busy digging and scratching even when they are cooped up. In addition, your floors should slope slightly toward the door in case you ever need to hose the coop out, leaving you with a clean coop and not lingering puddles.

Good Ventilation and Insulation Are a Must

Any farm building that houses livestock needs good ventilation, and a chicken coop is no exception. You want free movement of air but no drafts. Without the benefit of air movement, you will risk a buildup of high carbon monoxide and humidity levels. Your chickens will be uncomfortable and stressed, which will cause them to lay fewer eggs, and it can also promote the growth of mold in your coop and within the walls.

Insulate your walls. This helps your flock stay cool in the summer and warm in the winter. Insulation helps to regulate humidity levels inside the coop and will keep your chickens healthier.

Food and Water Placement Matters

Proper placement of the feeders and waterers is important and should be raised to about the height of a chicken's back. The reasoning for this is very simple: your chickens can reach up a bit to get their food and water, but they cannot get their feet in it. There is nothing more frustrating than setting out clean feeders and waterers only to have your chickens hop in and start scratching and pooping. Make sure that feeders and waterers are far away from roosts so that they don't get pooped in.

Chickens and Leftovers

Your chickens can eat a lot of your kitchen leftovers, but you should be sure to remove anything left uneaten from their coop. Any remaining pieces may mold or decay, bringing bacteria to your chicken's home, which could make them ill or bring rodents and predators. Food scraps should be limited and add up to 10% or less of their daily intake.

Not everything is going to be safe to give to your chickens, and some can even be deadly. Below, we have listed some common food leftovers that you should never give to your birds.

- Dry beans and lentils

- Dry rice

- Avocado

- Apple seeds

- Chocolate

- Tomatoes

- Eggplants

- Onions

- Lettuce

- Spinach

- Rhubarb

- Mushrooms

- Coffee

- Tea

In addition to these, you should avoid feeding foods that have been fried or seasoned to be salty or sweet. Too much excess fat, sodium, or sugar can make your chickens sick. Even though we eat these, they aren't really good for us either, so don't give them to your flock.

Keep the Elements in Mind

Design your coop with a good light source in mind. If you face your coop south, they should receive maximum sunlight throughout the day. You should plan on installing a light in your coop for the winter months when days are shorter, and the sunlight is fleeting. Added light in the winter will also help to keep your egg production flowing, and your chickens will remain happy.

Coops should always protect your flock from the elements. Think of this as their home, and just like yours, it should be properly sealed against drafts.

Don't forget that your coop should be elevated to keep out the dampness. When it rains, your coop should remain dry.

Predatory Dangers

Your coop should also protect your flock from predators. We already talked about this in the previous chapter, but look over those points so that you can keep your flock safe. After a predator attack, you should keep the flock cooped for a few days.

Always perform a bed check. Then, every night, count your chickens to ensure that some broody hen isn't hiding in the bushes, making her vulnerable to an attack from predators.

This may not be an obvious strategy, but if any friend visits with their dogs, they should always be leashed. Nothing is going to kill a friendship faster than having their dog kill your favorite chicken right in front of you.

Have a Poop Plan!

This may sound ridiculous to you, but when you install your roosts, there are some ways to thwart all the nighttime chicken droppings. It can be as simple as placing older cookie sheets underneath them at night and hosing them off each morning, leaving your bedding clean and ready for the next day.

Size Matters

Build it big enough. If you have plans of ever adding more chickens at a future date, always build a little bigger than your original plans.

Building a Coop

Gosh, where to start! There are so many directions to travel in regard to your coop. Just remember to build the hen house before you bring your chickens home to roost.

Prefab

There are many pre-built chicken coop designs that it can be tough to pick just one. When deciding, make sure that you keep your climate in mind. Prices can vary, but you can expect to pay anything from around $170 to $8,000, depending on what you want to spend.

- Apex house designs are proven and less expensive than other designs. They have wire floors that can stop both predators and your chickens from digging.

- Rectangular houses typically have a sloping roof to the coop and a flat top over the run area. The roofs are either sliding or hinged for easy access. These are usually raised over a section of your chickens' run, which can make it easier to clean, feed, and collect eggs.

Elevated chicken coops are typically around two feet off the ground, and your chickens can make their way in through a small ladder. While this is not a coop built for cold winters, if you live in a warmer area, this will keep burrowing animals out, and when placed in a run, this will provide your flock with some extra protection from the elements. Raised coops are usually a stationary construct, but some designs can lend themselves to add some wheel attachments, making them mobile. If you choose not to rotate areas, your chickens will likely turn the patch underneath their coop into their dust bath area.

These ready-made hen houses always look great in a catalog, but, if possible, you should try to see them in person. Be objective and determine if you can clean it out without having to dismantle the whole kit and caboodle. Does it seem sturdy? A raised structure can be easier to clean and collect eggs, but they can be top-heavy. If you live in an area with windstorms, you don't want your girls in danger. Always read online reviews of the product to see what other people have to say about the model and learn from their experiences.

While stationary homes tend to be a bit larger, the smaller units can be movable. If you opt for a movable house and run, you should plan on moving it about every three days as a minimum; more often is ideal. The concept is to never let your grass get too worn down. The aid of a tractor can move some larger portable coops and runs, but these can house as many as 25 chickens, and by the time you climb to a flock of that size, you are considered a serious chicken owner and should consider building something more permanent.

Many first-time chicken owners opt to begin with a prefabricated coop as a starting off point when deciding if chicken ownership is right for them. Once you are hooked, you can always design your own.

Build it Yourself

If you are handy or perhaps have a really good friend that can swing a hammer with the best of them, you can make the chicken coop of your dreams. If you can build a coop, make sure that you add an equally wonderful run to keep your flock happy and healthy. Regardless of how *eggstravagant* you make your custom coop, you will still need to include all the basic niceties for your flock. Keeping it safe and functional doesn't mean that it has to be boring. Follow your muse and add some style!

If you don't own a lot of tools, don't worry, it doesn't take many tools to build your coop, just a few common hand and power tools, and you will be all set. If you have to borrow tools from a friend, make sure that you invite them over to help. All you have to do is to promise to give them some fresh eggs, and most will be delighted to help. Make sure you offer them snacks and refreshments for the duration of the project.

Many of these tools you probably have laying around the house anyway and may depend upon the kind of coop you are planning to build. Here are a few tools you will need to create your coop.

- Safety gear like work gloves, hearing protection, and protective goggles.
- Tape measure
- L ruler
- Circular saw
- Hammer
- Drill

- Levels. Preferably a pocket-sized, two-foot, and four-foot model.

- Speed square

- Tin snips, because there is bound to be some wire involved somewhere in your coop or run.

When building your chicken coop, make sure that you take your time to think things through. If you are looking for ideas to incorporate, take a look at premade plans to see if they have any groundbreaking ideas that you want to include.

Write down all your steps and ideas. By doing this, you will be able to make a detailed list of all the materials and equipment you will need. Remember that cramped birds are unhappy, so the bigger the space, the better!

Repurposing

Perhaps your property already has an unused shed that you can repurpose? Conversion can be a fun project, and you can design the interior any way that you wish. This can save you a lot of time and materials since the shell is already there and all you need to do is customize it. When modifying an existing building, make sure to raise the flooring off the ground to prevent any possibilities of flooding or rotting of floorboards. You may need to also redesign the ventilation of the shed.

Have an old childhood playhouse on the property? This might also make a really cute coop! Tired of your she-shed? It can still be repurposed for chicks! Maybe you have access to some architectural salvage or even an old unused silo? You can decorate these any way you want too! There is no reason you can't make it look metropolitan, country chic, or even hang an old chandelier from the ceiling. The point is you can make anything that suits your tastes. We bet if you google custom chicken coops, you can come up with about 20 that you love. Just remember to consider your climate when you design your dream coop.

Nesting Boxes

It can be infuriating to build a dozen nesting boxes, and five hens will crowd into just one box! Don't laugh; it happens, especially since hens will often have favorite boxes in which to deposit their eggs. When figuring out how many nesting boxes you will need, plan on one box for every three to four hens. If you put them at floor level, they will not use them, so make sure they are always a few feet off the ground. The only exception to this might be if you have a breed that doesn't fly, such as a Silkie. They may prefer a ground-level box.

If possible, your nesting boxes should be in a darker area of your coop for privacy, far from feeding stations, and not directly underneath any roosts. If you are fortunate enough to have a spacious coop, you can put nesting boxes in a few different places. You can even place one or two out in the run; just make sure that you collect those eggs before any predators beat you to them.

If you are just starting out, you may find that you need to train your hens in the use of nesting boxes. When they start laying, which is somewhere around the 16-20 weeks of age, you may notice them wandering and looking restless. You can gently guide them to a nest that contains fake eggs or golf balls in the nest. If you have older hens, the younger ones will follow their lead and use a nesting box. Should they need some added incentive, you may need to sprinkle some cracked corn in the boxes, but make sure you keep the nests clean and fresh. If there is poop or dirt in it, they will not use it. Remember earlier in this book, we recommended that you close off these boxes at night so that your chickens won't poop in them and on the eggs. You may find that you have a hen that refuses to use nesting boxes, and you will never change their mind no matter what you do, so don't let it frustrate you.

Hens prefer a clean and cozy nesting box to lay her eggs in. If you don't want to build them, there are several you can purchase from farm stores or online. Just as there are plans online for your coop, there are do-it-yourself plans for nesting boxes as well. The size of your boxes is going to depend on the size of your chickens.

- Bantam chickens tend to prefer smaller boxes, roughly 10 x 12 x 10 inches

- Standard chicken size boxes are 12 x 12 x 12 inches

- Larger breeds need a bit more wiggle room, so plan on 12 x 14 x 12 inches

The preferred materials for nesting boxes are either wood, metal, or plastic since both are easy to maintain and wash. When attaching them to your coop walls, remember that wooden boxes are considerably heavier than plastic ones, so you should have some study walls or supports to hold them in place.

Some chicken owners are very creative when it comes to nesting boxes, and there are examples using wine barrels, five-gallon buckets, plastic milk crates, and even a nest built out of a covered tote.

Granted, some hens often decide to lay their eggs outside, under a large bush, but that makes them hard to retrieve, and predators will beat you to them.

If you are doing something of your own design, you may be able to build nesting boxes that you can access from outside of the coop as well as the inside.

When deciding upon nesting materials, below are a few popular choices. To cover all the hens' choices, you may want to vary what's in your boxes, so they have a choice.

- Pine shavings
- Straw
- Nesting pads (these are washable and inexpensive)
- Pine needles
- Leaves
- Sawdust

Roosting Bars

Roosts are elevated bars that are roughly two to four inches wide, and every coop needs them. They can be made from natural branches, narrow planks, ladders, or long wooden rods, and you should allow at least eight inches of space per hen. Metal bars can be harder to grip and be slippery, especially for an older chicken with arthritis. If you are in a region with cold winters, they could get frostbitten feet.

Chickens will instinctively perch at night, preferring to get off the ground as far as possible, so they remain out of the reach of predators. By sleeping up high, your chickens are also kept from sleeping on the floor of the coop, where they may be lingering bacteria or external parasites.

Having roost bars is highly recommended to keep your flock happy and stress-free. Roosts also allow your submissive birds to avoid their more dominant flockmates. Your bar length and sturdiness may vary depending upon whether you have a flock of bantams or one composed of Jersey Giants and how large your flock is.

You will want to position your bars so that they do not block any entrances, away from feeders, waterers, or nesting boxes, so keep them all clean. In addition, you do not want to position them in front of any ventilation areas in case of winter frostbite.

To appeal to your chickens, these can be placed as close as 18 inches from your coop's ceiling. If you have baby chicks, you can provide a small roosting bar in the brooder.

Dropping Board

This is a collective term that is used to describe placing a board below your chicken's roosts to catch those bedtime poops. This practice enables you to clean daily with ease. The whole idea of a dropping board is so that you clean that more and your coop less. It should just take a few minutes each day.

This isn't a new idea, but the concept leaves the execution open for interpretation. You can literally use anything that your chickens won't be able to tear apart, but there are a few things to keep in mind.

- It should be wide enough to catch all the droppings that fall from your roosting area.

- If you are using a wooden board, you can cover it with something easier to clean, such as scrap linoleum or peel and stick tiles.

- Trays can be filled with sand or Sweet PDZ to make it easier to scoop or scrape.

- It is helpful to have edges to hold the litter (and the poop) in until you can clean and remove it for use the next night.

- Whatever you use, it should be easy to remove for deep cleaning.

Besides making your cleaning chores easier, using a dropping board can have a few other benefits.

- Moisture will be reduced in the coop, which will keep your flock cleaner, healthier, and warmer.

- It will help with a reduction in ammonia, which can damage your chicken's respiratory systems. It can cut down on other odors as well.

- Reduces flies during the warm summer months.

- By keeping your coop clean, you will save money on bedding and also reduce how frequently you need a full coop cleaning.

- By observing overnight droppings, you may be able to identify an illness early.

Without the daily removal of the overnight poops, odor and flies can become a problem. You can quickly clean up a dropping board by removing it and hosing it off.

You can build your very own dropping board! Here's how.

Tools:

- Tape measure
- Pencil
- Handsaw
- Table or circular saw
- Drill with screwdriver bits
- Sandpaper

Materials:

- Plywood - since this will be used as the base of your tray, it should be wide enough to cover the drop zone of your chicken's nightly poops. Ideally, you want it to span the width, but if you have a sizable coop, you may want it in a few sections for more ease of handling.

- 1 x 2 or similar cuts of wood. These boards will be used to create the needed edges of your dropping board. You will need enough to cover the length of your board or boards.

- Vinyl tile or sheet vinyl

- Vinyl glue

- Screws

- Scrap wood to make supports for the dropping board while inside the coop.

Directions:

1. You will need to take your coops layout into account when deciding what size to make your dropping boards and keep them easy to handle.

2. If you don't own power saws or are uncomfortable using them, take time to pre-measure everything you will need to construct your drop boards and have the local home improvement store cut them for you. Some may charge a fee, but most will do this for no additional cost.

3. After the plywood is cut to the correct size, use sandpaper to smooth the edges and remove any hazard of splinters.

4. Measure and cut two pieces of the 1 x 2's and make them about two inches shorter than the length of your plywood board. Again, sand the edges to remove the risk of splinters.

5. Screw these pieces to the outer edges of your plywood piece, keeping the outside edges flush, and one end of the board should also be flush with these pieces (you will only frame the long sides making it easier to slide the boards in and out of your coop and to clean).

6. If you are using stick tiles, measure, cut, and install them on the tray you have just created. Should you decide to use sheet vinyl, you can trim any excess after it has been glued on.

7. If you want to elevate the trays, you can cut four blocks of your scrap wood to match the measurements of the short end of your tray and attach them to your coop sides so you can slide your tray in and out underneath a roost. Ideally, your tray should sit under the roost and be about halfway between the roost and the floor. These two boards will make it simple for you to slide the tray in and out for cleaning. Attach these boards using some screws.

8. You can fill your drop board with sand or sweet PDZ to help cut down on the smell in the coop. You do not need to use a lot, just enough to help clump us the droppings.

Tip: Remember that wood is subject to expanding and contracting depending upon the levels of humidity in the air, so don't design it to fit tightly.

It is all going to depend on how clean you want to keep your coop. If you are a neat freak like us, you can pick the clumps off these boards every morning and perform a complete clean once or twice a week. In between cleanings, feel free to add a little litter if you feel it is low. Every few months, you should plan on cleaning out all the litter and giving it a full scrub with your homemade cleaner (see Chapter 4). Let it dry completely, replace the board with new litter, and you are ready to begin another week.

Enclosed Runs

Providing an enclosed run still allows your chickens to run around but stay safe from those predators that mean to do them harm.

Just like your coops, you have an option of shopping for prefabricated chicken runs that remind us of outdoor dog kennels. They are available online or at your local farm stores. However, you may want to build your own. Just make sure that you use heavy gauge wire (not chicken wire) and build it to keep your flock safe. Even if you think you have everything perfect, you may find yourself face to face with a possum or snake in your hen house.

Your first step is to determine the dimensions of your run and design it to incorporate your coop, which should be flush with one side of the run. A good rule of thumb for a small flock is a run approximately four feet in width. Personally, we would cover it too, but we have been told that a hawk would never land in this narrow space, but we would rather be safe than sorry.

Choose sturdy materials and recall that we mentioned earlier that a raccoon can reach through a wire fence and still kill a chicken.

Space your eight-foot posts about every six feet by using a post hole digger for the holes. After placing the posts in the hole, fill it up with dirt and pack with a tamper. Roll out the fence, and before attaching it to your posts, you should make certain that the fence is at ground level. Recall that earlier, we mentioned burying some wire fences for extra protection against predators. If you wish to do that, make a trench about six to 12 inches deep and once you place it in the trench, wrap one end around your first post and then use some zip ties to keep it in place while you continue to work.

Pull your fencing tightly against the rest of the posts and wrap the other end around your final post, also securing it with zip ties. Before you begin the final steps of stapling your fencing to the post, make sure that you are happy with how your project looks. If so, then use ¾ inch poultry staples to attach your fencing to the posts you have in place.

Don't forget to cut out an opening and install a gate so that you can enter the run. We like to leave nothing to chance, so if you want to cover your run, cover it with heavy-duty C Flex 80 round deer fencing, and you can secure this with zip ties. Make sure that you routinely walk your fence line, looking for attempts at digging or areas that may need repair.

Are There Plants to Avoid in Your Run or Garden Area?

You have put in a lot of hard work by now and are ready to bring your first flock of chickens home, but have you considered your landscaping? If you plan on giving your chickens free access outside of your run or if they are free-range, you should be aware of any potentially poisonous plants that may harm your chickens. Make sure you read through the list below and check if you have any of these plants in their environment. If so, you may want to remove these plants before they cause an illness.

Poisonous plants can be a tough thing for an average homeowner to identify. We understand that there are apps available on your phone that can identify a plant for you by merely uploading an image of what is growing in your yard. If you cannot locate one of those, perhaps you have a friend or neighbor that has a green thumb. They may be able to tell you which plants are which. If you are still in doubt, you can check out books on plant identification from your local library or your local bookstore. Besides this list of plants, there can be some seasonal growth for you to combat. Keep an eye out for seeds, pods, or acorns that could cause your chickens some danger, and never feed them anything that has been treated with chemicals.

The list We have compiled below may only refer to a part of the plant, their seeds, or at a certain stage of growth, so you should really read up on the plants you intend to landscape with or those already in the area of your coop. The first time your chickens sample some of these plants may not be critical, but if they continue to consume them, there may be a residual buildup. If any of these are near to your coop, you should rip them out.

- Azalea
- Black locust
- Bladderpod/bagpod
- Boxwood
- Buttercup
- Castor bean
- Cherry laurel
- Corn cockle
- Crown vetch
- Daffodil
- Daphne

- Death camas
- Ferns
- Foxglove
- Holly
- Honeysuckle
- Hydrangea
- Ivy
- Jasmine
- Jimsonweed/thornapple
- Lantana
- Lily of the valley
- Lupine
- Mexican poppy
- Milkweed
- Monkshood
- Mountain laurel
- Nightshade
- Oak leaves
- Oleander
- Poison hemlock
- Pokeberry
- Rattlebox
- Rhododendron
- Sweet pea

- Tobacco

- Tulip

- Water hemlock/cowbane

- Wisteria

- Yew

In addition to keeping an eye on these plants, you should keep any weeds pulled from around your coop and maintain a short grass border. Rodents love to hide in the deep weeds and grass, so this will keep them sneaking into your coop area.

Ideally, you should build a 12 to 18-inch border around your run made up of dirt or stone because the running of a lawnmower too close to your coop could stress out your birds. A lawnmower can be loud and scary to your chickens, but you may be able to make it fun for them by mowing so that your first pass will aim the grass cutting directly into the run. They will happily make a dash for it and enjoy the surprise green gifts. However, if you treat your lawn with harsh chemicals, do not give them to your chickens.

Chapter 6:
The World of Chickens Beyond Eggs

The majority of chicken owners begin their hobby for eggs, but there are more choices in the chicken world. You can choose to show, breed, or raise meat birds. There is no wrong answer, only the path you wish to follow.

In our case, we just love being surrounded by animals. It doesn't matter if they are dogs, horses, or chickens. Some of our best therapists never say a word.

Show Your Chickens

Being able to show your chickens is not just for 4-H and local poultry club shows. There are poultry shows you can attend to learn about new breeds, study up on bloodlines, and even get some answers as to how to enter the show ring yourself.

If you want to locate an exhibition close to you, visit the Poultry Show Central's website, where you can search by state and mark your calendar for any upcoming poultry show dates. You will want to follow the same protocols when visiting these shows that you would when entering your own coop. Consider the following:

- Disinfect your footwear before attending your home flock

- Bag your shoes before entering your vehicle for the ride home as a biosecurity measure

- Always wash your hands and use hand sanitizer frequently

- Wear extra layers of clothes so that if they become soiled, you can remove them

Since you will have your phone with you, you will be able to take photos, but don't forget to bring a pen and notepad to write important things down. There is always something to learn, and you never know what great piece of information or tips you will come across. Most of these shows will last a day or two, and you may want to sit in on any seminars offered.

While you are admiring those chickens, take some time to study any comments the judges may have made on the cage tags. If this is your first time attending a poultry show, just take it easy and soak it all in because this can be an alien but exciting experience. Below We have listed some of the abbreviations that you might find written on the judging tags.

- AOCCL - all other combs clean legged

- AOSB - all other standard breeds

- AOB - any other breed

- AOV - any other variety

- B, BT, BTM - bantam

- BB - best of breed

- BV - best of variety

- C - cock

- CH - champion

- CONT - continental

- DQ - disqualification

- H - hen

- K - cockerel

- LF - large fowl

- MED - Mediterranean

- OT - old trio

- P - pullet

- RCCL - rose comb clean legged

- RB - reserve of breed

- RC - rose comb

- RV - reserve of variety

- SCCL - single comb clean legged

- SC - single comb

- SF - standard fowl

- WF - waterfowl (ducks & geese)

- YT - young trio

If you are just getting into the poultry show world, take time to view all the different breeds because there are hundreds. Don't worry about asking questions because chicken owners *love* to talk about their birds! Most of them are always happy to share secrets and tips for up-and-coming competitors. New interest keeps their world thriving.

Preparing for a Show

If you want to participate in shows, always start by investing in quality birds from a reputable breeder.

The key to success is preparation, and there are some things you should do before your show.

- Wash your birds around a week prior to your show

- Groom your bird

- Clip nails & beaks

- Shine their feathers

- Clean their legs & feet

- Relax & enjoy

Several shows run a raffle to win items like feed or other poultry products, and with any luck, they may draw your name. If you are interested in purchasing stock, you should hang out in the sales area because this is the time some vendors will be willing to make a deal on pricing. If you do end up bringing new stock home, you should quarantine them for at least a month before letting them integrate with the rest of your flock.

The desire to show chickens is primarily focused on improving a breed, and it is an interesting hobby for people of all ages. Most shows are free to attend, but if there is a small charge, it is usually to help support the organization. Shows are filled with great people who love chickens and have common goals, so go, have fun and explore.

Breeding Your Chickens

Whether you want to show, or you just want to sell chicks perhaps to other backyard chicken owners, you'll still need to know a thing or two about breeding your chickens. We are sure that you know this, but without a rooster on the property, there is no way to fertilize a hen's egg to produce a chick. Below are some insights on breeding.

- Follow selective breeding habits. Most likely, you have a plan already in place to develop a certain breed. It doesn't matter if you just want to breed your favorite chickens or further a bloodline. What matters is that your birds should be healthy, exhibit good temperaments, and have good production.

- While chickens can produce fertilized eggs all year, they are most prolific during the springtime. This is especially true if you reside in a colder climate region since your flock will spend more energy staying warm than anything else.

- Keeping more than one rooster for your hens is usually not a good idea because it can create a lot of competition between them. It may be possible to have roosters together if they have been raised together and you provide them with at least 4 to 5 hens each. The one benefit of keeping more than a single rooster is that there is a higher fertility rate within your flock.

- If you choose to single out a rooster for breeding, you will need to remove any other roosters from the flock. Observe your rooster with his harem and make sure that he is doing his job.

- There is a wait time if you have just introduced a rooster to your flock. A hen's reproductive cycle will not produce a fertilized egg for at least two weeks.

- Keep an eye on your rooster to make sure that he isn't harming your hens with his spurs and beak. It's normal for a rooster to jump on the hen's back and hold her in place by grabbing her comb. However, if you notice that your hens are losing feathers, appear stressed out, or looking bloody, your rooster might be overeager. If you are concerned about your hens, you can purchase a hen saddle to protect them, and when possible, trim your rooster's spurs and talons.

- If the rooster is harming your hens, you will have to decide to switch to a different rooster if you fear for your hen's physical or mental health. Without her, there will be no chicks.

- When your eggs are fertilized, you will start to notice them looking a bit different. If you see a small white splotch that puts you in mind of a bullseye, you will know that they are showing the signs of fertilization.

- Store your potential chicks at 50 to 60 degrees Fahrenheit for a week with the pointy end facing down. This is preferred to putting every egg into your incubator right away because this practice can cause some problems when it comes to hatching day. While in the incubator, your eggs need to be rotated and chicks removed when dry. This process can kill potential chicks that are still in the hatching process, so it is preferable to have all your eggs at the same stage of development.

There you go! Chicken breeding is not difficult. You just need to manage the safety of your girls and add all potential chicks to the incubator at the same time.

Hatching the Old-Fashioned Way

Many breeds of chickens make perfectly good mothers. However, sometimes, you may have a hen that doesn't want to sit on her eggs or raise her chicks. Now what? Luckily, you have had the foresight to add to your flock a couple of hens that are naturally broody and love nothing better than to sit on a nest of eggs.

If you are serious about breeding purebreds, then you may have those chickens separate from the rest or just start out with a flock of a single breed.

If your hen gets broody, don't make her feel uncomfortable about it. She needs to feel safe and protected, so she doesn't feel the need to abandon her eggs or chicks. During this time, you need to leave her eggs alone and place some food and water nearby. After hatching, your baby chicks will regulate their own temperature by positioning themselves under her, on her, or under her wings, depending upon the amount of heat they feel they need. You will still need to leave food and water nearby, and should you need to move them, try to do it in the evening when your hen is ready for sleep.

You should know that not all clutches of eggs will hatch even if the mother is dedicated. It is sad, but some chicks will either never make it out of their egg or pass away after hatching. After the first chicks hatch from the grouping, remove anything unhatched after four days have passed and *candle* them to check what is inside.

Candling Your Unhatched Eggs

You can check the inner contents of your hen's eggs by holding a light or lit candle near it. This process can help to determine if there is a chick in there ready to step into the world.

You should also candle the eggs that you are incubating to make sure that they are indeed fertilized and hold a growing chick inside. We suggest that you candle your eggs before placing them in the incubator initially. This can provide you with a comparison when you check them further. Any eggs with cracks do not necessarily need to be discarded, but you should monitor them closely. Unfertilized eggs will rot and begin to smell. It is also possible that any rotten eggs may burst and contaminate the other eggs in the incubator with bacteria.

You will need a bright light to look at your eggs, and the room you check them in should be dark. You can purchase a device at farm stores or cover the bright end of a flashlight with a piece of cardboard that you have fashioned a one-inch circular hole in.

When you are ready, pick up an egg and gently hold the larger end of the egg against the light, turning it slowly. Avoid looking directly into the light but look inside the egg to determine if there is an embryo inside. Do not keep the egg against the light for very long because you don't want the embryo to become too hot.

Growing embryos can be easily identified by a roadmap of blood vessels during the first week. After that, you can probably see an eye or a shadow indicating a body. If you are lucky, you may even see some movement inside.

An embryo that stops growing will often show a red ring around the yolk. These should be removed from the incubator and thrown away as they are not fit to eat.

After checking over your eggs, gently place them back in their spot inside the incubator. Your incubated eggs should not be away from the incubator for more than 20 minutes.

You can keep a log to keep track of your observations and even place a number on each egg. If you are unsure about the contents of an egg, you can place it back in the incubator and check it again.

Generally, you should candle your average eggs when you place them in the incubator, again on day seven and then a third time on the fourteenth day. The general rule is to not candle them again from day 16 until the day of hatching because moving or shifting eggs during this stage could result in harming your chicks.

Raising Meat Chickens

So far, we have covered a lot of information about taking care of your chickens and what to do with all those wonderful eggs, but there is another industry in the chicken world, and that is the meat chicken. There are different rules when raising meat chickens as opposed to laying hens.

The best chickens to raise for meat are Cornish crosses; these are the big, white chickens that you will find in supermarkets and restaurants. They are efficiently bred to grow quickly, basically following eight weeks to your freezer.

These chickens are not overly bright and should be kept separate from any laying hens you have simply because they will be picked on and even killed by the other birds. They are not known to have much of a personality, and they do just one thing, eat. They will start and never stop, causing them to eat themselves to death.

According to Twain Lockhart (2020), feeding a meat bird is a bit different from your layers because they will need a diet that is higher in protein. The meat bird feed is designed to help build the bird's skeletal system to hold its weight. Because of the way these birds are engineered to gain weight, you should restrict their diet to 12 hours on, 12 hours off. If you don't, the birds may outgrow their legs too early and suffer from broken legs, and at around seven weeks of age, they may suffer heart attacks.

While it is true that some chicken breeds can double as both layer and meat birds, these may not prove profitable for a side business producing meat birds. We admit that it's true that it will cost less to just visit your local supermarket and purchase your chickens already processed for your dinner table, but there is nothing quite as satisfying as producing your own food at home. In addition, with chickens now being processed for the US market in China, consumers may feel safer knowing where their food is raised and how it is processed.

You should know that there are ordinances that may allow you to raise chickens but prohibit the actual slaughter within city limits. You may be able to network with another person outside of the city limits that already processes their birds, and for a fee, may process yours as well. You will be able to load up your freezer and enjoy the fruits of your labor all winter long.

Conclusion

By now, you have become completely immersed in the world of chickens, and we bet you just cannot wait to get started!

We began by explaining why you need chickens in your life and the many benefits that they bring to you and your family. After that, we covered how to keep your chickens happy, their behaviors, and how they communicate either with us or each other.

The ability to know your chickens inside and out will help you care for them and know about common illnesses and pests. In addition to these tips, we have provided a list of chicken breeds that are fantastic choices for new chicken owners and indicated which ones were especially kid friendly.

Not that it will keep you from owning your own flock, but we would be remiss if we didn't prepare you for all the things that accompany chicken ownership. We cannot stress enough how important it is to understand chicken math. This rule that governs the universe will determine the size of your coop and run.

Besides your coop cleaning chores, we have given you options on buying a coop, building one, or repurposing an existing building. And your coop would not be complete without a protective run enclosure, nesting boxes, roosting bars, and the ever-growing importance of a drop board that enables you to keep a cleaner coop.

The world of chickens is more than just a huge pile of eggs (although that's the most attractive reason to enter the chicken world). Beyond eggs, there is the show world, investing in refining a breed, or even raising meat chickens.

Hopefully, we have inspired you to invest some time when planning your new chicken operation. Whether it's three chickens or 300, you will find them entertaining and personable. We wish you the greatest experience in your chicken endeavors because life is better with chickens around!

References

5 tips for clean eggs from your backyard chickens. (n.d.). Fresh Eggs Daily. https://www.fresheggsdaily.blog/2013/05/coop-to-kitchen-5-tips-to-ensure-clean.html

8 simple tips for breeding chickens. (n.d.). www.thehappychickencoop.com. https://www.thehappychickencoop.com/8-simple-tips-for-breeding-chickens/

26 sounds that chickens make and what they mean. (2019, March 18). Flip Flop Ranch. https://flipflopranch.com/chicken-talk/

Alectryon (mythology). (2021, April 29). Wikipedia. https://en.wikipedia.org/wiki/Alectryon_(mythology)

Arcuri, L. (2021, March 17). *Learn how to candle an egg.* The Spruce. https://www.thespruce.com/definition-of-candling-3016955

Are chickens really the closest descendants of t-rex? (2017, December 13). Earth Buddies. https://www.earthbuddies.net/are-chickens-really-the-closest-descendants-of-t-rex/

Armitage, N. (2020, February 12). *Dust baths for chickens and what to fill them with.* Cluckin. https://cluckin.net/dust-baths-for-chickens-and-what-to-fill-them-with.html

B, E. (2016, February 25). *Keeping dogs & chickens.* The Scoop from the Coop. https://www.scoopfromthecoop.com/keeping-dogs-chickens/

Barred rock chickens: complete breed profile. (2021, May 7). The Happy Chicken Coop. https://www.thehappychickencoop.com/barred-rock-chickens-complete-breed-profile/

Belanger, J. D. (2011). *The complete idiot's guide to raising chickens.* Alpha; London.

Biggs, Ph.D., P. (n.d.). *Kids and chickens Tips.* Purina Animal Nutrition. https://www.purinamills.com/chicken-feed/education/detail/backyard-chickens-are-a-kids-best-friend

Black copper marans: complete breed guide. (2021, March 18). www.thehappychickencoop.com. https://www.thehappychickencoop.com/black-copper-marans/

Brock, T. (n.d.). *Tools you need to build a chicken coop.* Dummies. https://www.dummies.com/home-garden/hobby-farming/raising-chickens/tools-you-need-to-build-a-chicken-coop/

Buff orpington all you need to know: temperament and egg laying. (2017, July 24). Thehappychickencoop.com. https://www.thehappychickencoop.com/buff-orpington/

CDC. (2018, May 8). *Outbreaks of human salmonella infections linked to backyard poultry.* Centers for Disease Control and Prevention. https://www.cdc.gov/media/dpk/food-safety/live-poultry-salmonella/live-poultry-salmonella.html

Chicken anatomy 101: everything you need to know. (2018, June 28). Thehappychickencoop.com. https://www.thehappychickencoop.com/chicken-anatomy/

Chicken nesting boxes 101 and 13 best diy plans. (2021, May 26). The Happy Chicken Coop. https://www.thehappychickencoop.com/chicken-nesting-boxes/

Chickens are cool! (50 chicken facts you will love). (n.d.). Backyard Chickens - Learn How to Raise Chickens. https://www.backyardchickens.com/articles/chickens-are-cool-50-chicken-facts-you-will-love.66963/

Cochin chicken: breed profile, care guide and more.... (2017, September 27). Thehappychickencoop.com. https://www.thehappychickencoop.com/cochin-chickens/

Damerow, G. (n.d.). *Raising guinea fowl: a low-maintenance flock.* Mother Earth News. https://www.motherearthnews.com/homesteading-and-livestock/raising-guinea-fowl-zmaz92aszshe

Damerow, G. (2019, March 22). *How Many Chicken Breeds Are There?* Cackle Hatchery. https://www.cacklehatchery.com/how-many-chicken-breeds-are-there/

Davis, T. (2017a, January 18). *Healthy Herb Garden Chickens Will Love - Top 16 Herbs.* The Imperfectly Happy Home. http://www.imperfectlyhappy.com/herb-garden-chickens/

Davis, T. (2017b, April 10). *Improve the Health of Your Chickens Naturally with 2 Things.* The Imperfectly Happy Home. https://www.imperfectlyhappy.com/chickens-naturally/

Davis, T. (2017c, October 5). *How to have happier chickens - 11 Tips to Make it Easy.* The Imperfectly Happy Home. https://www.imperfectlyhappy.com/how-to-have-happier-chickens/

Do I have to refrigerate my fresh eggs? (n.d.). Fresh Eggs Daily. https://www.fresheggsdaily.blog/2015/09/do-i-have-to-refrigerate-my-fresh-eggs.html

Easter egger: everything you need to know about this chicken. (2021, March 11). The Happy Chicken Coop. https://www.thehappychickencoop.com/easter-egger/

Fulghum, L. (2020, February 24). *How to build a Dropping Board.* Community Chickens. https://www.communitychickens.com/dropping-board-zb02002ztil/

Hatcher, M. (2010). *Keeping chickens: self-sufficiency.* Skyhorse Publishing.

Hirsch, V. (2003). *Brief summary of the biology and behavior of the chicken.* Animal Legal & Historical Center. www.animallaw.info. https://www.animallaw.info/article/brief-summary-biology-and-behavior-chicken

How much room do chickens need? (2021, March 9). www.thehappychickencoop.com. https://www.thehappychickencoop.com/how-much-room-do-chickens-need/

How to break a broody hen. (n.d.). Fresh Eggs Daily. https://www.fresheggsdaily.blog/2012/01/so-youve-got-broody-hen.html

How to do a chicken health check (checklist included). (n.d.). Www.thehappychickencoop.com. https://www.thehappychickencoop.com/chicken-health-check/

How to prevent and treat the 5 most common chicken diseases. (2019, July 12). Freedom Ranger Blog. https://www.freedomrangerhatchery.com/blog/how-to-prevent-and-treat-the-5-most-common-chicken-diseases/

Jersey giant: size, egg laying, colors, temperament, and more…. (2017, August 19). Thehappychickencoop.com. https://www.thehappychickencoop.com/jersey-giant/

Keene, B. (n.d.). *10 big mistakes first time coop builders make.* Building a Chicken Coop. Retrieved June 25, 2021, from https://www.oregon.gov/ode/students-and-family/childnutrition/F2S/Documents/10mistakes%5B1%5D.pdf

Leghorn chicken: all you need to know. (2021, March 18). www.thehappychickencoop.com. https://www.thehappychickencoop.com/leghorn-chicken/

Leonard, J. (2015, July 14). *20 convincing reasons to keep backyard chickens.* Natural Living Ideas. https://www.naturallivingideas.com/20-convincing-reasons-to-keep-backyard-chickens/

Lockhart, T. (2020, August 13). *The scoop from the coop.* The Scoop from the Coop. https://www.scoopfromthecoop.com/tag/meat-chickens/

Modern Farming Methods. (2015, November 9). *Araucana chicken breed information.* Modern Farming Methods. https://www.roysfarm.com/araucana-chicken/

Niemann, D. (2016, January 18). *11 reasons to keep backyard chickens.* Hobby Farms. https://www.hobbyfarms.com/11-reasons-to-keep-backyard-chickens/

Peterson, V. J. (2019, May 13). *How to get your chickens to like you.* www.acreagelife.com. https://www.acreagelife.com/hobby-farming/how-to-get-your-chickens-to-like-you

Poindexter, J. (2016, November 14). *How to clean your chicken coop & run: 9 tips to do it right.* MorningChores. https://www.morningchores.com/cleaning-chicken-coop/

Rhode island red: what to know before buying one. (2021, May 4). Thehappychickencoop.com. https://www.thehappychickencoop.com/rhode-island-red/

Rossier, J., & Steele, L. (2017). *Living with chickens: everything you need to know to raise your own backyard flock.* Lyons Press.

Schneider, A. G., & Mccrea, B. (2017). *The chicken whisperer's guide to keeping chickens: everything you need to know-- and didn't know you needed to know about backyard and urban chickens.* Quarry Books.

Shinners, R., & Lowin, R. (2021, January 22). *30 Chicken coop plans that are easy to follow.* Country Living; Country Living. https://www.countryliving.com/diy-crafts/g2452/diy-chicken-coops/

Smith, K. (2013, November 6). *Chicken care and maintenance.* Backyard Chicken Coops. https://www.backyardchickencoops.com.au/blogs/learning-centre/chicken-care-maintenance

Smith, K. (2014, March 18). *Natural homemade coop cleaner: citrus, apple cider vinegar, baking powder and more.* Backyard Chicken Coops. https://www.backyardchickencoops.com.au/blogs/learning-centre/natural-homemade-chicken-coop-cleaner-orange-peel-white-vinegar

Steele, A.: L. (2021, April 21). *Everything you need to know about chicken roosting bars.* Backyard Poultry. https://www.backyardpoultry.iamcountryside.com/coops/chicken-roosting-bars/

Sussex chicken: breed information, care guide, egg color, and more. (2018, March 31). www.thehappychickencoop.com. https://www.thehappychickencoop.com/sussex-chicken/

The egg float test for freshness. (n.d.). Fresh Eggs Daily. https://www.fresheggsdaily.blog/2012/10/the-float-test.html

The plymouth rock chicken: all you need to know. (2021, March 15). www.thehappychickencoop.com. https://www.thehappychickencoop.com/plymouth-rock-chicken/

Thesing, G. (2017, September 13). *Chicken predators – what you need to know.* The Scoop from the Coop. https://www.scoopfromthecoop.com/chicken-predators-what-you-need-to-know/

Vyse Arks, J. (2021, February 3). *Why keeping chickens is a great idea for families.* Jim Vyse Arks. https://www.jimvysearks.co.uk/why-keeping-chickens-is-a-great-idea-for-families/?doing_wp_cron=1618372147.0487859249114990234375

What is aspergillosis? plus how to prevent it in your flock. (2019, May 23). Freedom Ranger Blog. https://www.freedomrangerhatchery.com/blog/what-is-aspergillosis-plus-how-to-prevent-it-in-your-flock/

Winger, J. (2020, September 19). *How to build a chicken run.* The Prairie Homestead. https://www.theprairiehomestead.com/2016/08/build-chicken-run.html

Raising Goats For Beginners

A Step-By-Step Guide to Raising Happy, Healthy
Goats For Milk, Cheese, Meat, Fiber, and More

Small Footprint Press

Introduction

"Until one has loved an animal, a part of one's soul remains unawakened."

— Anatole France

It is often said that you can take the boy from the farm, but not the farm out of the boy. Many of us have an inborn sense of peace when we look out at our acreage and watch our animals at play, eating, and experiencing the joy of just being out in the sunshine and living in the moment.

Whether you are just head over heels in love with animals or merely wanting your life to slow down so that you can enjoy those simpler moments, the appeal of your own patch of land and many adoring eyes may be just the lifestyle choice you need.

The return to rural roots is devoid of cabs on every corner, elevated trains, or quick pizza delivery. You will be reliant on your own resources to get things done and plan for problematic seasons that bring with them weather challenges. You might never realize how good you are with tools until you have to repair your own tractor, but there are usually some friendly neighbors that can often lend a helping hand.

Rural areas might have fewer banks, dry cleaners, mechanics, babysitters, or even grocery store choices. However, you will become proficient at lists when you go to town.

While it may be an adjustment to relocate and become a member of the simpler country mindset and way of life, there are some outstanding benefits to be gained. More people realize that there are many advantages from living the country life that they never considered before.

For example, our recent pandemic has proven to us all that living in a heavily populated area can be a health risk.

When you live out in the rural areas, life tends to slow down, and you learn to appreciate all those little things you didn't realize were being taken for granted. Your air quality is better, and the rural setting is by far more healthy than living in any large downtown city. By switching to rural areas, you will find that you are able to live in a healthier way, resulting in far fewer health issues.

After moving to your little piece of heaven, you may discover that your brain changes the way it thinks, and you prioritize things differently. When you live in a more crowded area, you may find yourself over-stimulated and filled with anxiety. Rural living provides a more peaceful setting and every morning, you can still enjoy your cup of coffee, but instead of looking out of your apartment window and being flooded with honking horns of traffic, you can now look out upon animals enjoying their breakfast, playing, or even trusting to take a morning snooze in a sunbeam.

Tranquility has no price tag.

So, what animals appeal to you? If you are wondering about raising goats, look no further! There are many reasons to raise goats other than they can be fun to watch. They can provide you with meat, dairy, fiber, or entertainment. This book will discuss the benefits, tips, and pitfalls to avoid while raising your very own herd of goats.

You may have lived your entire life in the USA, and not know that goat meat is the most popular meat in the world. It is very high in protein, and goat meat is growing in demand annually. If you cannot face the goat meat industry, that's okay because there are plenty of other things you can do with them, including raising your goats for milk and by-products like cheese and yogurt. Were you aware that you can raise brush-eating goats? Believe it or not, there is always someone wanting to lease a herd of goats in order to clear brush and weeds from their fields.

Our goal here at Small Footprint Press is to help you sustainably survive and thrive while ensuring together that the world is a better place for future generations to come.

Born out of frustration with the planet's current state, we want to raise awareness about how we all affect the world we live in and what you can do yourself & collectively to make a real difference.

We know how important it is to start giving back to the earth and how true happiness can come from living sustainably. Furthermore, having your own backyard goats is an incredible way to put your worries to rest and become more self-reliant.

That's why we've taken the time to make sure that you feel safe and empowered in your own journey to sustainability. As the world gets more confusing each day, we are determined to keep life simple and ensure that everyone has the ability to survive off their own, homegrown food, no matter what situation they may face.

If you have a love for all things outdoors and truly want to make the Earth a better place, then we can help guide you through all the small chores associated with the raising of goats. Our planet needs people just like you who want to see our world improve, and learn to be the best version of ourselves. If you can make a living doing something that you love, what is stopping you?

Chapter 1:
Are You Properly Prepared?

Depending upon where you currently live, there can be some laws in place that govern the keeping, raising, transport, and welfare of any animal kept on your property. Since these rules will vary greatly, the first thing that you should do is some homework on what animals are allowed on your property and how many animals might be mandated per acre. The last thing any animal lover wants to do is get some critters, get attached to them, and then have to give up our dream before we even get started. Be prepared to do plenty of research before buying your first animal.

According to the Animal Welfare Act (2006), anyone owning an animal has a legal responsibility to fulfill the five basic welfare needs of their pets and farm animals. These needs are stated below:

- A proper diet

- A suitable shelter in which to live

- Any animal requiring a need to be kept separate from other animals should have those facilities available for them

- Any animal must be allowed to express normal behavior

- Any animal must be provided protection from and treatment for any illness and injury

Since goats are categorized as a farm animal species, all owners of goats must comply with some extra laws. There are laws that include, but are not limited to:

- The registration of the land on which you are keeping goats

- The way the goats are identified

- The transportation of goats

- The meticulous record-keeping of medicines and health issues

You should contact your local government officials regarding any law they may have regarding the housing of goats on your property and study your legal obligations.

- Always check any zoning or ordinances that might stand in your way. I know you have been daydreaming about goats and probably counting them as you fall asleep, but you first need to determine if your property is zoned for them. Many cities or towns will not allow goats and since it is probably not a largely requested topic, they may not be sure at first. Whoever you ask, preferably in writing, will most likely need to check out any zoning codes or municipal ordinances regarding the legalities of goat keeping on your property. It may be difficult to traverse some of the definitions when it comes to raising goats on your property. There are even codes that prohibit agriculture as a 'gainful business,' so you may be allowed to raise them for personal use, but cannot make them your livelihood. By checking town ordinances and bylaws, you should be able to determine if your goats would be welcome in the community or banned and labeled as a 'nuisance animal.' We all know that goats can be impressive escape artists and should they get into your neighbor's garden, there could be some damage that your insurance will need to cover. Always be prepared.

- Even if your city or town allows the ownership of goats, don't make the mistake of not checking your homeowner's association (HOA) should your property fall under their rules.

- Know all the rules. Even if you are lucky enough to live in an area that permits goats, there still might be some rules that you may have to follow. Some of these exceptions may include:

    - Goats must be dehorned

    - Male goats must be neutered

    - Size might make a difference - perhaps your area may only allow miniature goats such as Pygmy or Dwarf

- There might be a stipulation on how many goats you are allowed on your property. It might surprise you that there can be no less than and no more than rule in place when it comes to how many goats you are allowed.

- While your goats must be kept in a shelter, there may be specific design, size, and placement requirements that you must follow.

- There could be a rule in place about your shelter having direct access to an outdoor fenced-in enclosure. In addition, there could be specific designs, area, height, and other requirements regarding your pasture and fencing.

- Goats leave their droppings all over, and there will likely be rules about the removal and disposal of their waste so that it will not contaminate land, water, or cause potential health issues.

- Only personal consumption or benefits from goat-originated products may be allowed, in other words, no sales. This might be a problem if you wanted a goat-based business!

Just because this might fit your plans for today, don't overlook your future dreams. Anytime you commit to ownership of an animal, that is a responsibility, and you should keep in mind the lifespan of any animals you share your home and life with. Should you have an upcoming move in your future, the next property will also need to allow your goats. Before you sign on the dotted line for your new property, you should know all the rules and restrictions. If you have plans to add to your herd, make sure that your rules will allow you to add to your group without having to shop for another property if you want to expand.

Lastly, just because your area doesn't allow goats now, there are always steps you can go through to change your local laws in your favor.

- Do your breed research because it might surprise you to learn that some goats are noisier than others! If you rack up some noise citations, or your new neighbors complain of the smell or an overabundance of flies, this can reward you with some grief.

- As I mentioned above, make sure that your liability insurance covers property damage caused by your new goat herd. It seems that expensive landscaping is the tastiest morsel to a goat on the lam (if you will pardon the pun).

Size May Matter

Goats come in all shapes and sizes, and they also can differ in purpose and temperament. You may or may not be limited to smaller goats due to property restrictions, but now comes the hardest part; which goats are right for you? You are going to have to do your research before deciding on which goats are for you.

Full Size Vs Mini Goats

If you are looking for milking goats, many swear that the full-size goats are not only easier to milk, but they produce a higher yield. While this is true, larger goats can also be more difficult to handle. Despite the fact that some breeds can be more ornery than others, the amount of space you have available and the amount of milk you will need can be more of a deciding factor when deciding on a breed than their temperament.

Being a new goat keeper can sometimes seem difficult when it comes right down to making critical decisions, and that's why we will try to detail some scenarios below:

1. If what you desire is no-nonsense milk, and you want a larger yield, but have an acre or less, then you might want to look at a couple of full-sized does. One full-sized doe of virtually any breed will produce a gallon of milk each day. Two such does, will bring you 14 gallons of milk each week. This is an estimated amount, and you may experience a bit more or a bit less but what are your plans for this quantity of milk each week? Maybe you have a large family that consumes a lot of milk, but if you don't, are you planning to sell it? Maybe you are planning to get into cheese making? Remember, that with full-sized goats, you will need higher and sturdier fencing because they can be very destructive.

It's probably a good rule of thumb to plan on more food and more supplies in general.

2. This option will be very similar to number one, except you will want to proceed with two Nigerian Dwarf does. Instead of worrying about what you are going to do with 14 gallons each week, this pair of goats will provide you with half that amount, or 7 gallons a week. This provides you with a reasonable amount of milk each week, and the size of these goats will not impact your feed bill as much as the full-size animals.

3. Looking for something midway between these choices? Then perhaps you should look at two goats from a mini breed. Pygmies and Nigerian Dwarfs are considered mini breeds, and any crosses with Nigerians are still considered a mini breed. Any doe from these breeds or crosses typically produces just over a ½ a gallon each day. The amount of milk can vary because of the animal being crossbred.

Often it just takes some experience for people to learn how to plan ahead based upon individual milk production. Once you are blessed with extra milk, you end up finding ways to use it up. Products like soaps and cheese use a considerable amount of milk. You may not be ready to start production on these products just yet. However, if it is something you are thinking about for the future, instead of adding more goats to your start-up, then the full-sized goats may be your better solution.

We find that your choices are going to be made not only on the characteristics of the individual animals, but also on your ultimate goals. If you have never owned goats before, the Nigerian Dwarfs may seem like a better choice to get started. They are smaller and often easier to handle than their larger counterparts. Nigerian dwarfs are known for their great temperament and could be a great choice for a new goat herd owner.

Another reason this breed appeals to the majority of people is that their milk has the most butterfat ratio than other breeds. (This generally means it is tastier!)

Then there is the choice of keeping a buck. One smaller Nigerian buck can be easier to handle and contain versus a full-sized one.

Goat Dynamics

Goat herds can be found in a myriad of places, and not just on fertile dairy fields that we picture in Wisconsin or Minnesota. Goats are geographically the most widespread species of livestock. These animals are adaptable and herds litter the globe, from the deserts of Africa to the frigid mountainous regions of Siberia. According to Carol Amundson (2020), some studies show amid the world goat population, there is only a variation of about 10% in DNA results.

People have various reasons for choosing to raise goats. While one might just want to have some cute pets around to strut their stuff throughout their pasture, others may want to create a lifestyle of raising goats for sustainable income or self-sufficiency. Either way, if you are new to raising goats, there are certain behaviors that you will need to understand. You may have always thought of goats as mere farm animals or a favorite in the circle of chosen petting zoos. However, they also can prove to be good pets. If you are lucky enough to have a herd, you will find by watching them that there are a few key players that call the shots among your group:

- Herd Queen. There's one in every herd, and this one is the dominant female. No, she doesn't parade around with a crown on her head, but she might as well because this queen leads the way, deciding when the herd can go out to the pasture. She will always have the best sleeping spot, most likely right in front of the feeders. Should she be a dairy goat, she will be the first to be milked. Heaven help any goat that tries to change the pecking order because the herd queen will put them in their place quickly.

Any offspring of the herd queen are treated like royalty and are included in the queen's favorite eating spots. Like any mother, the queen will defend them if any other goats try to push them out of the way.

The herd queen does have some responsibilities because she is the first one to test any new plants and determine if it is beneficial for the rest of the herd. She is also considered the first line of defense against predators and will remain in her position until she dies or becomes old and sick. At this time, another doe will fight and take over the head position.

- Head Buck. Traditionally, this position is held by the biggest, strongest, and oldest buck. This buck will retain his position until he dies or a younger buck from the herd challenges him and wins.

Any intact males within your herd will have a certain smell. How shall we put this delicately? They stink! Your nose may find it very offensive, not to mention anyone who visits your farm that knows nothing about goats.

You may have already been aware that bucks will smell bad, but you may not know why. The musky odor that is specific to bucks comes from a combination of their urine and their scent glands. Just in case you need to know, these scent glands are located near their horns.

Bucks are a bit disturbing with their hygiene habits, choosing to spray their urine in their beards, chest, face, and front legs more than normal during the time of rut. You may find this surprising, but does seem to find the odor irresistible.

When you find out how badly they stink, you may decide to opt for artificial insemination or just lease a buck to breed your does and then send him packing for home.

- Kids. The survival and the increase of your herd depend upon the kids. If you want to perpetuate a thriving dairy, you will need kids in order for your does to provide you with milk. By raising kids, you will fortify your herd's bloodline and be able to replace aging animals.

According to legend, we even have goats to thank for the discovery of coffee. To this day, some goat owners will use it to stimulate labor.

No herd is complete without the antics of young kids. While most does are excellent mothers, there may be times when you will need to step in and lend a hand. Situations that may require extra support include:

  ○ In very cold or wet weather when the kid is born, they tend to lose body energy and heat quickly. As a result, they may become weakened and you will need to step in to ensure their survival.

- Maiden does may lack experience in the care of their newborn kids. The last thing you want to experience is a mother abandoning their kids, but it does happen, and you will need to take action immediately. If you have a doe with poor mothering abilities, you may want to cull them from your herd. Bottle feeding colostrum to kids may be necessary if they are not suckling.

- If your doe starts showing signs of poor health just prior to birth, they may show a lack of interest in their newborns. They may also not be able to produce enough colostrum and milk that is required by their new kids.

- Multiple births can prove difficult even for the most experienced does. When three or more kids are born, there may not be enough nourishment for all of them.

- Weak newborns may not be able to suckle or stand on their own.

- Your kidding area should be well protected from predators so that your newborns are not killed or injured by predators and the mothers are not stressed out.

- Overcrowding can cause aggressive animals in a herd to attack newborn kids, which is why you should have a separate kidding area.

If you are contemplating owning goats, you need to know that they are herd animals and will require at least one partner of the same species. In addition, they will need at bare minimum a large yard in which to roam and embrace their typical goat behavior. They will need and desire the same amount of attention that you would give to any pet or livestock animal you own. Just as any other pack or herd animal, you should never openly play favorites because, believe it or not, goats do become jealous and could display some aggression if not receiving their fair share of affection.

While you observe your herd interact, you will be intrigued by the way they communicate with each other. Here are some behaviors you will eventually become accustomed to:

- Biting: Goats will often communicate by biting.

- Butting: Why do goats butt? They tend to use their butting ability to bully others for a number of reasons. They may be establishing their place in the herd, pushing others out of their way, as a form of play, or to fight.

Butting is a very persuasive reason to dehorn your goats and, in addition, you should never keep horned and dehorned goats together because this is an open invitation for one of them to get seriously injured.

You will see an increase in biting and butting when a new herd member is introduced. Because of the newcomer, lower-status herd members are the first to initiate the fighting, primarily because they want to maintain or raise their position within the herd.

- Rut: What is a goat buck in rut? Rut, put simply, is a period of time in a buck's life when they experience a surge of hormones and become ready to breed. A buck can be ready to breed throughout the year, but when in rut, they can become more determined than any other time. Note to new goat owners: This is why you should not keep young bucks with their mothers for more than 3-4 months of age. Most goat breeds tend to go into rut during Autumn. Most of a buck's breeding is performed during the months that range from August to January.

- Mounting: You might be surprised to learn that goat kids will begin mounting each other at a very young age of a few days old. Even though this is getting a jump start in establishing dominance within the herd, they are also getting some practice before becoming grownup goats. Once they begin to age, the mounting games will take on a more sexual tone.

If you have a few bucks on the property, you may have to separate them during their rut periods so they do not harm each other. It is extremely important to note that you should never turn your back on a buck during a rut because they can be aggressive with humans.

Are Goats Intelligent?

Have you ever stared at a goat and wondered what they were thinking, and how smart they might be? Well, wonder no more because goats have a pretty impressive IQ! According to researchers for both the Queen Mary University of London and the Institute of Agricultural Science in Switzerland (2014), they found that goats might be more intelligent than they seem. During their studies, they learned that they dwell in complex social groups and are expert climbers. Because they live a considerable length of life, they believe that goats are able to build up a library of memories and skills more easily than other short-lived animals. Goats are adept at attaining hard-to-reach foods and despite the rumor that they eat garbage (although they do eat or nibble on things that surprise us), they can be picky eaters.

Researchers from the Queen Mary University of London went on to challenge 12 domesticated goats, believing that because of their domestication, they now lacked the ability to forage as well as their wild cousins. In a test designed to find out if goats had intelligence, researchers borrowed a page from primate scientists and placed some fruit inside of a box, which could only be accessed by the goats solving a puzzle. In order to solve this task, the goat would have to use their teeth to pull on a rope, thereby activating a lever. They would then have to use their muzzle to move the lever up, releasing their fruit reward for them to enjoy. Their end results showed that 9 of the 12 were able to master the task after around four attempts. The three goats that failed tried to circumvent the test by using their horns to pry open the box.

To test their long-term memory, researchers waited 10 months and presented the 9 goats that passed initially with the same food box puzzle to determine how long it would take them to repeat their success and obtain their snack. Every one of the 9 remembered how to receive their fruit and did so in less than a minute, showing long-term memory.

Be Prepared

Whenever you choose to add any animal to your life, you should always take its lifespan into account. No animal should be added to your life due to an impulse, and a goat is no exception. Goats breeds may differ on the length of life expectancy and of course, there will always be those exceptions that live far beyond a normal lifespan for that breed.

Generally, a doe can be expected to live 11 to 12 years when in good health. If you choose to breed your goat after the age of 10 it is likely to have a pregnancy-related death as opposed to does that retire from the breeding program early, thus enjoying a longer life expectancy. Due to the stresses centered around rut, it is unusual for bucks to live past the age of 10, while wethers (a castrated male goat), can live longer than bucks, usually between 11 and 16 years.

Below you will find lifespans broken down by breed and some of the more popular breeds—these may surprise you!

- Alpine goats live 8-12 years and are hardy and weather tolerant.

- Angora goats live over 10 years (generally into their teens) if they have received good care.

- Boer goat bucks have a lifespan of 8-12 years, while the does can live 12 - 20 years! This particular breed can attribute their long life to a natural resistance to disease.

- Kiko goats are a large meat breed of goat and have shown that they are disease and parasite-resistant. This breed often lives 8-12 years.

- LaManche goats are a dairy breed and have a shorter life expectancy than many other breeds. They live between 7-10 years.

- Myotonic goats (also known as *fainting* goats) can live up to 15 years and are quite hardy.

- Nigerian Dwarf goats are usually the go-to goat for smaller dairy farms. They have excellent quality milk and this makes them a frequent favorite by most owners. They live around 15 years.

- Nubian goats are used for milk, meat, and hides. While they don't produce a large volume of milk, it is higher in butterfat than most and more flavorful, making excellent cheese. One drawback is that they are very vocal, so get ready for 15-18 years of noise!

- Oberhasli goats are smaller goats with gentle and calm dispositions. They live 8-12 years.

- Pygmy goats are popular for smaller operations. This small and friendly breed is one of the most commonly kept for pets, but can be used for meat and milk production. They live for about 12 years.

- Pygora goats are primarily a fiber breed and were created by breeding white angora goats to purebred pygmy goats. If taken good care of, you can expect them to live 12-15 years.

- Saanen goats can live past 15 years and are associated with heavy milk production.

- Toggenburg goats live 8-12 years and are characterized as being friendly and curious. They will most often fit the role of pet or dairy goat.

By and large, goats are mostly sweet animals that grace your farm and clear your land, in addition, they can help you produce some excellent products. When there is nothing on television, just pull up a chair and watch your goat buddies entertain you.

Types and Breeds of Goats

What goat breeds you choose will depend upon your interest.

Dairy Goats

- Alpine goats originated in France and when they arrived in 1922, there were only twenty-one animals imported to the United States. They are hardy animals that thrive in virtually any climate.

- Guernsey dairy goats were developed from the rare Golden Guernsey goats. The Golden Guernsey is an English breed that is highly desirable by American goat lovers. The importation of this animal is currently impossible, but Guernsey-type animals are being bred by crossing Swiss dairy goats with Golden Guernsey semen. It is thought that these golden-haired dairy goats likely originated in Greece and Syria. This breed of goat is also considered rare (see below).

- LaMancha goats most likely originated from the Murciana, which was on exhibition at the 1904 Paris World's Fair. They arrived in California with Spanish missionaries, and by the 1920s, the descendants of the LaMancha had been crossed with Toggenburg bucks. They are known for their pixie-like ears and gentle, curious personality.

- The Nigerian Dwarf was originally introduced in the United States from West Africa by zoos to feed their large cats, but their gentle nature soon brought these minis to popularity as a pet. At one time, their future was at risk, but with their popularity as a dairy goat, they are well on their way to recovery from the Conservation Priority List.

- The Nubian goat was born from a combination of English goats and goats from other parts of the world. During the 1800s, some goats were brought to France from Nubia in North Africa. The Nubian-type goat came to America around 1896, but the first traceable animals were registered around 1918.

- Oberhasli goats at some point in the early 1930s were imported into the United States from the Oberhasli region of Switzerland. This breed was originally known as the Swiss Alpine, but in 1979, the American Dairy Goat Association (ADGA) recognized the Oberhasli as a separate breed. This breed was also listed on the endangered list, but is now growing in popularity and increasing in numbers.

- Saanen goats received their name from the Saanen Valley in the southern area of Switzerland. Between the years of 1904 and 1930, there were about 150 Saanens imported to the United States.

- The Sable goat was a late bloomer and only recognized as a separate breed by the ADGA in 2005. This breed was brought about by a recessive gene within the bloodlines of the Saanen goat, making the Sable a colored Saanen.

- The Toggenburg was among the first purebred dairy goats to come to the United States. The breed originated from the Toggenburg Valley of Switzerland.

Fiber Goats

- Angora goats journeyed to the United States in 1849.

- Cashmere goats are sheared once each year and can yield as much as 2.5 pounds of *fleece*. A cross between an Angora and Cashmere goat is called a Cashgora.

- Until fairly recently, Angora goats were only bred to be white, but recently, there has been some interesting breeding practices going on that has resulted in a Colored Angora goat.

- Nigora goats are created by crossing a smaller breed with their larger counterpart breed. Therefore, this cross between an Angora and a Nigerian Dwarf resulted in the Nigora. The breed association for this animal was formed in 2007.

- Pygoras are the result of another small-breed cross. Angora does were bred to Pygmy bucks in order to become a favorite with hobbyist breeders and pet owners. The Pygora Breeders Association was formed in 1987.

Meat Goats

- Boer goats were originally developed in South Africa and came to the United States by way of New Zealand because the USDA restricted the direct import of goats directly from Africa. By the year 1995, however, these restrictions were lifted, and the embryos were permitted to be sent directly from South Africa.

- The Kiko was bred in New Zealand by a group crossing Anglo-Nubian, Toggenburg, and Saanen bucks. Four generations later, a new breed of meat goat was created.

- Myotonic goats are also known as the fainting goat. This goat breed has a unique condition called myotonia congenita. What this means is that when the animal is startled, their muscle cells tighten and this can result in a momentary stiffening of the legs which causes them to *faint*.

- The Savanna goat was also a breed that was developed in South Africa around the year 1957.

- Spanish Meat goats have ancestral ties back to the sixteenth century and traveled with Spanish missionaries to the Caribbean Islands. For three hundred years this was the sole goat in the regions of the United States and Mexico.

Miniature Goats

- Pygmy Dwarf goats arrived in the United States from Sweden in 1959. The Pygmy comes in many coat colors and is popular for its playful mannerisms. Pygmies often display bowed legs and display a body that is disproportionate to the size of their legs.

- Mini Dairy goats are miniature versions of the larger dairy breed, but they require less space and feed, making them attractive alternatives to hobby farmers.

Rare Breeds

- Olde English Milche goats were initially brought to the South Pacific in the late eighteenth century. These goats are now extinct in England, but a feral group of goats has thrived in New Zealand for 150 years. According to the Arapawa Registry, there are only 175 of these animals present in the United States.

- San Clemente is a rare breed of goat that inhabits San Clemente Island. There are only about 500 of these animals in existence today.

So, Where Does One Buy Their Goats?

If you have never raised livestock before, you might be scratching your head wondering where you purchase livestock. Let's just assume that you have done all your research and know exactly what breed of goat you want to get started with. You have made some appointments to go look at some goats, but you want to make sure that you don't impulse buy just because they have some really cute goats in the front pasture.

Hopefully, you haven't been lured into a farm with a sign out front that simply states *goats for sale*. You should begin by looking for a potential breeder and make an appointment to go look at their operation and their animals. By checking out their farm, you will know what to look for by following some of my tips:

- Word of mouth. Don't be shy, ask around about the breeder's reputation. If you have a local feed store, strike up a conversation and ask what they think. Chances are excellent that they have a working relationship with the farm by delivering supplies. Local goat owners may have some input about the breeder in question too, and you might inquire if they have bought from this breeder if their animals were healthy and sound.

- Ask to see the entire breeding operation and take a tour, noting the cleanliness of their facility and if there appear to be only healthy animals on the property. Ask to see their breeding stock and any records that they might be able to share with you. Their records should show how well their sale animals perform, and they may even give you some references of buyers regarding their stock. Make notes on how their stock is managed and don't forget to shop around before buying.

- Avoid sale barns. Many times these animals are there for a reason and are being culled. What that means is perhaps that particular line has proven to be a poor dairy producer, they may have bad genetic physicalities, such as a genetically poor topline, poor udder attachment, weak pasterns, or perhaps they are just older animals who are no longer viable to use for breeding stock or have stopped producing dairy altogether.

- Join social media groups, especially if there is a local one that might be able to fill you in on the local breeders.

- Contact your local extension office to see if they might be willing to give you a referral.

- If possible, connect with a local livestock mentor and see if they would be able to share their insight. In my experience, most owners love to talk about their animals.

- Connect with veterinarians in your area that specialize in your intended livestock choice and pick their brain about red flags you should be looking for. (*Note: they will not talk directly about any customers, so keep to generic questions.*)

- Always ask questions.

  - Why are you selling these goats?

  - How old are they?

  - Has this goat ever been bred before, and what were the results?

  - Is the goat registered?

  - Is there any history of disease within this bloodline? Or with just this particular goat?

  - Is your herd CAE-free? (Caprine Arthritis Encephalitis) Any breeder should be able to provide documentation of this when requested. This is a viral disease spread by the bodily fluids of an infected animal and is much like HIV. The reusing of a needle can spread this disease, as well as spilled milk on the ground. CAE can cause severe arthritis in multiple joints, mastitis, and pneumonia.

  - Is your herd CL-free? (Caseous Lymphadenitis) This is a contagious bacteria-like disease that infects both sheep and goats. The organism itself can enter a goat through an open wound or mucous membranes. It will cause abscesses of the lymph nodes and will most likely display a thick yellow or perhaps green discharge that resembles toothpaste. These abscesses are not limited to just the lymph nodes and can also occur in a goat's organs, such as the liver, udder, or lungs. Once a goat has contracted CL, they will continue to battle with repeat abscess for the remainder of its life. The organisms that create the abscesses, when ruptured, will contaminate the environment and are very difficult to kill. Because of this, they may infect your goats for years. Should your animal experience internal abscesses, they may show signs of chronic weight loss, exercise intolerance, a chronic cough, difficulty breathing, or even sudden death. Once an environment has become contaminated with CL, everything should be burned. In theory, this can be transmitted to humans.

   o   Is your herd free from Johne's disease? Also known as paratuberculosis, is caused by an organism found in manure-contaminated environments. Even though kids can become infected from a dam through their milk or even in utero, clinical signs may not appear until the animal is 2-4 years of age. Infected animals will show progressive signs of weight loss even though they eat well and, in addition, the affected goats will appear weak, anemic, have a poor coat, and poor skin quality. It emulates chronic wasting disease that you see in deer species.

- When dealing with a breeder, you should always have papers in hand before you leave with your livestock. Registration papers should never be *mailed*.

Your goat business is an investment and should always be treated like a professional business transaction. Reputable breeders will never have any problems producing the necessary paperwork you will need to register your goat, nor will they be offended by any questions you might have.

Reasons to Buy a Registered Goat

1. If you want to be able to breed as part of your operation, you will be able to connect with more people that own registered goats. Even customers that are just starting their first herd, will typically want to buy a registered animal. Without a registered herd, you will risk reducing your customer base.

2. Registered goats will have generations to back up their bloodline, enabling potential owners to track their lineage.

3. Registered goats will have the ability to be entered in shows and contests, for example, county fairs and 4-H competitions.

4. Your registered goats will always be able to command a higher price than an unregistered equal.

Questions to Ask a Breeder Before Purchasing Your Goat

1. THE most important question (see above for why) to ask of your breeder is if their herd has been tested for CAE, CL, and Johnes. They should be able to supply you with all results.

2. You should ask for pictures of the goats being purchased from all angles.

3. Confirm that all the registered paperwork will be included at the time your sale is finalized. You can always request that they email you a copy or take a picture and include it in a text message.

4. Ask them what goat organizations they belong to and which one their herd is registered with.

5. Always ask them about their feeding practices, health practices, worming, and any general maintenance they follow with their herd.

Reasons to Look for Another Breeder

If you are feeling uncomfortable about a deal, or you are feeling pressured by the breeder, you always have the option of walking away and calling it a day. Learn to listen to your intuition.

1. Lack of important testing papers for CAE, CL, and Johnes

2. No photos

3. Lack of or insufficient paperwork

4. An inability to list what is included in your purchase

5. Poor information regarding the goat's Dam and Sire

6. Do you notice that the living conditions for the prospective goats and their herd seem unhealthy?

Do You Have Reservations?

Do you have reservations about getting into goat ownership? If you are a novice, goats can seem extremely less intimidating than jumping headfirst into cows just by size alone, but many people get into goats without thinking everything through. While it's true that goats are less expensive than cows, there are some things to consider before making that final commitment. You should be aware of every aspect of ownership before you dive right in. Make sure that you are committed!

1. Were you aware that goats need their hooves trimmed on a regular basis and that this can also play a part in their overall health? Overgrown hooves can make it hard for your goats to get around and could end up causing them arthritis and lameness issues. If you are planning on performing this yourself, you may need to look into the best methods out there.

2. Fencing challenges can arise because every goat is a reincarnation of Harry Houdini. If you think that your fence line is perfect, think again. Goats will always be able to escape, and it can happen on a daily basis. Even providing them with an enticing playground and ample pasture will still not always be enough to keep them on the correct side of the fence.

3. Deworming. One thing that goats are prone to get is intestinal worms, and you will need to stay on top of their overall health by practicing deworming regularly using herbal or chemical options. By the same token, you must be careful not to over deworm your goats because worms are becoming more resistant to all of our market chemicals.

4. If you want to have goat milk, you have to have a buck. Without breeding your does, you will not get milk, but the downside is that you have to deal with a buck. Your buck, to put it mildly, will smell. If I put it honestly, they will stink to high heaven, but only during their *rut*. It seems that the true ladies' man will stink bad enough to make you vomit because they rejoice in playing in their own pee and that of others.

5. Say goodbye to your landscaping and vegetable garden once you have goats. Not only will you have to remove any toxic plants that might injure or kill your goats, but everything else will be eaten down to the ground. If the promise of homemade soft goat cheese outweighs your green thumb, then you may be alright embracing their quirky behavior.

6. Castration. If you are a beginner, you will probably need many more miles under your belt before you are ready to contemplate performing this action. If you are unsure or just plain don't want to deal with castration, you can always lean on your veterinarian.

Any young bucks that are not considered as replacement bucks for your future breeding program should be castrated between the ages of 2 to 4 weeks. Young bucks are fully capable of breeding does as early as 4 to 5 months of age. There are three common ways to castrate your bucks, and we have listed these below:

1. An elastrator is an inexpensive and quick method of castration that is a bloodless method. You would put a heavy rubber ring around the scrotum near the goat's body. This ring will block any blood circulation reaching the scrotum and testicles, causing them to dry and shrivel, sloughing off in 10 to 14 days. This method can only be done when the scrotum is small (from three days to three weeks of age, depending upon your breed's size). This method will rely on the fact that the scrotal muscles and tissues are still underdeveloped.

Your first step is to put the rubber ring on the prongs of the elastrator and while the male kid is restrained, you will pass the scrotum through the open ring, and you should see the prongs of the elastrator facing the kid's body. You must be able to feel the scrotum and make sure that both testicles are in the scrotum below the ring. The rubber ring that is positioned close to the goat's body should then be slipped off the elastrator prongs. When performing this, you must not inadvertently injure the rudimentary teats of the male kid.

There should be minimal discomfort to your animal until the area becomes numb, however, you should always monitor your kids during the period prior to the sloughing off step. This method does run a higher risk of tetanus than other castration methods. Should the banded scrotum not fall off within an appropriate amount of time, then it will need to be removed manually.

2. Burdizzo® is another quick and bloodless method of castration using a Burdizzo clamp that will emasculate, or crush and rupture the spermatic cords. While this method can be used on older animals, if you follow my advice, you will castrate your animals when they are young.

The spermatic cords must be crushed one side at a time, and you should have your animal restrained during this process. Grabbing the scrotum, you will need to manipulate one of the testicles deep within the scrotal sac and locate the spermatic cord. You will then place the clamp over the spermatic cord one-third of the way down the scrotum. After you have performed this, clamp down and hold for 15 to 20 seconds. Afterward, release the clamp and reposition it over the spermatic cord one-half inch lower and repeat the procedure. You will then mirror these steps on the other side to crush the other spermatic cord. ALWAYS check the position of the spermatic cord before and after each clamping to make sure that no mistakes are made. When using this method, the scrotal sac will not slough off but will remain on your animal. The testicles on your kid will atrophy and disappear.

During fly season, this method works well because there are no open wounds. The goats should be between four weeks and four months of age, with an ideal window of 8 to 12 weeks being optimal. It can be difficult to tell sometimes if the spermatic cords have indeed been crushed. Therefore, this method may be less reliable than other methods.

3. A knife is the third method of castration and often results in less stress for the animal. Ideally, the animal should be restrained and the scrotal area washed. The hands of the person performing the task should be washed and sanitized with alcohol. The scrotum is then gripped, and the testicles should be pushed to the upper portion and the lower third of the scrotum is then cut off. The removal of the lower third allows for wound drainage and helps fight against infection. Each testicle is slowly pulled down and away from the kid's

body until the cord breaks. If your subject is more than 4 to 5 weeks old, you should take the knife and scrape through the cord rather than wait for it to break (this creates less bleeding). The remaining part of the scrotum is then sprayed with an antibacterial spray that will repel or kill flies. It will not be unusual for your kids to be lethargic for a few days, but they will recover and be their normal bounding selves. Following common sense, your kids should not be in an area that is muddy or filthy while they recover from this procedure.

Housing Needs

Every animal needs shelter and there are always going to be general shelter tips that will work almost anywhere, but sometimes regional ideas will apply, so we would recommend to always study what people who live around you do. For example, if you live in Texas, you probably wouldn't build the same kind of building needed for severe winter weather in another part of the country. Ideally, if you have a large herd, you may want to practice pasture rotation in order to rest a field, but you would still need shelters that could move easily without tearing up your fields. Of course, if money is no object, you can build two separate permanent shelters and just move your goats.

There is no one correct way to build a shelter, but they should provide protection from drafts and elements like rain, sun, or heavy winds. Running water makes it easier to refill buckets, water troughs, or perhaps you want to splurge and install an automatic waterer.

Having electricity is beneficial when it starts getting dark early or if you want to power water heaters for winter, run some clippers, or add a needed heat lamp for your newborn kids.

If you live in a northern climate, you will need a shelter that can protect your herd from snow, ice, and the eventual flooding when wintry precipitation finally melts. Having your shelter face the south will provide the best protection against winds.

Believe it or not, the breed you choose to raise can also make a difference in what kind of shelter you invest in. Dairy goats tend to have a lower body score condition (more on that later) than a meat goat breed because they use up most of their body's energy-making milk instead of staying warm.

While there are some ingenious inventions out there to improve your goats' comfort, we recommend touring some local goat shelters to help you make up your mind on what to build. One thing that is important no matter where you live is ventilation. Without proper airflow, you can run the risk of an ammonia build-up, which can cause respiratory issues within your herd.

According to Jodi Helmer (2020), you should avoid building materials such as plywood, plastic, or areas with unprotected insulation. The floors should be made of dirt, concrete, sand, or gravel. We do not recommend wood flooring as this will soak up urine, and besides being impossible to clean, will hold in the ammonia smell.

Shelters are usually located on the highest point of your property, so rain and melting snow will drain away from the building. Keep in mind whether you are utilizing a shelter or barn, it should be accessible for the delivery of supplies. For this reason, many hobby farmers opt to keep the shelter and their herd closer to their homes for convenience.

Starting with a smaller shelter is easier for new owners so they can get some experience with running their small operation before making decisions on a grander scale. Starting smaller with a preexisting barn or shed of some kind will give you a chance to construct more permanent housing.

Avoid Overcrowding

Just because you are starting small, you still need to offer your animals space. To avoid overcrowding, your basic shelters should have a rear eave height of 4 - 6 feet and the front eave should stand around 6 - 8 feet. You should figure that each goat requires between 8 - 10 square feet of floor space as a minimum. A better standard for measurement would be 12 - 25 square feet per animal (especially if you have larger goats instead of the dwarfs or minis). So, if you have, for example, a herd of 10 goats, your starter shelter would measure between 120 - 250 square feet.

Again, ranges in shelter size can be greatly affected by the climate that you live in. If your herd is found in a place where you have a considerable amount of winter weather or rainy weather, your goats will be spending more time inside versus a dryer climate. Should you have a large pasture and a milder climate, your goats will likely spend more time outside on their playground equipment than inside the barn.

Animal Welfare can also dictate how much space you must provide. Animal Welfare Approved (2020) rules dictate that any dairy goat weighing no more than 44 pounds must have a minimum of 4 square feet of space per animal. If you provide less than adequate space, the less dominant or smaller herd members may be pushed out into the elements if there is a shortage of space. Overcrowding can also play a part in health issues, like mite outbreaks. With the goats all snuggled up in smaller areas, it can cause the spread of various health concerns, and it will also be more difficult to keep clean.

You should take the size of your goats into consideration and build a tall enough roof accordingly. Should you build too short of a shelter, your goats might decide to jump on the roof, which will cause damage not only to your shelter but also to members of your herd. Another problem that you may not consider when building a lower roof is that a human needs to be able to fit underneath in order to effectively clean the shelter.

Speaking of clean shelters, it is essential to your herd's health to remove any manure and soiled bedding. You should plan on cleaning and disinfecting your shelter regularly.

Adding Kids?

The best-laid plans are often tossed out the window when you suddenly find out that you have kids on the way! Even if you don't plan on keeping any offspring, you still need to provide certain amenities for their health and well-being.

Pregnant does and newborns come with their own specific shelter needs. They will need a secluded pen that provides them with extra protection from the elements and a safe outlet that can be used for a heat lamp.

Kids can be extremely fragile and if not provided with adequate shelter requirements, they can succumb to respiratory infections and hypothermia due to cold, wet weather. In extreme cases, the elements can even cause their death.

Does and kids should be separated from the herd for a minimum of 3 - 5 days after birth. This private space not only provides them with adequate shelter needs but will allow you to assist with deliveries should that be necessary, and the private area also gives the does and kids time to bond without interference from the rest of the herd.

Adding the Essentials

Ideally, your shelter will be more than a house for your herd; it should also be a storage building for your hay, grain, minerals, equipment, and any other supplies. Goats will always need access to their feeders, free-choice minerals, and of course, water, but you may want to incorporate a milking station into your design, or a designated area in which you will attend to their hoof trimmings or shearing.

While many people share housing between goats and other livestock, it is always best to provide a separate shelter for your goats. Chickens can add additional mess to goat quarters and if your hay is not covered properly or up high enough, the chickens can poop on the hay, causing sanitation issues and health problems. We have even heard stories of finding a dead chicken in a goat area. What happened we will never know, perhaps they trampled her or head-butted her, but the result was a sad one.

Sheep and goats can get along, but each species exhibits different behavior from the other. Both of these species can share the same diseases and parasites, so it may be more beneficial to keep them separated. Also, when feeding, sheep will not tolerate copper, which may be found in your goat feed and minerals. Since they are different animals with different mannerisms, they will probably not be happy together. If you are fortunate, they will merely ignore each other. Sheep, like goats, are herd animals and will need another of their species. There have been people I have known that say that their goats were just pesky bullies and acted aggressively toward their sheep.

How to Survive the Winter

If you happen to live in an area where you are subject to severe winter weather, then there are some other plans you will need to make. All of your livestock will find winter more stressful than other times of the year, but being a great owner, you will be able to give supportive care by adjusting your care, feeding, and overall management of your herd.

The most important winter adjustment to make to protect your goats is to block any cold north winter winds and keep them warm and dry. If you have been following good nutritional practices for your animals, then they will have grown a thick coat of hair to help them survive the winter chill. In addition, you will have to provide plenty of clean, dry bedding, and if you have goats kidding in the cold weather, they will require extra shelter because the young goats will not be able to maintain their body temperature. Most in these situations will require a heat lamp, but these will need to be monitored with caution because of the added risk of barn fires or if your animals can reach and chew on electrical cords. Your herd will grow furry coats to help keep them insulated through the winter, and most breeds will have a two-layer coat consisting of longer hairs on top and a fluffy cashmere layer underneath. It is important to provide your herd with mineral supplements that support healthy fur growth, like copper and zinc.

It might seem like a large investment, but insulation is key for areas that experience winter months. Keeping your animals safe, warm, and comfortable will make it all worth it.

Along with insulation, you want good ventilation while keeping drafts at bay. Cold air can accumulate at the floor level of your barn and can create toxic gases, but with proper ventilation, those unhealthy aspects will be pushed out, bringing warm clean air from the barn ceiling downward. Improper ventilation will cause cold air to blow on your goats, and those drafts can make your herd susceptible to illnesses, such as pneumonia.

Fresh clean water is a constant need for all livestock and if you do not have some sort of heating source, you will need to change their water several times each day to remove ice. Any sort of heating device will need to be monitored for chewing. Should you be fortunate enough to have a heated automatic waterer, those cords will be encased in the unit and the only thing you will need to do is freshen the water when it becomes dirty.

Your goats will require more roughage to help them maintain their body temperature during cold winter months. You may need to add feedings of alfalfa or mixed hay. Alfalfa hay, in particular, is a great source of both energy and protein for your livestock. However, when feeding bucks and wethers, the extra protein can cause urinary calculi. This disease can affect both goats and sheep and will prevent urination and breeding; this illness can and does have the ability to kill your animals.

Unless you have splurged on radiant heat (and yes, there are some that have!), you should provide your goats with a resting or sleeping place that is up off the ground on platforms. Fresh deep bedding and platforms will give your goats somewhere to lie down on a surface that isn't cold, dirt, or concrete, which can pull heat from their bodies.

Even if there is snow on the ground, but the sun is shining, make sure that your goats go outside and move about and play, even if it's only for a few hours. Activity helps them create heat and remedies the boredom that they may experience when it is bitterly cold and conditions prevent them from going outside. Providing multiple feeding stations is a good way to get your goats moving around and jockeying for position.

Eew, Lice!

Goat lice tend to be more prevalent during the winter months and these strains of lice are host-specific, meaning that they only attack goats and species that are similar, such as sheep. The lice strains that will plague your goats are divided into two groups: the Anoplura (sucking lice) and the Mallophaga (chewing or biting lice).

You can recognize the signs of lice by your animal's dull coat and excessive rubbing, itching, scratching, and biting behavior. If your goat is suffering from sucking lice, you may also see scabby, bleeding areas that can quickly turn into bacterial infections if not treated quickly.

It is recommended that you work together with your veterinarian to plan ahead for any treatments needed to keep a lice outbreak under control. They will recommend either topical or systemic treatments depending upon which kind of lice you are addressing. Biting lice can be controlled with a liquid or powder applied topically and while sucking lice can be treated in the same fashion, it usually requires a systemic treatment (oral or injectable). Since there is no treatment currently labelled for or approved for goats, you must treat under the advice of your veterinarian. Remember to follow your vets directions exactly as there may be specific waiting times for milk or meat harvests.

If you suspect that your animals have lice, one of the best places to look for the parasite is just behind the foreleg on the skin. The lice may look like dirt between the hair and the skin. You have to wait and watch for movement to properly identify it. You may also see some eggs attached to your goat's hair follicles.

Telltale signs of goats that might be infected include dull coats, exhibit excessive biting, scratching, rubbing, and grooming behavior. You may even notice patches of missing or thinning hair. If you are raising goats for fiber, this can greatly affect the value of their harvest due to low hair quality. Bites from the Anoplura can develop into bacterial infections, but the greatest threat to your herd because of lice is anemia, which can cost them their lives.

The presence of lice can add stress to your animals because they will feel anxiety and discomfort. As a result, they may even go off their feed, causing weight loss and an increased inability to stay warm in the cold months. If you have dairy goats, they will likely experience a drop in milk production up to 25 percent.

Don't feel like you have let your animals down because any herdsman can have infected animals; cold climates and being confined are unfortunately ideal conditions for a lice infestation. Certainly, don't let this discourage you about your care because lice are typically seasonal and show the highest amount of activity during the late winter to early spring. When extended sunshine and warmer temperatures return, lice tend to disappear, but don't believe that you can put off treatment because the health issues will not leave with the lice.

Don't Fence Me In

Oh, give me land, lots of land under starry skies above, don't fence me in."

— Cole Porter

What would a habitat for your goats be without an enclosure to keep them and the rest of your property safe? Chaos, that's what! And while your goats might enjoy their freedom, they will not be safe.

Fencing is incredibly important to get right since goats are such escape artists. What you read about their abilities might give you some second thoughts about bringing them home, but here are some tips I have gathered to make your fencing efforts more solid:

1. All design aspects of your fencing should target keeping your goats inside the area. We all like nice-looking things, but when it comes to fencing, functionality is of the utmost importance. What we are hinting at here is that you might have to let the idea of adorable fencing be saved for another day and for another purpose. The fact is that if a goat really wants to get out, it probably will. What you ultimately decide to use should at least put up a good fight.

Wooden posts placed in the ground are best supported by concrete overshoes. After that, livestock fencing is a good choice and smaller mesh typically is a better choice than the larger mesh. The smaller the holes, the harder time they will have passing through it. To be honest, no matter how well you plan, if they really want to get out, they will find a way.

2. Besides keeping your goats in, it should also keep predators out. Even if your area seems devoid of predators, it is in your best interest to plan like you have an abundance of potential predators. With that in mind, your fence should be sturdy and tall. Frankly, the best defense against coyotes is to put a donkey out in the pasture with your goats because, even at 6 feet tall, coyotes can still find a way to jump in and get to your goats.

Donkeys will attack a predator and can be extremely aggressive while using both their teeth and hooves to confront an attacker. Often your sheep or goats will perceive the donkey as their protector and will gather nearby if they think there is a threat. Should you choose to add a donkey or two and integrate them with your herd, you should keep in mind that the shelter will need to be taller to accommodate the bigger animal. If you add a donkey to your herd, be aware that they should never have access to Rumensin, or any other feeds or supplements intended for your ruminants.

3. Electric fencing can be a good option, especially if you are located near a rather busy road. It is a small inconvenience to shock your goats until they get used to it and figure out they should stay away from it. Depending on how large of an area you need to electrify, it can be a bit expensive, but if you live close to a busy road, it might be worth it, so you don't worry so much about your goats getting loose and getting hurt or causing an accident.

While you may experience some initial internal struggles about shocking your animals, it is not that strong of a current, and if it keeps them from being harmed or killed, it is worth the expense.

If you are relying on electric fencing alone, the recommended number of strands is seven. Your best option is to use a single strand with a mesh fence. Apparently, there is a new electric fence on the market that features woven wire that you may want to look into.

4. Your fence must be strong. Especially if you have male goats, you should consider the smaller mesh livestock fencing or even invest in more expensive livestock panels.

5. Maintaining your fencing is imperative. Regular fence maintenance should be made part of your routine. Walking the fence line will help you notice any holes or other areas that need your immediate attention and mending. When you do this, you should always check the gates and latches to ensure that nothing needs repair. If you have installed electric fencing, you should periodically use a fence tester to make sure that the current is still working properly.

6. Keep your goats happy on their side of the fence! If they love their play areas, their bed, and their feeding schedule, then they are far less likely to roam. If you find that your goats are trying to escape a lot, you may want to change things up in their pasture.

Woven wire and chain link can also be good options for your fence. The heavy gauge of a chain link can last for some time, but it must be heavily secured.

Goats Love to Climb

Get ready to watch endless rounds of king of the mountain between your goats. They love to climb on anything and everything (including cars). Your goats will probably perform some impressive things, and some goats can even climb trees.

Over the years, goats have evolved to perform tough climbs and daring jumps and this is primarily because they possess two toes on each of their hooves, which has given them an advanced sense of balance for scaling things that amaze and astound us. There's a good chance that when you see a photo of a goat standing in a tree, it has not been photoshopped.

Planning Ahead

Advance preparation is key when you are bringing home your first herd. It can be a very exciting time for you, but the last thing you want to happen is to discover that you forgot an important supply for your new herd and the local farm store is closed. We suggest that you make some checklists regarding your new shelter and supplies to make sure that you have everything that you need.

- Shelter
    - Secure fencing should be in place. Netting and wire will both work, but the key is to make sure that it will (ahem) keep your goats in and possible predators out. Electric fencing may create some added protection.
    - Hay mangers, because once a goat drops hay on the floor, it will not eat it.
    - Hay
    - Water buckets, small water trough, or automatic waterer
    - Salt
    - Free choice minerals for goats (always choose *chelated minerals*)

- Free choice baking soda, which should always be offered to prevent indigestion or bloat in your herd.
- Kelp is an option for your pregnant or lactating does. Always pick *chelated mineral-free* varieties.

- Medical Kit (a more detailed list is found in chapter 6)
  - Digital thermometer
  - Pepto Bismol
  - Electrolytes for dehydration (can use Gatorade)
  - Probios probiotics for gut health, especially after an illness
  - Drench syringe for the administration of oral meds
  - Aerosol antiseptic bandage protector (Blu-Kote, AluShield)
  - Dewormer
  - Bandages
  - Gauze
  - Medical tape
  - Alcohol swabs
  - Iodine
  - Hydrogen peroxide
  - Healing salve like Neosporin
  - High-potency B complex in case of goat polio
  - 6 cc syringes and needles

- Additional Supplies (many of these focus on kids)
  - Milk replacer
  - A clean bottle, a wine, or soda bottle will do
  - Nipple(s)

- ○ Grain or alfalfa pellets to offer as a weaning adjusting supplement

- ○ Vaccinations: CD&T (This is a goat vaccine for use in healthy goats to aid in the prevention of enterotoxemia which is caused by Clostridium perfringens and provides long-term protection against tetanus. USDA approved.

- ○ Straw bedding

Feeding Your Goat

If you don't know much about goat nutrition, that's okay because that's what we are here for! For the record, goats do not eat tin cans, but they might check out inside to see if there is something yummy leftover. The closest animal that goats resemble for nutritional needs is the deer. Goats are considered ruminants and eat plants, digesting them through a four-compartment stomach system. This is not to be confused with the misinformation that goats have four stomachs. What they have is one stomach with four compartments.

Contrary to popular belief, goats are actually picky eaters. They may taste many things but not eat the entire stalk. There are some goats that harbor suspicions regarding their new foods and might be on the verge of starving before they give in and try out the new taste. Unlike their livestock counterparts, sheep and cattle who tend to eat mostly grass, goats should not eat a diet composed entirely of fresh grass.

Proper attention to feeding will ensure that your herd lives longer, produces more, and has fewer health issues. Any changes in diet should be made slowly so that you might be able to spot any red flags regarding the recent changes. The best practice is to not make any sudden or drastic changes to your herd's diet because this can lead to digestive upset.

Hay

Hay is the main source of a goat's nutrients besides their range, and the hay can be a grassy bale or can include legumes like clover or alfalfa. Always purchase the best quality hay you can locate. Good hay will always be expensive, but the better the hay, the less need you will have for supplementation or added grains. Especially if you are running a dairy barn, good-quality hay will influence the amount and quality of milk you receive from your animals. Hay can be fed freely or just twice a day. The average goat will ingest about 4.5 pounds of hay a day per 100 pounds of body weight. Remember to limit hay to smaller feedings in mangers if you have great pasture since once the hay touches the floor the goats will not eat it.

Tip: If you feed your goats a low-quality forage, all they will do is play with it or pee on it.

Goats require additional hay to boost their roughage intake in order to keep their rumen functioning properly. You should never expect to feed your herd solely on pasture. The rumen is their first stomach compartment and this uses long fiber-like hay to keep the rumen rich in live healthy bacteria. Alfalfa hay or grass alfalfa mix is a popular hay choice for feeding goats and provides them with more protein, vitamins, and minerals than most grass hays. Alfalfa hay will also provide more calcium for feeding your milk-producing goats.

For those of you unfamiliar with a product described as chaffhaye, this is made by using an early cutting of alfalfa or grass and chopping it into fine pieces, and then mixing it with molasses and a probiotic culture for gut health, called bacillus subtilis. After the ingredients are combined, the end product is vacuum-packed. The hay will further ferment while contained, which will add beneficial bacteria that target the goats' ruments. You can feed chaffhaye as an alternative to hay, but realize that this product will be more nutrient-dense than hay. For example, a 50-pound bag of chaffhaye will roughly equal 85 to 100 lbs of hay.

Educate yourself on hay quality found within your region. Hay stored under the roof of a protective barn will retain most of its nutritional value for up to a year. Watch for hay that has been baled and put up still wet or damp because not only is this a fire hazard, but it can lead to mold and microorganisms. These, in turn, will release toxins that can cause your animal to become ill. Never feed your goats moldy hay!

Grain

A good rule of thumb is to have your hay tested for nutrient values because hay is going to differ depending upon where you live and the soil content. It can also differ from year to year due to drought and other environmental issues. Since there is no such thing as perfect hay, this will provide you with what is lacking in your pasture and hay that you can then take the results to an animal nutritionist to devise a plan of attack for your herd's diet. Depending upon the size of your herd, you may want to have a custom feed designed by your livestock nutritionist.

A grain feed or a pelleted mix will add protein, vitamins, and minerals to your goat's diet. Your use of grain will vary, but unless it has been a terrible year for hay production and your pastures are empty, grain products are only a supporting player in your nutritional foundation. There are always exceptions, such as does that are raising multiple kids or a rash of bad weather, but the basis of your herd's nutrition will always be obtained through foraging.

Overall, grain should never be overfed as it can lead to overweight goats and open them up to illnesses. Your grain bag should provide you with a guaranteed analysis and feed rate that gives you guidelines on how much to feed per body weight. Many feeds will include ammonium chloride to promote a healthy urinary tract.

Besides balancing out a hay deficiency, grains are regulated to show animals and growing, breeding, or lactating animals.

There are medicated feeds that are designed to be fed to young goats for the prevention of coccidiosis (see chapter 6). **MEDICATED FEEDS SHOULD NEVER BE FED TO GOATS THAT ARE PRODUCING MILK USED FOR FOOD.** These are usually very palatable to encourage early-weaned kids to eat.

Loose Free Choice Minerals

There are loose minerals formulated for goats that you should always offer free choice to your animals. When possible, always opt for chelated because those are more bioavailable for your animals. Loose minerals are more desirable since the blocks often contain an overabundance of salt and molasses.

Loose Free Choice Baking Soda

Goats can benefit from free choice baking soda, and many goat breeders offer this to their herd. Most herdsmen feed this to their goats to keep their digestive tract in check. There is no need to mix it into their feed because your herd will self-dose when they feel they need it. According to Manna Pro (2020), baking soda can not only aid in digestive issues, but can help prevent bloat when your animal has overeaten or ingested the wrong food. A goat that is offered baking soda on a daily basis can help balance the pH levels found in the rumen, which works similar to how heartburn relief works with us humans. Since goats are typically escape artists, they may be more prone to eat something that causes stomach upset.

The true goat's diet is not just pasture, but a diet that includes shrubs, weeds, and brambles (which is why they make excellent living bush hogs). Since we keep our herds contained in a pasture, our animals will resort to eating grass once all the brambles are cleared away. Should they consume too much grass, it can overpower the bacteria found in their rumen and cause a case of bloat.

Offer baking soda in its own container and replace it when your goats soil the container.

Kitchen and Garden Scraps

Typically, your goats will generally do fine eating kitchen compost, but eggshells can be a problem. If they are used to it, you should be okay, but you should never overdo amounts or frequency. Raisins, corn chips, stale popcorn, or even a slice of bread might make a nice special treat, but we are not an advocate of providing this to your animals with any frequency. A consistent diet keeps a healthy gut, and adding too many extras can upset the animal's digestive tract.

Meeting the Nutritional Needs of the Older Goat

Goats are considered to be of age at around five-years-old and by eight, many exhibit signs of aging. Your older goats may have some special needs because as they age, their teeth will wear down or even fall out. The elder goat may require support in the way of additional grain or some liquid supplements. Your senior goats may need easier access to food and water, and their stiff joints may prevent them from eating or drinking enough to support themselves. If you are unable to separate the younger and older animals, you will have to watch to make sure that the older goats are getting what they need in order to remain healthy.

Feeding Equipment

Nothing fancy is necessary. In fact, many goat keepers make suitable containers from items found at your local farm store or home improvement center. The Internet is full of many such ideas for you to copy. As we have mentioned, you should have some sort of manger that helps your stock access the hay, but not waste it.

You should also invest in metal or plastic containers with tight-fitting lids to keep any grain or minerals in. This will keep pests, like mice, out of your supplies and keep them free from contamination. You may want to consider:

- Feed storage containers
- Food buckets
- Water buckets
- Hay mangers
- Mineral feeders

You Can Build Your Own Manger

There are almost as many designs for building your own mangers as there are stars in the night's sky. It can be as simple as some hog wire nailed into some sturdy two-by-fours or a store-bought manger that hangs over a stall wall or bolted to a wall. It all depends on how handy you are or how comfortable you are around saws.

There are so many designs for mangers inside and outside. Our best recommendation is to surf the web a bit and find one that works for your farm. If you are as handy as one of my good friends (snicker), you will be ordering them from a supply house.

Body Score Conditioning Chart

Score	Condition	Backbone & Ribs	Loin
1	Very lean	Easy to see and feel Can feel under the ribs	No fat
2	Lean	Easy to feel Smooth Need to use a little pressure to feel ribs	Smooth fat
3	Good	Smooth and rounded Even feel to the ribs	Smooth fat
4	Fat	Can feel backbone with firm pressure No points on spine and no ribs felt Indent between ribs felt with pressure	Thick fat
5	Obese	Smooth No individual vertebra felt No separation of ribs felt	Thick fat Lumpy Jiggles

Chapter 2:
It's Going to be Goat-tastic!

Did you know that goats are fantastic at clearing overgrown bits of land? There is no need to rent a bush hog anymore because your goats can take care of that for you, and they are much less labor-intensive.

Goats for Land Management

If you have heard that goats are capable of clearing unwanted vegetation, invasive plants, and overbearing brush, then you have heard correctly. These little dynamos can clear a lot of unwanted vines and weeds, and the best part is they eat all of it, preventing unwanted regrowth. Mowers will cut weeds down and allow seeds to scatter and reestablish said weed in more places, while your grazing goats will eat the weed, seeds, and often the roots.

Goats will go out in the heat of the sunshine and save you many labor-intensive hours using machinery to clear your land. You will not have to invest in extra fuel, spare parts, and repairs if the machinery is yours; rental fees and transportation issues if you are renting equipment. You will also be able to keep your land clear from toxic herbicides that can cause health concerns with the animals, humans, and pollinators that have access to those treated pastures and the goods potentially grown upon them. Your goats will provide a natural solution and will most likely fertilize as they go.

I already mentioned that grass is not a goats' favorite choice for when they get the munchies, and they are unique in the fact that they have special gut enzymes that enable them to digest any number of plants that would prove toxic to other animals.

So, what plants will they clear? They will completely clear overgrown vines and clear any and all weeds, but you should always be aware of anything growing that might transfer to you or your goods, such as poison ivy and poison oak. The fact is that goats love to eat these, but it will transfer to you if you pet them or milk them. Besides overgrowth, you will have to watch them if they begin to destroy something you don't want them eating, such as young apple trees. You will have to devise protection for any plants or trees that you don't want them to clear.

Believe it or not, there are professional goats that are hired to eat excess vegetation. Wouldn't it be great to get paid to just eat all day? There are actual goat landscaping businesses that will drive their herd about in their own trailer, bringing their convenience to you for a price. If you are struggling with growing goats for food, then starting a goat landscaping business might be a good alternative for you, and many companies that provide this service find that they are booked solid from April through November and clear public and private properties.

The goat grazing business will not utilize fossil fuels, even though the goats do emit a greenhouse gas called methane. All you need is a herd of goats and land to keep them on to get started. As with any herd, probably your biggest expense is hoof trimming (if you don't perform this yourself) and veterinarian bills. Depending upon where you are, most cities don't even require a permit to let a herd of goats chow down on an overgrown field.

Truthfully, people hear about goats clearing land, and not only will it be a novelty for them, but they can practice being green, and possibly placate protestors of other less favorable methods. In any case, it can just be fun and entertaining to watch a herd of goats chow down on unwanted overgrowth. A herd can prove to be the perfect group of employees because they love their work. Should they need a bathroom break, they go right where they are eating, which spreads fertilizer.

According to Rachel Manteuffel (2019), a herd of 28 goats can clear an acre of brush in 10 to 12 days. The average charge from a goat landscaping company can cost 2,500 to 3,000 dollars per acre, plus any unseen expenses. The humans from these companies will dig post holes and put up a fence for their herd, but the prep work is anything but glamorous. It can be a hot, sweaty, buggy day and everyone is in high-top rain boots to protect against chiggers and ticks. It is not a huge moneymaker, but it is a business that you can have all to yourself and enjoy the perks of your goofy goats.

Your Goat Herd Will Help You Deliver Amazing Milk and Cheese

Your herd is going to surprise you, when you realize that your friendly and intelligent goats are going to reward you with some outstanding milk. Your animals will be able to thrive on sloping or flat land, and two does will be able to produce enough fresh milk to feed your family all year long. If you add a few more does to your herd, you will even be able to make your own cheese, yogurt, and ice cream. When you walk through your local grocery store and look at all the cow's milk lining the shelves, it may be hard for you to believe that the world's people overall consume goat milk more than cow milk. Since goats tend to appreciate a varied diet composed of what is available in your pasture, you may want to double-check some of the plants growing in your pasture. For example, if they consume some wild onions, it can really alter the flavor of your milk. Roughage from twigs, bark, or leaves is a good source as well as regular pasture, corn, sunflower stalks, and fine stemmed hay filled with alfalfa or clover.

Milking does should receive 2 to 3 pounds (depending upon feeding recommendations) of a commercial feed. If milk production is important, you will want high-quality hay balanced with a dairy grain ration that provides protein, minerals, and vitamins to support quality milk production.

In order to keep your milk flowing, you will need to breed your does once a year. Dairy goats are usually bred in the fall. However, they can have heat cycles from August to January. Their heat cycle lasts three days, and you should put the buck and does together during this time. Once they have been bred, you should again separate the buck from the does. Kidding will occur around 145 to 150 days after the initial breeding.

Interestingly, does will usually have twins or even triplets depending upon the breed. Your doe will begin producing milk after the kids are born and will continue to produce for up to 10 months. You should give each doe a 'dry period' of about two months before she is again bred and delivers new kids, restarting the milk production.

There should be no problem sharing the milk with the kids. After the kids are two weeks old you can confine them overnight and this will allow you to milk the doe in the morning. After you milk, you can return the kids to the doe, so they can nurse. A great way to get the kids used to being handled by humans is to milk the does twice a day and give the kids bottles.

We have found that the milking process is easier if you feed your does grain while you milk them. Milking will be easy to learn, and you should milk out both udders completely at the same time each day. If you choose to milk twice a day, you should separate your milking times by 12 hours. You should keep your milking equipment and area clean and once you have completed milking, you can cool the milk-filled container quickly by setting it into a large pan that you have pre-filled with cold water for the duration of about 15 minutes. If you stir the milk occasionally with a clean utensil, it will help you cool the milk evenly. After your milk has cooled, you can pour it into clean glass containers and immediately refrigerate it. Remember that everything that touches your milk must be sterile. If you plan on hand-milking, you will need the following equipment:

- Milking Stand
- Stainless-steel milking pail
- Stainless-steel strainer and milk filters
- Dish soap or dairy soap
- Bleach or sanitizer
- Acid detergent
- Clean-up brushes
- Strip Cup
- Mastitis indicators
- Paper towels or dairy towels
- Teat dip, such as Fight Bac®

You will find that people who are used to commercial cow's milk will find the taste of goat milk richer and sweeter.

Goat milk is naturally homogenized because the butterfat globules are smaller than that of cow milk, so they will disperse more easily. But unlike cow milk, the cream will not separate on its own, making goat milk products smoother and creamier. If you want to try your hand at butter, you will need to buy or borrow a cream separator. We will have more on milk products in chapter 3.

The Advantage of Meat Goats

Meat goats can be a profitable avenue to follow for a livestock business. However, meat goats are not for everyone. There is no shame in the discovery that meat goats are not your cup of tea.

If you have decided to raise meat goats, you should know upfront that the most difficult thing about them is giving your managed herd proper nutrition. Just like the human saying, you are what you eat.

As we have mentioned before, you should always buy the best hay you can find and afford. Goats have the quickest metabolism of all the ruminants, so proper nutrition is the building block of the best milk, meat, or fiber that you wish to produce. You should never consider feeding a grain-only diet, believing that you will add weight quickly to your animals. Goats can become bloated or develop enterotoxemia from an imbalance of rumen flora due to feeding an improper amount of roughage in your goat's diet.

You will only require a small amount of acreage to test the waters of the goat meat industry.

Meat goats are a staple in many cultures and are extremely popular in Mexican, Greek, African, and Arabic cuisines. It may surprise you to learn that when taking into consideration all the red meat eaten around the world, 70 percent of it comes from goats! I bet you didn't know that! Within the United States, the largest meat goat operations are found further south, where there seems to be more of a demand for the product. Even though the consumption of goat meat is on the rise, the average American has never eaten goat meat.

The production of goat meat tends to increase when there is a trend in ethnic cooking and when people start to analyze the nutritional content of the meat of the goat when compared to that of other livestock.

Changes in food choices are driven by people becoming more conscious of the environment and the health impacts of what we are eating. Educated consumers are learning to look for grass-fed meat raised under humane conditions. Many of these customers will seek out local products from neighborhood farmers.

Goat meat, when roasted, has the same number of calories as chicken, but the meat contains more minerals and less fat. It will contain the same protein content as beef, but provides 10 percent more iron. When goat meat is a product of grass-fed animals, the result is higher omega-3 fatty acids.

Fiber Production

When you raise goats for their hair coat, these breeds are referred to as fiber goats. People always think of sheep or even rabbits when we talk about products of fiber and have no idea that goats are used to produce natural fibers.

Advanced technology may try to duplicate the comfort, strength, and durability of animal fibers, but fiber artisans and educated people know that man-made fibers are no match for those that nature provides us. Natural fibers are amazing when it comes to their ability to insulate you and keep you warm. Natural fiber will absorb perspiration and will wick it away from your skin, discharging it into the air. Another bonus is that all goat fibers are inherently flame-resistant.

Goats that provide us with fibers, such as angora, cashmere, or mohair will grow a new coat every year. The large commercial angora herds are found primarily in the Southwest, and they produce more than one million pounds of mohair each year!

Cashmere goats through selective breeding have finally become viable in the United States, but because only 4 to 6 ounces of this undercoat are produced each year per goat, this drives up the price of cashmere.

If you are looking to dive into ownership of fiber goats, confirmation should always be one of your top considerations. You will need to look for strong legs and feet, as well as a well-formed mammary system for raising kids.

Animals should always possess a good set of teeth and a strong jaw for maintaining proper nutrition.

After confirmation, the next consideration is the fleece, and it should cover as much of the animal's body as possible. You should learn as much about fiber goats as possible before taking the step into ownership.

Types of fiber include:

- Cashmere is produced from the Cashmere goat and their fiber is well known for the lightness, warmth, and softness that this fiber creates.

- Mohair - Angora fiber is called *mohair*. Angora goats are the most efficient fiber-producing animal in the world, and there isn't another animal in the world that produces this product. Angora goats are usually sheared twice a year

- Cashgora is a product made from crossing an angora buck and a cashmere doe, and this fiber is favored by many of the world's top fashion designers.

- Kemp is the long, straight, and brittle hollow hair that can show up on the thighs or the backbone of a fiber goat. These fibers break easily and do not take to dye well. The representation of kemp is one criterion for culling a goat from a fiber-producing herd.

When caring for your fiber herd, the majority of these animals will be raised using range-like conditions. This method of husbandry can create challenges for meeting the nutritional needs of your herd. Once they are sheared, these goats can be prone to becoming chilled from cold or damp weather. These animals should never be exposed to sudden temperature drops, increased winds, or humidity. The end result may be the animals falling ill or even dying.

Even the Goat Manure Can be Used

If you want to create the best growing conditions for your plants, then adding goat droppings can be a great choice, since their dry pellets are easy to collect and tend to be less messy than other types of manure. You can even compost it and use it for mulch.

There are several advantages when using goat manure instead of cow, chicken, or horse manure. One of the best benefits that goat manure has is that it doesn't attract insects or burn plants when fresh. It is relatively odorless and has beneficial properties, such as nitrogen, for better fertilizing.

The best time to add goat manure fertilizer to any garden is in the fall, allowing your soil to absorb the nutrients over the winter. As a goat farmer, many people are happy to come and get it out of your way, so it's likely a simple sign offering it for free will find your pile going down quickly.

If you have an extensive garden, you may want to compost your goat manure, and it is neither hard nor messy. A composted product produced in a bin-type structure will be dry and very rich when you mix in some other materials, such as eggshells, straw, grass clippings, leaves, or even kitchen scraps (though most prefer to leave any meat products out of their compost). It's a good practice to keep your compost moist, and you should turn the layers of your pile on occasion to help increase airflow and break down your materials.

Because goat manure is pelletized, their droppings allow more airflow, which aids in how rapidly the compost mixes. The advantages that composted manure brings is:

- Promoting healthier plant growth
- Adding missing nutrients to your soil
- Increased crop production
- The ability to circumvent harmful chemicals

Goats Can Make Great Companions

You may have no aspirations of raising meat or dairy goats, but you will probably discover that many urban households are keeping their goats merely as pets. Goats can display some very charming attributes and because of their good personalities, they can become a good company for other animals, too. Pygmy and Kinder goats are prone to make excellent companions, and even though all sizes of the goat clan can make a good pet, the smaller breeds are the more popular choice.

Like any animal that graces your life, goat owners are finding that their goats bring them stress relief and their barnyard antics are fun to just sit, watch, and relax to. Pet goats are just as messy as their productive counterparts and owners will still face all the basic goat challenges, such as climbing, destructiveness, and being a picky eater. No matter what job your goats perform, they are all fun and social animals that become very attached to their owners.

Most of these pet goats don't have many demands made upon them other than eating, sleeping, playing, and general entertainment. However, some have learned to be therapy animals and will accompany their humans to assisted-living facilities, battered women shelters, schools, and orphanages.

If you are interested in a therapy goat, you can research The Delta Society. This organization registers many different pets, including goats, for therapy work. Any goat in question must pass a test to show that it is a reliable, predictable, and controllable animal that will pursue visiting with strangers. A registered pet with the Delta Society will always display good manners in public places.

Raising a goat as a pet is not as easy as your typical dogs, cats, or even chickens. They can have requirements that you may not be fully aware of, such as the need to roam, hoof trimming, or the fact that you probably will need another of the species. The best way to prepare is to soul search as to why you want to raise goats as pets. You should always look for goats that have been well handled and therefore, well-behaved. Wild or feral acting goats will not be appropriate to shape into pets.

You may not even want a goat for human companionship. Were you aware that many horse racing stables use goats as companions for their higher-strung equine athletes? It's fairly common to find some goats napping in horse stalls, even at Churchill Downs! Owners and trainers agree that goats can have a steady and calming effect on jumpy racehorses.

Regardless of your goat's vocation, they will still need to follow a good diet, receive annual vaccines, and should see their veterinarian regularly. Keep in mind that all baby animals will grow, and a baby goat is no exception! Even the smaller breeds can mature to be about 60 pounds, so be prepared for the adult goat.

The best choice for pet goats are the wethers or castrated males, and you will find that not only are pet goats affectionate and loving, but they will respond to their name, lay their head in your lap (a good reason to remove horns), and they enjoy being massaged and petted. My suggestion is to stick with the castrated males as the best choice for a pet. Since you will need two, we would recommend two castrated bucks.

There are a few tips we would like to give you if considering owning or raising goats as pets:

- Don't buy kids if they are too young. We recommend you wait until they are over 4 to 5 months of age.

- If you want to have castrated bucks, don't perform this when they are still too young. Sometime after 6 months of age would be appropriate.

- Because castrated bucks tend to get urinary calculi, you should feed them only a small amount of grain.

- DO NOT ROUGHHOUSE WITH YOUR GOATS. Playing rough, especially with young kids, can make for some rude behavior when they are older. Too many games of pushing can make your goat aggressive and dangerous when they are older. Always play gently with your baby goats.

- Never allow your baby goats to jump on you. When they become adults, this can become a very dangerous habit.

- Spend quality time bonding with your goats. They enjoy having their muzzle massaged gently and find it calming to have a physical nearness to you. You may even see them roll back their eyes in pleasure.

- Walk around with your goats on occasion. Both parties will find this pleasurable, but make sure that there are no aggressive animals around that might hurt your goats.

- If you plan on taking your goats anywhere in the car, you should get them used to a pet carrier. Always practice safe driving and give them a good experience, so they don't feel apprehension the next time. Slamming on your brakes will tend to alarm your animal. Always get your goat out of the car immediately after arriving at your destination.

- Always communicate with your vet about your goat's health issues. Any noticeable change should be addressed as soon as possible.

- Take good care of your goats and treat them with the love and respect any living creature deserves.

- Have fun with them!

When all is said and done, goats can be a tremendous benefit to you and the upkeep of your land. Even better, is the fact that they can help you profit from having them around. There are so many options. All you need to do is figure out which direction you want to go!

Chapter 3:
Endless Milk and Cheese

Did you know that August is National Goat Cheese Month?

We have already discussed several aspects of milking goats, their nutritional needs, and their milking schedules when balanced with the needs of their kids, but you probably didn't know that your does can experience their first heat when they are seven-months-old!

When Do Does Stop Milk Production?

If you breed her at 12 months of age, your doe will have her first kid around 18 months of age. Your doe will begin to produce milk immediately after giving birth to her first kid. Any milk production will require a birth cycle to get things rolling. Does will continue to produce milk for many years to come, right up until they are 8 to 10 years old; some even up to 14 years of age. There is no specific age that does will stop producing milk, but a good rule of thumb is whenever you stop milking them or allowing them to be bred.

Do All Does Produce Milk?

Theoretically, all goats that can become pregnant will be able to produce milk, but that doesn't mean that they will all be top producers. If you are looking for a meat breed of goat that is also capable of producing milk, they usually only have enough milk to feed their kids and milk production will drop off for meat goats after a few months following the birth of their kids.

Obviously, dairy goats will be the best milk producers for your farm, and they will produce it for longer periods of time, which will allow you to create some amazing things.

As mentioned earlier, balance milking with kids present, but your kids should always have their mother's milk for at least a couple of weeks after their birth. Goat kids can be bottle-fed if needed, but first, they MUST receive their colostrum.

The first milk that goat kids drink from their mother will contain colostrum. The reason this is important is that this first milk will provide them with needed nutrients and antibodies that will aid in their newborn survival. Without this, they will not thrive.

Should you decide to leave the kids on their mother for the duration of their time together, then the mom will begin to wean the kids on her own around the 6 to 8-week range. At around this time, the kids will be proficient at eating solid foods, such as grass, hay, and grain. When they can do this, they can be weaned off their mother's milk entirely.

How Long Will a Doe Produce Milk if They Are Not Bred Again?

You may intend to hold off breeding your goat once their most recent kid has been weaned, and that's okay because a doe will continue to produce milk up to 10 months after the birth of their kid. However, if you cease milking them routinely (daily), you will run the risk of their milk supply either decreasing in yield or drying up completely.

You can always encourage better milk production by keeping your does happy, and that is a fairly simple thing to do.

- Keep them healthy - watch for any signs of mastitis or other viral condition that causes the mammary glands to become inflamed. If you see red, swollen, or otherwise painful udders you should contact your vet immediately

- Feed a high-protein grain, that little bit of extra energy really helps keep their cycle going

- Always provide plenty of high-protein hay

- Provide high quality chelated free choice minerals

Is There a Benefit to Breeding a Doe Who is Already Producing Milk?

Many goat owners who produce dairy find that rebreeding their does help to increase milk yields and keeps their does natural hormones in check. A doe will always produce the most amount of milk right after giving birth and while their baby is growing up. Should your milking does dry up completely, the only way to restart their production is to once again breed them.

How Much Milk Should You Expect?

In nature, there is never an exact number. Some does will produce more and some will produce less. No matter what your yield, you can be facing some large milk quantities if you have a large herd. Below you will find some average yields for the dairy breeds that are based on a single lactation cycle (275-305 days).

Breed	Average Gallon Production
Alpine	272
LaMancha	252
Nubian	218
Oberhasli	257
Saanen	309
Toggenburg	253

How to Milk a Goat

If you are an old hand at owning a dairy herd, you probably already know not only how to milk a goat, but likely you have some of your own innovations to make the process easier. For those of you just starting out, we included information for those just raising their first herd or who are in the process of buying their first herd.

You may feel overwhelmed by the thought of milking your goats, but really, once you get the gist of it, you will find it quite easy. If you recognize going into this venture that you may be a bit uncoordinated with your hands, your first experience may not go as smoothly as you wish. Don't give up! We have all been beginners at one point or another, and you can always get better. One day, you will look back on your experience and laugh. Let's get started:

1. Begin by having some goodies ready for your does. A mixture of alfalfa pellets and a small amount of grain should do the trick, but you can always add other incentives such as alfalfa hay, fresh weeds, or sprouted barley grass. This will keep them distracted and happy.

2. One really good piece of advice is to keep your doe's udder shaved. This can make it much easier to milk and is also easier to keep cleaned off.

3. Always clean up the udder and teats. We prefer to create my own stash of homemade udder wipes (see below) because they circumvent all the online wipes that contain many chemicals. You want to be sure to squeeze the teat so that you can also wipe that opening well.

4. Perform one squirt out of each teat to flush out any blockages or bacteria present.

5. Take time to inspect that first squirt from each teat. What you are looking for is to make sure there is no sign of blood or clumps of milk, which could be an indication of mastitis.

6. You are now ready to begin milking your first goat. The technique you want to use starts with you taking a hold of the teat as high as you can (which is a couple of inches into the udder).

7. You will use your thumb and forefinger, squeezing the teat hard, so you can trap the milk in the teat.

8. The hard part to grasp is that you need to keep your thumb and forefinger tight, you will bring the rest of your palm and other fingers together. The pressure this causes is what will squirt the milk out to be collected. If you experience a tiny stream or no milk at all, it's probably caused by not keeping your thumb and forefinger pinching hard enough. Milking is not about the tugging, but rather the pinching and the squeezing.

9. You will continue with these last few steps until you have gotten all the milk out that you can.

10. Here's one tip: when you think you have gotten all the milk you can, take a break for a few seconds, then punch into the does udder lightly to help release any other milk that might be trapped there. This movement simulates what a baby kid would do to help get more milk from the mother. Milk out any more product that you can.

11. When your doe is finished being milked, the udder will have a wrinkled and deflated look.

12. Afterward, you should apply some udder balm to the teat and udder to keep them from becoming sore or chapped.

Homemade Udder Wipes

These wipes contain no chemicals, so you always look for the most holistic alternative if you are uncomfortable with harsh chemicals. If you have several species on your property, good news, they can be used on goats, cows, and sheep!

Ingredients

- 1 package (100 wipes) dry disposable wipes

- 2 C filtered water

- ½ C On Guard® Cleaner Concentrate or Castile Soap Natural cleaner concentrate

Instructions

1. Place the package of disposable wipes in a Ziploc bag or reusable plastic container

2. In a bowl, mix the water and cleaner thoroughly

3. Pour your mixture over the wipes and seal

4. You can store these right by your milking area and keep them handy!

When comparing cow's milk to goat's milk, you will find smaller butterfat globules. What this means is that the goat's milk will be more digestible and contain less carotene than cow's milk.

When making products like cheese, goat's milk will produce a softer cheese than that made from cow's milk, even though the butterfat content will be relatively the same.

Homemade Udder Balm

Your does udders are super important when it comes to milk production, and it is essential to keep her teats and udder healthy. That's why it is critical to keep those teats and udders clean, healthy, and soft. Depending upon where you live, your does can become dried out, for instance, in the state of Arizona. This recipe deserves a permanent spot in your milking supplies. Just a note on essential oils, make sure that you are buying 100 percent pure so that it is not contaminated by chemicals.

Ingredients

- ½ C coconut oil
- ¾ C olive oil
- 1 C beeswax
- 1 t raw honey
- 10 drops lavender 100 percent pure essential oil
- 10 drops tea tree 100 percent pure essential oil

Instructions

1. Combine coconut oil, olive oil, and beeswax to the top of a double boiler.
2. Slowly melt these over a low flame, then remove them from the heat
3. When the mixture is warm (not hot), add in your honey and essential oils
4. Chill your mixture in the refrigerator for an hour.

5. Remove the mixture and place it under a mixer to whip for 10 minutes or until the mixture appears fluffy.

6. Place the mixture in a mason jar or clean glass jar to store.

Goat's Milk Composition

Most people assume that since cow's milk doesn't freeze well because of the cream separating after the freezing and thawing process, that you should also resist the practice of freezing goat or sheep's milk, but that's not entirely accurate. Goat and sheep's milk can be frozen for up to 30 days and can be used for drinking. Frozen milk should not be used to make any type of cheese. Also, when you compare goat's milk to cow's milk, you should remember that it is lower in fat, calories, and even lower in cholesterol levels. As a bonus, it provides more calcium. Surprisingly, goat's milk and cheese tend to be easier on the stomach than their cow counterparts. So often, people with digestive issues with cow products may be able to consume the goat version without incident.

The average composition of goat's milk is as follows:

Water	86.0 %
Albuminous Protein	1.0 %
Casein	3.3 %
Lactose	4.4 %
Butterfat	4.5 %
Minerals	0.8 %
Total Solids	14.0%

When making cheese from raw goat's milk, you may find that it will have a distinct peppery hot smell to it that is caused by naturally occurring fatty acids and lipase enzymes.

In any recipe, not goat milk specific, you may want to reduce a recipe's temperature by five degrees since goat's milk curds tend to be more delicate. Always remember that goat curds will need to be treated more gently.

Using Raw Milk

Raw milk is not pasteurized and contains a higher vitamin content than any heat-treated milk. Raw milk embodies the fullness and richness of flavors.

Should you choose to utilize raw milk, you should do so within 48 hours of being milked. If you are pulling milk from your own herd, you should wait at least 2 or 3 hours before using the product.

If you are making cheese with raw milk, please remember to top-stir when you see any butterfat rising to the surface. By doing this, you will mix the butterfat back into the body of the milk.

When using raw milk, it is typically not necessary to add calcium chloride, since the calcium of the milk has not been changed by the pasteurization process or any other long-term cold storage. Since many cheesemakers use calcium chloride in their product to help compensate for any seasonal variations in their collected milk, I still like to use it. It will not hurt your cheese.

There are natural floras contained within your raw milk that can be useful in the making of cheese. However, you should be aware that if you consume and produce products that use raw milk, you should be 100 percent certain that there are no pathogens contaminating the milk.

Raw milk should only come from tested animals that are kept clean and never, under any circumstances, should raw milk be used from an animal suffering from mastitis or receiving antibiotics. Even though raw milk cheeses are some of the best worldwide, make sure that if you are buying or producing raw cheeses, all precautions are being followed on a regular basis.

Top-Stirring

When you top-stir, this action takes place just below the surface of your raw milk. Should you be using raw milk, top-stir it for another 30 seconds when adding rennet. Note: rennet is an enzyme used to set the cheese during the process of making the product. When stirred into a vat of cultured milk, it can cause the mile to separate into solids (curds) and liquid (whey). Rennet can be found at any health food store near you or online.

This will mix any butterfat that has risen to the surface of your product back into the body of the milk. Top-stirring is using the bottom of a slotted spoon to stir the top ¼ of the milk.

Pasteurizing Your Milk at Home

Pasteurized milk goes through a heat treatment to destroy any pathogens. However, it reduces the availability of proteins, vitamins, and milk sugars, in addition to destroying some enzymes. It is a very easy process and can be done on your stove top.

According to Ricki Carroll (2018), if you want to pasteurize your milk at home, just follow these steps:

1. Pour your raw milk product into a double boiler to protect it from becoming scalded.

2. Slowly heat the milk to 145°F (63°C) for precisely 30 minutes while stirring occasionally. The temperature during this cook time must remain constant, so you may find you will need to raise or lower the flame accordingly.

3. Once done, remove the pot of milk from the heat and place it in a sink filled with ice water. Stir constantly until the temperature of your process drops to 40°F. This step of rapid cooling is important to eliminate any conditions that would support the growth of unwanted bacteria.

4. Store your milk in a sealed container in the refrigerator until you are ready to use it.

How to Make Goat Cheese

Now that you are an expert goat herder and have all the milking processes and handling down pat, you are probably itching to whip up some homemade goat cheeses to impress your family, friends, and neighbors!

It is easy to make cheese at home and one of the great things is that you can flavor them how you want and the best thing of all is that you will know exactly what went into your tasty cheese products.

Even if you are still relatively new to goat herding, milking, and now cheese making, you will be amazed that the process is much simpler than what you have built up in your mind.

This creamy goat cheese that we used as an example uses what is called a coagulation method. What this basically means is that you will combine the goat's milk with heat and acid. By doing this, the ingredients break down into curds and whey. For this simplistic method, you will need no special equipment except for some cheesecloth and a thermometer. You will collect any curds and drain to become cheese - Voilá!

Equipment

- A large saucepan

- Measuring cups and spoons

- Cheesecloth

- Thermometer

- Beeswax wrap or cling wrap

Ingredients

- 8 ⅓ C Fresh goats milk

- ½ C Water

- 1.5 t citric acid (you can also substitute ⅔ C fresh lemon juice or ½ C vinegar, if you are using lemon or vinegar you will not need to add water)

- 1 t cheese salt (kosher salt)

Optional ingredients:

- Add dried herbs, such as chives, thyme, rosemary, etc. This should be added at the same time as your milk so that it is distributed evenly throughout the cheese

- You can add fresh herbs or chopped nuts to the outside of your cheese log

- Drizzle with honey and a little cinnamon

Instructions

1. Prepare your citric acid by dissolving it in water. There will be no need to heat the mixture.

2. Heat your goat's milk by pouring it into a large saucepan. Add the previously dissolved citric acid and carefully stir. This should be heated slowly and over medium heat until the contents reach 185°F (85°C). When this is achieved, remove the pan from the heat source.

3. Let your milk curdle while it sits aside and rests. Cover it with a lid or tea towel for 10 minutes. You will notice that goat's milk will not curdle in the same manner as cow's milk and the curds will be smaller and less *formed,* which simply means that your mixture will still look like liquid after 10 minutes.

4. Drain the cheese by placing cheesecloth inside of a sieve and pour the milk into the cheesecloth, draining it for about an hour. During this time, you can leave the sieve over a large bowl and collect the leftover whey to use in other recipes that you have in mind.

5. Add the salt to the drained cheese and mix it well. At this time, you will form your cheese by either placing it into a mold or rolling the product into a log. You can easily roll the product into a log by placing it over a piece of beeswax wrap, plastic wrap, or even wax paper, and use these products to form the cheese into a log. Twist or fold in the ends to secure your cheese roll. Move this to your refrigerator to chill and set up. After that, your homemade goat cheese will be ready to eat!

6. Optional: If you want a smoother, creamier cheese, once your product has set, you can blend it with some water (2-3 T as needed) to produce a smooth and creamy end product.

Goat Milk Cheeses Are Made Worldwide

Goat cheese comes in many different textures and flavors. There are always options to add that can give your cheese a mild or tangy flavor. Goat cheese is versatile and once you make your own, you may find it habit-forming. Below is a list of cheeses that are all made from goat milk:

- Anari cheese
- Añejo cheese
- Anthotyros
- Ardagh castle cheese
- Ardsallagh goat farm
- Banon cheese
- Bastardo del Grappa
- Blue Rathgore
- Bluebell Falls
- Bokmakiri cheese
- Bonne bouche
- Bouq Émissaire
- Brunost
- Bucheron
- Cabécou
- Cabrales cheese
- Caciotta
- Capricious

- Caprino cheese
- Caprino dell'Aspromonte
- Castelo Branco cheese
- Cathare
- Chabichou
- Chabis
- Chaubier
- Chavroux
- Chèvre noir
- Chevrotin
- Circassian cheese
- Circassian smoked cheese
- Clochette
- Clonmore cheese
- Cooleeney Farmhouse cheese
- Corleggy cheese
- Couronne lochoise
- Crottin de Chavignol
- Dolaz cheese
- Faisselle
- Feta
- Formaela
- Garrotxa cheese
- Gbejna friska
- Gbejna tal bzar

- Gbejna mghoxxa
- Geitost
- Gevrik
- Dunlop cheese
- Gleann Gabhra
- Glyde Farm Produce
- Graviera
- Halloumi
- Harbourne blue
- Humboldt Fog
- Jibneh Arabieh
- Kars Gravyer cheese
- Kasseri
- Kefalotyri
- Kunik cheese
- Leipäjuusto
- Majorero
- Manouri
- Mató
- Mizithra
- Nabulsi cheese
- Pantysgawn
- Payoyo cheese
- Pélardon
- Picodon

- Picón Bejes-Tresviso
- Pouligny-Saint-Pierre cheese
- Queso Palmita
- Rigotte de Condrieu
- Robiola
- Rocamadour cheese
- Rubing
- Sainte-Maure de Touraine
- Santarém cheese
- Selles-sur-Cher cheese
- Snøfrisk
- St Helen's
- St Tola
- Testouri
- Tesyn
- Tulum cheese
- Valençay cheese
- Van herbed cheese
- Xynomizithra
- Xynotyro

According to Analida (2021), the use of goat cheese and goat milk dates back to the fifth millenium BC, when goats were kept by shepherds and herders. Goat cheese even made an appearance in Greek mythology, set in Homer's epic tale The Odyssey. Even ancient Egyptian tombs depict cheese-making drawings. By the rise of the Roman Empire, cheese-making was a well-established practice.

Recipes

Soft Goat Cheese

Ingredients

- 1 gallon goat's milk
- ½ t calcium chloride, diluted in ¾ C of cool non-chlorinated water
- 1 packet buttermilk direct-set culture
- 1 drop liquid rennet diluted in 5 tablespoons of cool non-chlorinated water
- 1 t cheese salt (optional)

Instructions

1. Heat your milk to 86°F (30°C) and add the calcium chloride solution. Stir well. Sprinkle the buttermilk starter over the surface of the milk, then wait 2 minutes for the powder to rehydrate. Stir well to combine.

2. Next, add the diluted rennet solution and gently stir the mixture with an up and down motion for a total of 30 seconds.

3. Cover and allow the milk solution to set at 72°F (22°C) during a time frame of 12-24 hours or until you notice firm coagulation.

4. Place 4 to 8 soft-cheese molds on top of a draining mat and then set on a wire rack set up over a basin to collect your whey.

5. Gently ladle the curds into the molds, taking care to not break up the curd.

6. Fill the molds and wait 15 minutes for the curd to settle, then ladle more curd into the molds until the mixture is completely used up. Allow the cheese to drain for 18-24 hours. During that time, turn once to help with drainage. The final result will settle by one-third to one-half of its original amount.

7. Unmold your cheese. If desired, you can take the optional salt and sprinkle it lightly after unmolding. You are now ready to eat the

finished product, or wrap it up in a cheese wrap and store it for up to 2 weeks in your refrigerator.

Goat's Milk Cheddar

Ingredients

- 2 gallons of goat's milk
- ½ t calcium chloride diluted in ¼ C cool non-chlorinated water
- 1 packet direct-set mesophilic starter culture
- ½ t liquid rennet diluted in ¼ C cool non-chlorinated water
- 2 T plus 1 t cheese salt
- Cheese wax (optional)

Instructions

1. Heat the milk to 85°F (29°C) and add the calcium chloride solution. Stir well to combine ingredients. Sprinkle the starter over the surface of the milk mixture and wait 2 minutes for the power to rehydrate. Stir well, then cover and allow the milk to ripen for 30 minutes.

2. Next, add the diluted rennet and stir gently with an up and down motion for a total of 30 seconds. Cover the pot holding the mixture and let it set for 1 hour at 85°F (29°C).

3. Cut the curd into ½-inch cubes and allow them to sit undisturbed for 10 minutes.

4. Gradually heat these curds 2 degrees every 5 minutes until they are 98°F (37°C). Stir gently every 3 minutes to prevent the curds from matting. Maintain this temperature for 45 minutes while stirring gently every 3 minutes.

5. Remove the whey and add 2 tablespoons of the salt to the curds and then mix.

6. Line a 2 pound cheese mold with cheesecloth and ladle the curds into the mold. You will need to press the cheese at 20 pounds of pressure for 15 minutes.

7. Remove the cheese from the mold and gently peel away the cheesecloth, then flip the cheese, rewrap it, then place it back into the mold. Press at 30 pounds of pressure for about an hour.

8. Unwrap. Flip. Rewrap and press at 50 pounds of pressure for 12 hours. At this point, you can remove the press and gently peel away the cheesecloth. Rub salt on all the surfaces, then place it on a cheeseboard.

9. For the next 2 days, turn your cheese once daily while rubbing salt on it once a day at room temperature. When the surface is dry, you can wax it to create a moister cheese or age it for something drier.

10. Age the cheese at 50-55°F (10-13°C) for 4-12 weeks

Dry Cottage Cheese

Ingredients

- 1 gallon goat's milk
- ¼ t calcium chloride, diluted in ¼ cup of cool non-chlorinated water
- 1 packet chèvre starter culture or 1 packet direct set buttermilk starter culture
- 3 drops liquid rennet, diluted in ¼ c of cool non-chlorinated water (use this only if using the buttermilk starter culture).
- Cheese salt (optional)
- Herbs (optional)

Instructions

1. Heat the milk to 72°F (23°C), then add the calcium chloride solution. Stir well to combine the ingredients, then sprinkle the starter over the surface of the mixture. Wait 2 minutes until the powder rehydrates. Stir well.

2. If you are using the buttermilk starter instead of the chèvre starter, then add the rennet solution and stir gently with an up and down

motion for a total of 30 seconds. (If you have used the chèvre starter, then skip all of these instructions.)

3. Cover the mixture and let it set at 72°F (23°C) for 24 hours.

4. Cut the curd into ½ inch cubes and allow them to rest for 5 minutes.

5. Gradually heat these curds to 116°F (47°C) by raising the temperature 5 degrees every 5 minutes for 40 minutes. Stir every 3 minutes to prevent the curds from matting.

6. Allow your curds to rest for 5 minutes at 116°F (47°C). When the curd is ready, it will be slightly resistant when pressed between your fingers.

7. Remove the butter muslin and submerge the colander of curd in a pot of cold, sterilized water in order to remove the lactose from the curds. When the water appears to be milky, then drain it off and replace it. You are ready to drain and store the cheese when the water runs clear. You can put this in your refrigerator for up to 10 days.

8. Should you want to add salt or herbs to boost the taste, mix these in just before eating.

Goat Milk Vanilla Ice Cream

Ingredients

- 3 large, whole eggs
- 2 ounces fresh goat cheese (chevre) preferably smooth and spreadable
- ½ C sugar
- 6 T dry, full-fat goat milk powder
- Pinch of salt
- 2 C whole goat milk
- 1 T tapioca syrup
- 2 t vanilla extract

Goat Milk Chocolate Ice Cream

Ingredients

- 3 large, whole eggs

- 2 ounces fresh goat cheese (chevre) preferably smooth and spreadable

- ½ C sugar

- 3 T Dutch process cocoa powder

- 6 T full fat, dry goat milk powder

- ⅛ t salt

- 2 C whole goat milk

- 2 T tapioca syrup

- 1 t vanilla extract

Instructions for Either Ice Cream

1. In a medium-sized bowl, whisk the eggs until yolks and whites are combined. Set them aside.

2. In a small bowl, warm the goat cheese until soft and whisk it until smooth. Set this aside too.

3. For the chocolate ice cream only: whisk together the dry ingredients until the mixture is free of lumps. Set aside.

4. Add the 2 cups of milk and tapioca syrup to a 3 or 4-quart saucepan. Heat this over medium-high heat. Stir frequently until the ingredients reach a simmer.

5. Add the dry ingredients (vanilla or chocolate) to the hot milk and whisk this until dissolved. Remove the mixture from the heat source.

6. Add a generous portion of the hot milk mixture by drizzling it into the eggs. Whisk briskly while adding.

7. Now, carefully pour the egg mixture into the saucepan with the balance of the hot milk. This should be done while continuing to whisk the milk.

8. Cook this over medium-low heat and stir constantly, if possible with a heat-proof spatula, but if you do not have one, a spoon will suffice). Scrape all portions of the bottom of the pan until the mixture thickens and reaches a temperature of 170-175°F. It should appear thicker than uncooked milk, and this process should take about 7-14 minutes. Remove mixture from the heat.

9. You will gradually add some of the hot custard into the softened cheese (about ½ cup to a cup). Whisk after each addition until the mixture is smooth.

10. Pour the cheese mixture into the saucepan and continue to whisk until combined.

11. Pour through a fine-mesh strainer and into a clean bowl.

12. Cool in a cold water bath for about 30 minutes, or if you want, you can place the mixture directly into the refrigerator. Stir occasionally during those first 30 minutes of cooling.

13. Cool completely, which would be a minimum of 4 hours, but preferable to be overnight.

14. Stir in the vanilla extract, then churn in an ice cream maker following any manufacturer instructions for the equipment.

15. Transfer the contents to a 1-quart freezer storage container. At this time, you can stir in any desired additions you wish.

16. Store in your freezer and enjoy!

Goat Milk Candles

- Beeswax

- Double boiler

- Goat's milk

- Vanilla 100 percent pure essential oil

- Wick

- Scissors

Instructions

1. Place 2 lbs of beeswax into the top of a double boiler and heat the water in the bottom over high heat until the wax melts.

2. Add ¼ cup of goat's milk into the wax and stir this thoroughly with a spoon until both are combined, and the ingredients bind together.

3. Add any scents to the mixture, for example, the vanilla essential oil. Use only pure essential oils, as cheaper blends contain chemicals that may be toxic to burn.

4. Cut wicks at least two inches longer than your desired candle height. If you want, you can tie a metal washer to the end of one side of the wick.

5. Either way, you lift the wick out of the wax and hold it in the air. Once the wax has begun to solidify, you can dip it back into the wax. Remove it after it's been covered. Repeat these steps until the candle reaches your desired thickness.

6. Once you have reached this stage, place your candles on a sheet of newspaper until they become completely cooled.

7. You can give candles to friends, decorate your home, even make them to sell for charitable events.

Frequently Asked Questions

When making recipes, we all have questions regarding the making of cheese products. Here are a few common questions and some sensible answers.

- **Why did my cheese turn out crumbly?** The milk may have been heated too quickly. Try heating your mixture slower because that is the key.

- **What kind of vinegar should I use?** White vinegar.

- **What type of milk can I use?** Use a fat-type milk and avoid the use of anything ultra-pasteurized because the high heat will affect the proteins, and you will notice that the curds will not form well. You should always use the freshest milk possible.

- **Can I rinse my curds before storing them?** Yes. Gently rinsing your curds will remove some of the tangy flavors of the acid you used to coagulate the milk. It all depends on the taste you desire. Stir in any salts and herbs after the rinsing procedure.

Chapter 4:
The BEST Meat

Without a doubt, the highest cost of raising meat goats is the feeding program. Any animal that is raised for meat requires a high level of nutrients that support meat production.

Where goats differ from cattle or sheep is their ratio of weight gain and if you are new to the management of goats for meat then you should be aware that they do not fatten like sheep or cattle. The general ratios of meat goats range from between 0.1 to 0.8 lbs per day.

In order to achieve a profit, they must be fed a high-quality forage and often be supplemented with an expensive, but effective concentrated feed. (A concentrated feed will generally have higher nutrients packed into a pellet where the feed ratio is less than other feeds.)

If you have exposure to other people who also raise goats for meat, perhaps they will share some of their philosophies on their year-round forage program. Most of these will include as much grazing as possible throughout the year.

There are people trying to raise meat goats that honestly believe a low-quality feed is sufficient, but keep in mind that you have to feed muscle to make muscle and if you are a human athlete, ask yourself the following question: can I compete in a triathlon with a diet of junk food? I am sure that you already know the answer to that question!

Feeding Requirements

You may have some previous experience with cattle, but a goat does not digest plants as well as a cow. The reason for this is that the feed stays in a goat's rumen for a shorter period of time. There is also a distinction between what forage will work best for your animals. While trees and shrubs do not provide quality roughage for a cow, the same cannot be said for your goat herd. A cow might graze through some straw and be able to use some of that low protein that it offers, but straw will not even provide nutritional maintenance in a goat. Why? Simply, because goats do not use the cell wall of straw as effectively as a cow.

Another reason that goats should consume a higher quality diet is due to the size of their digestive tract. It is considerably smaller, but in relation to their body weight, the amount of feed needed by meat goats is almost twice that of cattle.

Nutrient Requirements

Protein, minerals, and vitamins, along with water are all essential in the nutritional needs of your meat goats. Without these critical nutrients, it will be difficult for your meat goats to remain in good flesh, be able to reproduce, support a pregnancy, or support the production of meat, milk, or hair.

In a pasture, your animals will have access to lush leafy forage, but during winter months or in times of drought, you will have to provide the highest quality hay you can find. You should always have your hay and pasture tested annually to know what nutrients you can count on. Just because your pasture was lush last year, the following year is a whole new growing season and the nutritional content can be affected by many things, such as too much rain, too little rain, or even an invasive insect. No two growing years are going to be exactly the same.

No matter if your goats are grazed, barn fed, or a combination of the two, your animals should be offered a supplemental concentrated feed to cover any nutritional deficiencies in your grazing program.

Total digestible nutrients (TDN) will give you an idea of where your forage will fall in regard to its nutritional content. Below is a chart that reflects the daily nutrient requirements for feeding your meat-producing goats provided by NC State Extensions (2015).

- Low-quality forages are 40-55 % TDN
- Good quality forages are between 55-70% TDN

Daily Nutrient Requirements for Meat Producing Goats	Young Goats		Does (110 lb)				Bucks (80-120 lb)
Nutrient	Weanling (30lb)	Yearling (60lb)	Pregnant (early)	Pregnant (late)	Lactating (avg milk)	Lactating (high milk	
Dry Matter, lb	2.0	3.0	4.5	4.5	4.5	5.0	5.0
TDN. %	68	65	55	60	60	65	60
Protein, %	14	12	10	11	11	14	11
Calcium, %	.6	.4	.4	.4	.4	.6	.4
Phosphorus, %	.3	.2	.2	.2	.2	.3	.2

Protein

The attainment of your protein levels will be the most expensive part of your goat's diet. You will find protein in lush, leafy forage, tree leaves, hay, and grains. Feed grains provide high protein by using whole cottonseed, soybean meal, wheat middlings, and corn gluten. Proteins are required and provide a source of nitrogen for the ruminal bacteria and needed amino acids to build muscle, bone integrity, and how the muscles adhere to the bone.

When levels of protein run low in your animal's diet, their digestion of carbohydrates in the rumen will slow down and their intake of feed will decrease. In a domino effect, this will continue to lower your levels of proteins in your animal's diet and will, in turn, affect your animal's growth rate, milk production, reproduction, and the ability to fight off diseases. You do not need to worry about extra protein being stored in your goat's body because any excess will be excreted out in their urine.

Proper amounts of protein are vital to cover your herd's nutritional needs.

Minerals

Goats, like all other members of the animal kingdom, need minerals to support basic body function. A free choice complete goat-specific loose mineral mix will cover any major minerals that are likely to be deficient in your herd's diet. Chelated minerals are always a better choice as they are more bioavailable for your animals. The major minerals these typically cover are:

- Sodium chloride (salt)

- Calcium

- Phosphorous

- Magnesium

- Selenium

- Copper

- Zinc

Calcium to phosphorus ratios in any animal's diet is important and for your goats, they should be kept in the 2:1 - 3:1 ratio.

Depending upon which area of the country you live in, your soil may be deficient in selenium. Predominantly North Carolina and most of the Southeast are the areas most affected by this deficiency and for that reason, many commercialized trace mineral salts do not contain selenium. For your herd, you should provide trace mineral salts that do include selenium.

While goats tend to accept copper more readily than sheep, you should be aware that young, nursing kids are more sensitive to copper toxicity than their grown fellow herd members. For this reason, you should never feed cattle milk replacers to nursing kids. It is also worth mentioning that the maximum copper level for a goat to tolerate has never been established. Therefore, you should always use caution when choosing proper supplementation for your goats.

Vitamins

We all need vitamins, and your goats are no different. Because of their size, most will be needed in very small quantities. The vitamins that your herd may be deficient in are A and D.

Because a goat's rumen will form bacteria responsible for all B and K vitamins, these are not essential vitamins required in goat nutrition. Vitamin C needs are met by the synthesized quantities made within your goat's body tissues.

Those green, leafy forage pieces that your goat consumes contain carotene, which their bodies convert into vitamin A. Goats are also capable of storing vitamin A in their liver and fat when they consume more than needed. If, however, your goat is not taking in sufficient vitamin A, they will need support for that vitamin level.

If your herd is confined in barns for long periods during the winter, they should still have access to frequent sunlight. This exposure creates vitamin D to be produced under their skin. If not, they will need to receive supplemental vitamin D. Good quality sun-cured hay can be a good source for your animals to intake vitamin D. When an animal experiences a deficiency in vitamin D, they will not be able to absorb calcium and this can lead to an animal developing rickets (this is a condition where young animals or even people will grow abnormally in their bones and joints).

Water

Water is the life force for every living creature. It is necessary and the cheapest of your feed ingredients. Your lactating does should always have access to high-quality water. Always provide fresh, clean water for your herd. Always have your water tested to make sure that there are no unhealthy levels of nitrate in your properties drinking water.

Tip: A smaller water container is easier to maintain, keeping the water clean and fresh for your herd. This will require changing and refilling more often.

Energy

Your animal's energies come from carbohydrates found in sugars, starches, fats, and fibers in their diet. If your herd is struggling with finding sufficient sources of energy, then you might want to add a grain that will provide for the deficiency. Grains that are high in energy contain whole cottonseed, corn, wheat middlings, soybean hulls, soybean meal, and corn gluten. Any added fat should not represent more than 5 percent of your animal's diet. If it ends up representing too much of your animal's diet, that extra fat will be stored in your goat's body around many of their internal organs.

Which Are the BEST Meat Goats?

Frankly, goats from any number of breeds end up getting slaughtered for their meat. However, not every breed is bred specifically for meat production. The one breed that stands out more than the rest is the Boer, which is a breed best known by the people living in the Upper Midwest of the United States associated with meat production. Developed in South Africa, the Boer is one of the few breeds selectively bred for meat harvesting. Incredibly, the Boer is a newer addition to the United States and was first imported in 1993 from New Zealand.

Other goat breeds that are generally acknowledged as meat producers are Spanish, Pygmy, Kiko, and the Myotonic (fainting goat).

Even if you primarily raise dairy goats, sooner or later, most owners will decide to cull the herd's least productive animals. Those targeted will be low milk producers, poor mothers, and the least valuable of the newest bunch of kids. Especially if you are a dairy producer, you may want to consider culling if you have had a bumper crop of male kids because typically, you only keep one out of every 100 bucks in the eventuality that you need to replace an aging patriarch buck.

Navigating the Goat Meat Industry

Meat goat production usually includes the owning, breeding, raising, and selling of your animals and does not always mean that you will be processing the animals as well. You can become involved by raising them and caring for them until their time of sale.

You can get started by purchasing several does, getting them bred by your buck, a buck you have leased, or AI (artificial insemination). You will care for your does all through their pregnancy and make nutritional decisions. When their kids are delivered, you will care for them until their time of sale. The production of these animals is a year-round commitment, and you should establish a budget for how and where your investment monies will be spent, especially when just getting started.

Just like any business, you will need to know where your animals will be sold. Because the meat goat industry is fairly new, it might be difficult to find the best place to sell your animals right away. This can be frustrating for beginners to navigate through leads in order to find your best market. You should develop a marketing plan that details your targets.

Regional Auction Market

This is typically an auction barn that will sell goats for you, the producer.

- **Advantages**
  - ○ There is no need for you to find buyers.

- **Disadvantages**
  - ○ This type of market can be unpredictable, causing you to lose money or break even.
  - ○ You, as the seller, will have to pay a percentage of the final price to the auction barn as a commission.
  - ○ Depending upon the auction house, or the sale, your goats might be sold by the pound instead of a per animal basis. This can make it difficult to determine what the most profitable animals are to produce.

Niche Markets

These are markets developed by you, the producer, and others like you to reach a specific demand. Perhaps a country farmer's market type of event.

- **Advantages**
  - The producer (you), can obtain better value.
  - The customer base can become regulars, and they are looking for specifics.
  - The product you offer is well-defined.

- **Disadvantages**
  - These types of markets can be seasonal, so you cannot count on them for year-round support.
  - You become dependent upon the demands shaped by the customer base, and you are subject to their current needs.
  - You will need to work hard to market and maintain your market to ensure any levels of success.
  - These are markets developed by you, the producer, and others like you to reach a specific demand. Perhaps a country farmer's market type of event.

Seedstock Markets

This particular market will involve the selling of high-quality breeding animals.

- **Advantages**
  - The type of market will allow you as a producer to capture more value for your high-end replacement breeding animals.

- **Disadvantages**
  - To survive in this market, you will have to survive trends in the breeding industry and popular opinions.

- This outlet is only for animals that are quality enough to be used as breeding stock, and therefore not a good choice for marketing the majority of your herd that is for sale.

Show Prospect Markets

This market targets only the show industry. However, this can provide a name for your farm.

- **Advantages**
  - Prices tend to remain stable
  - Goats shown in different ranges of shows will provide publicity for your farm and your brand.
- **Disadvantages**
  - This is only an outlet for the goats you have bred that are of a high enough quality to be competitive in the show ring.
  - Just as with any show ring featuring animals, this makes your sales prospects subject to any trends and cycles in the industry. This makes it necessary for you to keep up with what is trending and keep your quality goats in high demand.

Youth Livestock Sales

This market is solely for goats that are exhibited in youth shows.

- **Advantages**
  - The market is well established.
  - Sellers tend to receive a premium over the market value.
- **Disadvantages**
  - Buyers may be limited in this market.
  - The seller must find their own buyers, typically.
  - There is no guarantee that your animal will be accepted into the sale.

Keep Records

You are going to want to keep track of your successes and failures in order to decide what methods work the best for you and to weed out any methods that don't produce the desired results. It doesn't matter which goat type of business you pursue, but records are the only way for you to keep track of your expenses and keep track of what methods and outlets are working for you. Make sure that you record all useful information, no matter how small it might be.

Keep your record-keeping methods easy and simple to understand so that when you revisit them, there will be no confusion.

Here are some things we recommend keeping track of:

- Expenses
- Income
- Animal Inventory
- Feeding Records
- Animal Health Records
- Emergency Vet Care
- Breeding Records
- Birthing Records
- Weaning Rates
- Weight Gain Chart
- Goals

Breeding and Raising Your Flock

Just like anything you create, you want to start with the correct quality ingredients. While it may take time to develop your intuition about the selection of your breeding stock, learning the fundamentals will only help you in the end. Never be afraid to ask questions of anyone that you feel can give you excellent tips and advice.

Picking Your Breeds

While it's true that all goats can be harvested for their meat, there are certain breeds that are more predisposed for top meat production. For that reason, you should always make the best decisions possible when choosing your breeding stock. Top chosen breeds include:

- **Boer** - This breed excels as a meat producer and carries a high fertility and growth rate.

- **Spanish** - Are known to be breedable, even when outside of the typical breeding season. Their appeal is that they are very hardy and do well in difficult environments. With some recent changes in breeding toward better meat production within this breed, they have increased in suitability to sustain a goat meat herd.

- **New Zealand Kiko** - This breed is a result of crossbreeding heavier muscled wild does with Saanen and Nubian bucks. The end result was developing this breed to be a larger framed animal that is capable of early maturing.

- **Tennessee Fainting Goat** - Besides exhibiting the condition called myotonia, these goats have the ability to breed out of season and will kid up to twice each year. They are chosen for meat breeding production because they tend to be a very muscular animal.

The above breeds are not your only choices for meat production, but we have mentioned them because they are most suited to drive a farm's meat production business. When you start to do your research, you will find that there are further crossbreeds to consider using these breeds and certain dairy goats that ramp up meat production. Your location may be a deciding factor on which goat breeds you think will work best for you.

If you are purchasing your foundation herd, you should probably take age into your equation. If you are looking to build your kid crop right away, you should purchase goats that will be old enough to breed. Males will reach their breeding capabilities between 4 and 8 months of age, while females tend to age a bit slower, and they are ready for breeding between 7 and 10 months. These ages can vary between breeds, so do your research before making your final decisions. Many producers tend to hold off breeding during their first year, preferring instead to let their animals mature during their first year, so their bodies are better able to withstand the demands of pregnancy.

Evaluation

It can take practice to become knowledgeable enough to make practiced decisions when it comes to evaluating your potential livestock additions. The goats you choose for your herd will have a direct impact on your end breeding results. You can be the best manager in the world and show infallible instinct regarding the running of y0ur operation, but the bottom line is that you need to begin with good livestock.

There are many people out there that have excellent track records regarding the development of a great meat-producing herd, and most of them are willing to help out a greenhorn. They will use terms like condition or finish, which indicates the amount of fat covering the spine and ribs. When more knowledgeable people use terms like style or balance, this refers to growth, appeal, production, or muscle. When an animal has style, they have an appealing look that will catch a buyer's attention. A female should appear to have a long, thin neck, a smooth shoulder line, and be more refined than a male. Within the same breed, a buck should appear more masculine and have a heavier bone structure.

There can be a fine line regarding weight for your market animal because a thin layer of fat is necessary to produce a more tender, and fresher selection of meats, whereas too much fat will make the meat unappealing to potential customers.

Take time to study a goat's body structure to enable you to better understand the evaluation process. The biggest problem areas of confirmation are the shoulder, pasterns, and hip areas and these can impact your herd ideal. Problems that are apparent when the animal is younger will only worsen with age, making it difficult to keep your animals producing for many years to come. You should always select animals that are heavily muscled to develop a more production-oriented herd. Obviously, the muscles that produce the most meat are the most important to focus on (These would be the shoulder, leg, and loin).

Tip: Goats that are better muscled generally stand and walk wider. Also, when attempting to evaluate a potential animal, muscle creates a goat's shape and the fat should be smooth and flat.

Here are some helpful hints when learning to evaluate your potential animal's structure:

- The animal's top and bottom jaws should align. Over or underbites are not a desirable trait.

- Shoulders should demonstrate a 45-degree angle.

- The goat's topline should be mostly level and not appear tented.

- The angle from hooks to pins (you can discover these by viewing a goat's skeletal structure) should seem to be gently sloping.

- The animal's hock should display enough angle to allow for easy movement.

- All four pasterns should demonstrate a 45-degree angle.

Chapter 5:
Fiber for the Win

If you are new to the fiber industry, you may not be aware that this industry has been in existence for over 100 years. Unfortunately, the fiber industry has seen some recent struggles in regards to the amount of product available because many producers of fiber have either changed breeds or products. Today, efforts are being made to regrow some of the recent losses of producers.

Especially if this is your first time as a goat owner, you should start small with your fiber business and not overwhelm yourself with everything you need to know and a huge herd that might make you feel pressured. Joining local and national fiber goat organizations is one of the best ways to get started in the ownership of fiber goats. By doing this, you can meet others involved in the industry that have more experience than yourself.

Fiber Goat Associations and Registries

We want to provide you with a list of possible organizations you may want to look into:

- American Angora Goat Breeders Association (AAGBA)
- American Colored Angora Goat Registry
- American Nigora Goat Breeders Association
- Australian Cashmere Growers Association
- Cashmere Goat Association
- Colored Angora Goat Breeders Association (CAGBA)
- Eastern Angora Goat & Mohair Association (EAGMA)
- Cashmere and Camel Hair Manufacturers Institute (CCMI)
- Northwest Cashmere Association

- American Goat Federation (AGF)

- Pygora Breeders Association (PBA)

- The Angora Goat Society (U.K.)

- Miniature Silky Fainting Goat Association (MSFGA)

In chapter 1, we briefly introduced you to the best choices of goats to buy when pursuing a fiber goat herd. Let's briefly revisit those breeds:

- Angora goat's origins date back to early biblical history. These goats are sheared twice a year before breeding (Fall) and before kidding (Spring). They are a bit unusual because both sexes display horns, but they are best known for their long, wavy hair and their relaxed and docile nature.

Meeting the nutritional needs of the angora goats will be a producer's main concern since these goats have very high nutrient requirements.

Tip: When your does kid, they should be moved into stalls. Kids that are cold will not suck, and they may require a heat lamp. The Angora does and kids should be left as undisturbed as possible for several weeks because does have a tendency to abandon their kids.

- Cashmere goats have been bred selectively to produce a more significant amount of cashmere fiber. The truth is that any goat grows cashmere because that is the goat's soft undercoat. It should be noted that the American cashmere industry has very high standards regarding the quality of any cashmere fiber. Raising healthy animals is a good start to maintaining the quality needed. Cashmere goats are described as being flighty and high-strung. Cashmere breeds are:

  o Australian Cashmere goat

  o Changthangi (Kashmir Pashmina Cashmere goat

  o Hexi

  o Inner Mongolia Cashmere goat

  o Liaoning Cashmere goat

  o Licheng Daqing goat

- Luliang black goat

- Tibetan Plateau goat

- Wuzhumuqin

- Zalaa Jinst White goat

- Zhongwei Cashmere goat

- There are several various crossbred goats with no specific name. Generally, Angoras can be crossed with many different breeds. Depending on the goat you choose, there can be significantly less fiber availability, so before you jump into cross-breeding, do your homework.

- Nigora goats are a smaller breed of goat and created from breeding a Nigerian Dwarf buck with Angora does. The breeding of these goats began in 1994. They have calm temperaments and also make excellent pets.

- Pygora goats are a cross of a registered Pygmy goat with a registered Angora goat. This is a relatively new breed, established in 1987. They are easy to handle and considered to be good-natured.

All About Shearing

Each breed of goat may have some specifics to follow when shearing, and some breeds will need periodic combing during the year. You will be able to determine this by speaking with other fiber farmers, visiting your breed association, or studying up on your breed or breeds within your herd. Not all goats will have the same shearing requirements. For example, you don't shear a cashmere-producing goat. The process is achieved by combing or plucking the fiber once a year.

If you are practiced, you can shear an animal in 1 to 3 minutes. However, when you are just starting out, you will need to practice, practice, practice. It can be tough and dirty work, and experts say that this is not a job for anyone with a temper.

The general care of your fiber goats is going to be very similar to that of your dairy and meat goats. Without good nutrition, you will not get a good coat on your animals and that is the most important thing you need in order to provide quality fibers. Fiber goats will need extra fats in their diet to help provide the lanolin necessary to protect their coats. You can achieve this by adding some black oil sunflower seeds to their high-end hay and commercial feed. Even adding a little beet pulp can prove beneficial, and it can be fed dry or soaked to provide some extra calories. Should you soak your beet pulp, you can factor in that this will be giving your goats extra water intake, so don't panic if they drink a little less.

General Shearing Tips

- A clean animal is going to be much easier to shear than an animal that is dirty. The dirt will collect in your clippers and dull your blades.

- Prepare your goats for shearing by performing the following:

  - During the few weeks before shearing, you should use a pour-on insecticide that contains either permethrin or pyrethrin to kill any existing lice or ticks.

  - If you are due for rain or show, you should keep your animals confined inside for 24 hours prior to shearing, so they remain dry.

  - Clean and add new bedding to your dry shelter for the time following your shearing process. After being shorn, your herd is more susceptible to health issues due to losing their protective coats.

- Your goats should always be completely dry for the shearing process.

- For beginners, clipping is much easier to perform than shearing.

- It is advised that you not cut the same area twice, so you are only offering the higher quality product.

- When shearing, use long, smooth strokes because this keeps the goat's *fleece* in longer pieces. Not only will this make the piece easier to work with, but its value will be higher.

- Take care when shearing so that you do not cut their skin. Be extra careful on their belly area, areas where the body meets the legs, and the scrotum and teats. Accidents always happen, but if you do happen to cut one of your goats during the shearing process, you can treat it with antibiotic spray.

- Begin with the youngest goats and work your way through the herd based upon their age, since the youngest usually has the best fiber to offer.

- Shearing isn't necessarily difficult to do, but it can be very hard on the back because of all the time you spent bent over. If you have a bad back, you may want to hire someone to do this step for you.

- If you only have a couple of goats, you can probably perform the shearing with scissors or a pair of hand shears, but if you can afford it and want to perform this action yourself, you can always invest in some electric shears. These will range in price starting at 300.00 dollars and up.

- Gather up these supplies to help you shear:
  - Blow-dryer
  - Sheep shears
  - Grooming stand or stanchion
  - Scissors
  - Clean paper bags, pillowcases, or even baskets to hold the fiber
  - A hanging scale to weigh the fiber

Ready, Set, Shear!

1. Secure your first goat on the grooming stand.

2. Use your blow-dryer on your goat and get rid of any hay, loose hairs, or other pieces of debris that may be in your goat's coat.

3. Shear the goat's belly by starting at the bottom of the chest and move back toward its udder or scrotal area.

4. Shear both sides by working from the belly up to the spine and back leg to the front leg.

5. Shear each hind leg by working from the beginning of the coat, traveling upward toward the spine.

6. Your next step is to shear the neck. Begin at the bottom of the goat's throat and work toward the top of the chest and then on to the ears on the top and sides.

7. By working from the crown of the head and traveling back toward the tail, you will shear the top of the animal's back.

8. Go back and remove any excess hair that you might have missed with your scissors. One area often overlooked is the area of the udder or testicles.

9. Give your goat a treat and release your animal to frolic.

10. Go through your fiber and separate out any stained or soiled particles. Weigh any unsoiled product, then roll it up and put it in a paper bag. Make sure that you mark each bag with the goat's name, their age, the date sheared, and the weight of the product. Store in a dry area.

11. Thoroughly sweep your area so that the next goat will start with a clean environment.

Finding a Shearer

Generally, someone that shears sheep will also be able to shear your goats as well. Remember that if you are not doing your own shearing, to include this in your business expenses.

Fiber Goat Terminology for Beginners

It doesn't matter if you are getting a job in a new industry or getting invested in a new hobby. There are always buzz words or terminology that pertain to that interest. Try to make yourself familiar with these terms, so when you are talking with others, you have a better understanding.

- **Angora Goat** - is a breed of goat that produces mohair.

- **Angora Wool** - this is a textile that actually comes from Angora rabbits, not goats. The only fibers that come from goats are Cashgora, Cashmere, and Mohair.

- **Cashgora** - is a high-quality goat fiber that lies somewhere between Angora fibers and Cashmere fibers. Cashgora goats are cross-bred goats between Angora and Cashmere goats.

- **Cashmere** - This product can come from any goat that grows a quality downy undercoat in the winter. This textile is noted for its softness and warmth.

- **Fiber Goat** - This is a general term for any goat that produces Mohair, Cashmere, or Cashgora.

- **Goat Fiber** - There are several stages of fiber:

  - Raw is what is combed out of the goat's coat before any processing occurs.

  - Processed fiber has been washed, and carded.

  - Virgin fiber has been made into yarns.

  - Recycled fibers are reclaimed from scraps or fabrics.

- **Guard Hairs** - This hair stays all year long and grows through the undercoat; remaining even when the undercoat molts or is combed out.

- **Mohair** - A fleece and silky fiber that is created from the long hair of the Angora goat. Mohair is found in a number of textile products, including yarns for handcrafted products and fabrics.

Chapter 6:
General Health & Diseases

Prevention is key when developing a health program for your herd. You should always practice being observant, and often you can notice the start of any illness before it has a chance to become serious.

Be familiar with diseases common to goats and by using prevention. You can head off most problems before they get a foothold in your herd. It can be as simple as giving each of your animals a once over every morning or evening.

Normal Goat Health Data

Temperature:	104 ∓ 1°F, 40°C
Heart Rate:	70 to 80 beats per minute, faster for kids
Respiration Rate:	12 to 15 breaths per minute, faster for kids
Rumen Movements:	1 to 1.5 contractions per minute

There are some signs to look for when checking your animals, and they include:

- Poor appetite
- Diarrhea
- Limping
- Labored breathing
- Grunting or groaning
- Grinding teeth

- Behavior that is out of character for that animal

When conversing with your veterinarian, it is important that you be as precise as possible and use correct body parts when possible if describing a wound or a limp. When you first acquire your herd, you should question your vet about any common diseases common to your locale.

1. Observe the animal in question from a distance. Jot down their overall condition and age. When making further notes, your checklist can include things like its ability to stand. Is it able to walk normally? Is it staggering or bumping into objects? Does it appear to be able to see? Does it appear to be bloated or exhibit targeted area swelling? If you are able to, can you count the respirations per minute?

2. If you have a helper, they should hold the goat for you to check over. Avoid making the animal run as this can cause false readings regarding pulse, respiratory, and temperature.

3. With a digital thermometer, insert it into the goat's rectum and leave it there for 3 minutes. Make notes on the reading.

4. Place your fingertips, or palm, on the left flank and feel for any rumen movement. Always relay to the vet if your goat reacts in pain, the rumen feels mushy or appears to be filled with water.

5. Place your fingertips on both sides of the lower rib cage and feel for a heart rate, count the heartbeats that take place for one minute, and make a record of it. Your goat's pulse can also be taken by feeling the large artery in the inside of the upper rear leg.

6. You can pull back the lips of your goat's mouth to check the color of the animal's mucous membranes. Pink is the norm unless the animal's dark skin colors naturally extend into the areas of the mouth.

7. Gently run your hands over the animal's body to search for any swelling or signs of pain.

8. Listen for any out-of-the-ordinary sounds emanating from your goat. Any wheezing or coughing may indicate body pain being present in the chest or abdomen.

9. Test your animal for blindness. Move your hand toward your goat's eye, but resist the urge to merely fan the air. Even a blind goat will blink if it feels air movement on its face. Instead, move your hand steady and straight toward the suspected eye. Any blinking will indicate that the goat can see.

10. Observe if your animal shows any signs of diarrhea, a runny nose where the discharge appears to be cloudy or clear, crusty eyes, runny eyes, or excessive salivation. Let your vet know what you are noticing.

11. If you are examining a doe, always check her udder and notice if there are any hard knots, heat, clots, or signs of bloody milk. Note if the udder seems painful.

12. A stethoscope should be in your first aid kit because you will be able to use it in the detection of abnormal sounds emanating from the chest or abdomen area. If you do not have a stethoscope, place your ear against the animal's chest or abdomen and listen, making note of anything you hear.

By keeping detailed notes about your initial examination, you will have a list of symptoms to help you identify what is wrong with your animal or relay those findings to your vet. Having detailed records will help you identify if your animal is improving during treatment. You can utilize a simple spreadsheet to help you keep track of specific readings or information.

Always consult with your veterinarian before administering any treatments, and remember to read all the label instructions for any drug you are using on your animals.

Your animals will need periodic blood tests, vaccinations, and constant observation while you monitor them for any signs or symptoms of health issues.

Disease Descriptions

- **Acidosis** can occur when a goat has eaten too much feed that contains high levels of starch and sugar. This list includes grains, grain by-products, and vegetable parts. Any of these will make the rumen create more acid, giving your goat a stomachache.

Symptoms are bloat, dehydration, a weak pulse, increased respiration, and appear to be weak. There will be no rumen movement and the stomach will appear full and watery.

Treatment includes the administering of mineral oil via a stomach tube to help break up any excess gas.

- **Enterotoxemia** is caused by an organism that is found in the intestines of goats, however, when a feeding schedule drastically changes or large amounts of grain are eaten, this will cause the organism to grow rapidly, producing a toxin that can cause death within a few hours.

Symptoms are a full stomach, a fever, star gazing, convulsions, and tooth grinding. Sudden death is common for this.

Treatment includes the administration of immediate antitoxin. Prevention is two doses of vaccine.

- **Caprine arthritis-encephalitis (CAE)** is a virus that spreads from an older, infected goat to kids. An example of how this can be spread is from an infected doe to her kid through milk. Even though the testing for this virus yields a high percentage of positive tests, only a small number of animals ever show signs of this disease.

Symptoms for young goats include becoming weak in the rear legs with progressive weakness until death. Adults will exhibit swollen joints.

Unfortunately, there are no treatment procedures, and the prevention of this is to test your bloodlines and use culling for any positive stock.

- **Caseous lymphadenitis (CL)** is contracted by consuming a contaminated feed or through an open wound. There is some speculation that this can even enter through unbroken skin. The bacteria that cause this disease is commonly found in soil.

Symptoms include large knots and abscesses located on the goat's body around their lymph nodes. The animal will start losing its body condition and exhibit a fever.

The treatment is to lance the abscesses and rinse with 7 percent iodine and injectable antibiotics.

- **Chlamydiosis** is one of the causes of reproductive failure in goats. The disease manifests as abortion, stillbirth, and weak kids. Abortion usually manifests during the last 2 to 3 weeks of the doe's gestation and does not necessarily become apparent when the animal was originally infected. It is important to note that this CAN be spread to humans, so caution must be observed.

Treatment includes antibiotics as advised by your veterinarian. Prevention requires herd testing.

- **Coccidiosis** is caused by a parasite that is found within the cells of a goat's intestines. Depending upon the number of parasites present in the intestines, it can dictate how severe a case may be. If this animal becomes stressed, you will notice the symptoms become worse and lower the animal's resistance to other diseases.

Symptoms include bloody diarrhea, a loss of appetite, weight, and a possibility of sudden death.

Treatment is the sulfa drug, isolating the sick animal, and good sanitation practices on the property.

- **Flystrike** is fairly rare in goats, as the primary target is typically sheep. This occurs when maggots of blowflies hatch on the skin and feed on the animal's living tissue. This occurs when adult flies lay their eggs in a moistened coat from urine or fecal staining. Skin wounds, weeping eyes, or lesions from footrot can be targeted by the adult flies.

Symptoms will include agitation, secondary bacterial infections, picking at infected areas, exhibiting a foul smell, and flies targeting one particular animal.

Treatment for this includes close clipping of affected areas, removing the affected animals from the balance of the herd, cleaning and dressing any area showing infection, and the application of antibiotics at the discretion of your veterinarian.

- **Internal parasites** generally cover the various worms that your goat can be exposed to by grazing in pastures. Each distinct type of worm will have its own lifecycles and can appear at different times of the year. Worms are typically indicated by a decrease in body weight, body muscling, or a loss of appetite.

Symptoms include increased pulse, increased respiration, swelling under the chin area, and severe weakness.

Owners should consult with their veterinarian to determine the most effective dewormer to use. All animals should follow routine deworming practices as well as being dewormed at purchase and when put on any pasture.

- **Pinkeye** is identified by redness and watering in the eye. You may see eyelid swelling or a clouding of the pupil. Besides being transmitted from goat to goat, pinkeye can hop species and even infect humans, so it is important to follow protocols and head off an outbreak to your herd or other animals. Pinkeye will remain contagious for as long as symptoms remain and for a period of 24 hours after administering antibiotics.

Treatment includes injectable antibiotics and the application of eye ointment.

- A **ringworm** is actually not a worm, but instead a skin fungus that looks circular and scaly. This can be caused by unclean conditions or even be found after living dormant in your soil. Consult your vet immediately, as with pinkeye, this can easily hop species and be contracted by humans.

Symptoms include rough circular patches over the body.

Treatment includes consulting with your veterinarian to find the safest treatment available to you.

- **Sore mouth** is a viral disease common in sheep and goats, and the virus that causes it can also lay dormant in your soil or on the surface of barn equipment. Symptoms include thick and scabby sores that are typically found on the lips or gums of the suspected infected animal. If the case is severe enough, you may find these scabs on the udders of does. This condition is very painful and does will be unable to nurse. Always monitor your animal to make sure that they are eating and drinking enough.

Treatment includes a vaccine for kids and the use of a softening ointment to help with existing sores on the animal's body. Use extreme caution around your goat's eyes.

- **Urinary Calculi** is specific to male goats and is best compared to kidney stones in humans. It is the formation of stones in the male's urinary tract. Calculi is caused by an imbalance of calcium-phosphorus levels found in your feed ratios.

Symptoms include being unable to pass urine, kicking at the belly, restlessness, and stretching while attempting to urinate.

Treatment involves paying strict attention to your feed ratios. They should have a 2:1 calcium-phosphorus ratio, and 10 t0 15 pounds of ammonium chloride per ton. Following these guidelines and supplying plenty of clean, fresh drinking water will help stop the formation of calculi.

Basic First Aid Supplies

- Thermometers
- Disposable gloves
- Scissors
- Surgical Scissors
- Needles (22g, 20g, 18g)
- Syringes (3cc, 6cc, 10 cc, 20cc)
- Red top tubes. These are used for blood collection for mail-in tests for CAE & CL
- Vet Wrap, elastic bandage

- Gauze Pads
- Cotton Balls
- Alcohol prep wipes
- Triple Antibiotic Ointment
- Vetricyn Spray
- Betadine or Iodine scrub
- Rubbing alcohol
- Terramycin eye ointment
- 7% Iodine solution spray
- Antiseptic spray like Blu-Kote
- Di-Methox powder or liquid for coccidiosis or scours
- Epinephrine, for reactions to injections
- Procaine penicillin
- LA-200 or Biomycin
- Tetanus antitoxin
- Probiotics like Probios
- Powdered electrolytes
- Fortified vitamin B
- CDT antitoxin
- Milk of magnesia for bloat
- Kaolin pectin for scours
- Aspirin
- Activated charcoal product, for example, Toxiban, for accidental poisoning
- Green goo animal formula (for wound care)

- Drench Syringe

- Weight tape

- Scalpels

- Tube-feeding kit to feed sick or weak kids

- Small clippers for shaving wounds

- Blood stop powder or cornstarch

- Children's liquid Benadryl

- Mastitis Test Strips (if you are milking)

- Heat lamps (kidding), heating pad

- Notepad & pen

- Headlamp and flashlight

Conclusion

There are many people out there that are looking to start up their small business on their own land or becoming more self-sufficient. Equally, there is something satisfying about building something with your own two hands.

You may have dreams of starting your own small herd and creating goods from their gifts, such as milk or fiber. If you have never done this before, it may be difficult to navigate how to get started, where to purchase your seed stock, and what animals to choose.

That's why we have put this book together, to help you determine where to get started and why. Besides details about the more popular breeds of goats today, this book addressed detailed questions to ask, information that should be given to you, and how to prepare your property to house your new investment.

Goats are adventurous, and it can be difficult to keep them fenced in because they are such proficient escape artists. The key is to keep them happy on their side of the fence and provide them with a proper and safe environment filled with tasty weeds and shrubbery overgrowth, since those are their favorite snacks.

If you are new to caring for goats, we have given you insight into how to feed them, so they stay healthy and continue producing goods for you.

Dairy goats are probably the most popular herd today, and there is so much more than just getting goat's milk involved with your new venture. This book has given you a small sampling of recipes that you can create using your new homegrown supply, and there are so many more choices out there! We hope that you will enjoy making cheese, ice cream, and more!

If you choose to start a meat goat herd, you now have a list of some of the best breeds to use to solidify your business. It can be difficult getting started, but once you are in the eye of a recurring buyer, you may receive a contract if you continue to improve your herd's confirmation and your reputation for raising the very best animals.

It can be challenging and a bit scary taking that leap and getting started in your chosen goat business. With determination and quality, you will find your niche in the market.

We have explained how important it is to keep records of your venture. This way you will know how much you are spending and how you are improving the bloodlines of your herd.

Another choice, of course, is raising fiber goats. With them, you will enter the world of textiles, and right now, there is more demand than there is production. You received tips on shearing and terminology associated with the industry that will make you sound like a pro.

Lastly, you now have in dept information about keeping your herd healthy and some challenges that you may face. We never want to, but it helps to be prepared for any emergency! Along with those disease descriptions, this book has included a basic first aid kit supply list that you will want to assemble and keep handy.

Raising your own herd will help you become more self-sufficient and teach you about living off the land. They will give you milk to drink, food to eat and provide you with entertainment and companionship.

They can be instrumental in clearing land of unwanted vegetation, they even clear poison ivy!

By reading through all the materials, you can knowledgeably decide which goats are right for you. Happy Herding!

References

Alphafoodie, S. (2020, July 29). *How to make goat cheese (plus FAQs and tips)*. Alphafoodie. https://www.alphafoodie.com/how-to-make-goat-cheese/

Analida. (2020, January 7). *How to make goat cheese recipe - Chèvre*. Analida's Ethnic Spoon. https://ethnicspoon.com/how-to-make-goat-cheese-recipe-chevre/

Bradshaw, A. (2015, March 5). *Goats for sale - 6 mistakes to avoid when buying goats*. Common Sense Home. https://commonsensehome.com/goats-for-sale/

Carroll, R. (2018). *Home cheese making : recipes for 75 homemade cheeses*. Storey Books. (Original work published 1982)

Castration | Agricultural Research. (n.d.). www.luresext.edu. Retrieved June 5, 2021, from http://www.luresext.edu/?q=content/castration#:~:text=Three%20comm on%20ways%20to%20castrate

Fiber Goats – The american goat federation. (n.d.). American goat federation. Retrieved June 8, 2021, from https://americangoatfederation.org/breeds-of-goats-2/fiber-goats/#:~:text=The%20Fiber%20Goat%20industry%20has

Garman, J. (2020, January 4). *How long do goats live? - Backyard Goats*. Backyard Goats. https://backyardgoats.iamcountryside.com/health/how-long-do-goats-live/

Griffith, K., Rask, G., Peel, K., Levalley, S., & Johnson, C. (n.d.). *Raising and showing meat goats! A youth manual for meat goat projects in Colorado!*. Retrieved June 8, 2021, from https://www.meadowlark.k-state.edu/docs/4h/resources/Meat_Goat_Manual.pdf

Harlow, I. (2015, February 13). *Goats for land management*. Farm and Dairy. https://www.farmanddairy.com/top-stories/goats-land-management/240237.html#:~:text=If%20you%20want%20to%20clear

Helmer, J. (2020, December 7). *Tips for providing your goats the shelter they need.* Hobby Farms. https://www.hobbyfarms.com/tips-providing-goats-shelter-they-need/

Kopf, A. : K. (2021, January 19). *Goat lice: are your goats lousy?* Backyard Goats. https://backyardgoats.iamcountryside.com/health/goat-lice-are-your-goats-lousy/

Manteuffel, R. (2019, August 13). *Are goats the new weed whackers? Plenty of people want them to be.* The Washington Post. https://www.washingtonpost.com/lifestyle/magazine/using-goats-to-clear-land-is-way-more-labor-intensive-than-anyone-can-imagine/2019/08/13/acc17608-b78e-11e9-b3b4-2bb69e8c4e39_story.html

Manuel, A. (n.d.). *How to make goat milk candles.* Home Guides | SF Gate. Retrieved June 6, 2021, from https://homeguides.sfgate.com/make-goat-milk-candles-74284.html

Metzger, M. (2018, December 14). *Winter management tips for goats.* sheep & goats. https://www.canr.msu.edu/news/winter-management-tips-for-goats#:~:text=Goats%20that%20are%20properly%20cared

Nutritional feeding management of meat goats | NC State Extension Publications. (2015). Ncsu.edu. https://content.ces.ncsu.edu/nutritional-feeding-management-of-meat-goats

Nuwer, R. (2014, March 26). *Never underestimate a goat; it's not as stupid as it looks.* Smithsonian; Smithsonian.com. https://www.smithsonianmag.com/science-nature/never-underestimate-goat-not-stupid-looks-180950265/

Pesaturo, J. (2014, February 10). *Goat milk ice cream bases |.* Our One Acre Farm. https://ouroneacrefarm.com/2014/02/10/goat-milk-ice-cream-bases/

Ploetz, K. (2013, July 16). *The law | rspca.org.uk.* Rspca.org.uk. https://www.rspca.org.uk/adviceandwelfare/farm/farmanimals/goats/law

Poindexter, J. (2017, March 22). *Goat fencing: 6 important tips to consider to build the perfect fence.* MorningChores. https://morningchores.com/goat-fencing/

Roy's Farm. (2021a, May 17). *Raising goats as pets: beginner's guide for raising pet goats*. Roy's Farm. https://www.roysfarm.com/raising-goats-as-pets/

Roy's Farm. (2021b, May 17). *Why do bucks smell so bad: the secrets of the goaty smell*. Roy's Farm. https://www.roysfarm.com/why-do-bucks-smell-so-bad/

Sartell, J. (2018). *Feeding baking soda to your goats*. Mannapro.com. https://www.mannapro.com/homestead/feeding-baking-soda-to-your-goats

smallholderhollow. (n.d.). *Dairy goats: full size vs mini goats*. Retrieved May 27, 2021, from http://smallholderhollow.com/dairy-goats-full-size-vs-mini-goats/

Smith, C. (n.d.-a). *Creating a first aid kit for goats*. Dummies. Retrieved June 8, 2021, from https://www.dummies.com/home-garden/hobby-farming/raising-goats/creating-a-first-aid-kit-for-goats/

Smith, C. (n.d.-b). *How and when to shear your goats*. Dummies. Retrieved June 8, 2021, from https://www.dummies.com/home-garden/hobby-farming/raising-goats/how-and-when-to-shear-your-goats/

Smith, C. (n.d.-c). *What is normal goat behavior?* Dummies. Retrieved May 31, 2021, from https://www.dummies.com/home-garden/hobby-farming/raising-goats/what-is-normal-goat-behavior/

The Hay Manager. (2018, October 31). *Keeping goats warm in the winter*. The Hay Manager. https://www.thehaymanager.com/goat-and-sheep-round-bale-hay-feeders/keeping-goats-warm-in-the-winter/

The Law | rspca.org.uk. (2017). Rspca.org.uk. https://www.rspca.org.uk/adviceandwelfare/farm/farmanimals/goats/law

Tilley, N. (n.d.). *StackPath*. Www.gardeningknowhow.com. Retrieved June 4, 2021, from https://www.gardeningknowhow.com/composting/manures/goat-manure-fertilizer.htm#:~:text=Goat%20manure%20is%20virtually%20odorless

Treehugger. (n.d.). *Learn how to feed and tend goats on the small farm*. Treehugger. Retrieved June 1, 2021, from https://www.treehugger.com/feed-and-tend-goats-3016793#:~:text=Hay%20is%20the%20main%20source

Vet, S. C. (2019, February 11). *Three diseases all goats owners should be aware of, test for, and work to prevent.* Sale Creek. https://salecreek.vet/three-diseases-all-goats-owners-should-be-aware-of-test-for-and-work-to-prevent/

Wetherbee, K. (n.d.). *Raising dairy goats and the benefits of goat milk.* Mother Earth News. Retrieved June 2, 2021, from https://www.motherearthnews.com/homesteading-and-livestock/benefits-of-goat-milk-zmaz02jjzgoe

Wikipedia Contributors. (2019a, February 27). *Cashmere goat.* Wikipedia; Wikimedia Foundation. https://en.wikipedia.org/wiki/Cashmere_goat

Wikipedia Contributors. (2019b, October 27). *List of goat milk cheeses.* Wikipedia; Wikimedia Foundation. https://en.wikipedia.org/wiki/List_of_goat_milk_cheeses

Wolford, D. (2014a, February 16). *Homemade udder & teat wipes.* Weed 'Em & Reap. https://www.weedemandreap.com/homemade-udder-teat-wipes-milking/

Wolford, D. (2014b, April 5). *How to milk a goat: step by step pictures.* Weed 'Em & Reap. https://www.weedemandreap.com/how-to-milk-a-goat/

Wolford, D. (2016, April 27). *Homemade udder balm recipe {with free printable label}.* Weed 'Em & Reap. https://www.weedemandreap.com/homemade-udder-balm-recipe/

Wright, A. (2013, September 18). *No, goats do not eat tin cans.* Modern Farmer. https://modernfarmer.com/2013/09/goats-eat-tin-cans/#:~:text=They%20can%20be%20pets%2C%20they

Backyard Beekeeping for Beginners

Step-By-Step Guide To Raise Your First Colonies
in 30 Days

Small Footprint Press

Introduction

Does being in nature bring you unparalleled joy and contentment? When you think about the world of bugs, insects, and other critters, do you find that you are constantly captivated, and you find yourself interested in learning more? Maybe you are concerned with what humanity is doing to the planet and want to explore the various ways in which you can give back to mother nature?

If you answered yes to any of these questions, becoming a beekeeper should be right up your alley!

Humans are hardwired to build, create, and work for things that give us joy. As we have become bogged down with office work, jobs that do not challenge us or stimulate our minds, that joy has begun to diminish. We spend far too much of our time sitting around doing menial tasks that do not have much of an effect on our world or our spirits. Nowadays, we find ourselves feeling disconnected from nature and not properly understanding how we can return to a rightful balance with the natural world around us.

It is understandable if you feel this way in today's world, but there are many things you can do to reconnect. One of the most powerful and impactful ways to give back to Mother Earth and build a fun new hobby for yourself at the same time is to start your very own beehive. Bees are nature's most precious asset, and without them, the world would truly never be the same again.

Becoming a beekeeper is an excellent way to fulfill the primal need that we talked about above. It gets you out and about and lets you create and do things for yourself rather than being reliant on others. It lets you become more self-sufficient and return to the land, rather than buying products from corporations that mass-produce the food in chain stores—no step of that process is great for the Earth.

Becoming a beekeeper is very rewarding, but it is not for the faint of heart or those following a whim. It takes time, sweat-inducing effort, and money, but the rewards are numerous. Not only are you getting a captivating and fun new way to pass the time, but you are also getting quality one-on-one interaction with nature and giving back to it at the same time. And of course, you get the reward of honey at the end. Store-bought honey is OK, but it cannot beat the quality or the satisfaction that comes from that first bite of honey you produced yourself.

Along with that sense of pride, beekeeping is a great pursuit for those who are interested in bees or other insects. Becoming a beekeeper will increase your knowledge of the small but vital part of the ecosystem. You will also get another bonus of being able to observe the little critters to your heart's content and see how they interact with the world around them.

Or maybe you want to get into beekeeping for reasons other than just giving yourself something to do other than work. Bees are a vital part of our lives, as they play a role in every single part of our planet's ecosystem. Around 90% of all plants in the world need to be cross-pollinated to survive, and in North America, bees are the most important movers in pollination (Home and Garden, 2021).

As is well known by now, bee species all over the world are dying at a truly alarming rate. It might be tempting to think of that as a "somewhere else" problem, but it's affecting us close to home as well. In Ontario, Canada, one common species of bumblebee was put on the endangered species list in 2009 and has not been seen in the wild since then (Wildlife Preservation Canada, 2021). And it is not the only bee species to be disappearing—between October 2018 and April 2019, the University of Maryland reported that 40% of bee colonies in the United States died, making it the highest winter loss in 13 years (Woodward, 2019).

The reasons that the bees are dying are numerous and happen all over the globe:

- Climate change has created later growing seasons, so bees cannot get the pollen they need to survive early enough in the year.

- They have lost their natural habitat and spaces to city development, resulting in fewer spaces for bees to live.

- With large areas of land dedicated to growing a single kind of crop (monoculture), bees lack the plants and flowers that sustain them.

So, what do the bees dying mean to us? Remember, bees are the major source of pollination for both wild and cultivated plants. So, if all the bees were to die, plant life on our planet would stop growing. Or at least stop growing in the manner with which we are most familiar. We might be able to come up with artificial methods of pollination for crops, but replicating what nature has already perfected is never easy or cheap. What if that method was not cost-effective and plants that corporations could not make a profit from were no longer being pollinated? Would that leave us with a barren post-apocalyptic-style world?

Maybe things would not be that dire, but it is a concern all the same. Thinking about those kinds of things might be why you are interested in becoming a beekeeper.

The good news is that by providing a place for bees to live and be safe, you are also providing up to one acre of pollination per hive you run (Government of New Brunswick, 1996). That is a pretty good area of coverage and would contribute a lot to your local flora. Even small steps, done all together, impact the wider world and make it a better place.

Everything presented in this book will help guide you in your first steps toward your end goal—being a full-fledged apiarist. To make all the information as accessible as possible, everything that you read here will be presented straightforwardly and simply.

That way, you can get the best knowledge you can without getting bogged down by terms or information that a beginner does not need to know. The tips, tricks, and advice presented here are all gathered from beekeepers with years of experience and are designed to set any newbie up for success rather than failure.

As a company, Small Footprint Press is focused and determined on providing the best help possible. We want to make it easy for people to return to the land and live more sustainably for the long term.

We do this by doing in-depth research for all our books, with topics ranging from survival training to various self-sufficiency methods and prepping for disasters (natural or human-caused). We work our hardest to teach you how to care for the planet Earth and its inhabitants in the most holistic and mutually beneficial manners possible. Our team is made of dedicated and enthusiastic nature lovers, who altogether have over three decades of combined knowledge of outdoorsmanship and conservation. We can't wait to pass it all along to you.

Our goal is to help empower you to achieve the sustainable lifestyle that you want. Like you, we feel that giving back to our planet is crucial for our continued survival as a species. We full-heartedly believe that being outdoors (in a sustainable manner) makes us humans happy, and we want to share that happiness with you as well.

We know that the idea of starting a beehive can be intimidating, but we are here to help you take it one step at a time. This book is designed to help you know how to follow your path—both before starting on the road and during your first year. We emphasize building a proper knowledge base and understanding before getting started so that you can avoid as many pitfalls as possible.

By the time you are done with this book, you are going to be feeling much more confident in your knowledge and abilities. As long as you have the right knowledge and tools, getting started and succeeding in beekeeping is not as hard as you might imagine.

In this book, you will learn about:

- The benefits of joining a beekeeping club and the many ways that doing so will help make you a better apiarist.

- An accurate estimate of the time and money that you are going to be investing in your first year.

- What to look for in choosing the location of your beehive and why this is vital for your success.

- Preparing your hive for success and happiness, both for yourself and for your bees.

- How to install bees into your hive and set it up so everything goes swimmingly right from the start.

- Common mistakes and pitfalls that befall beekeepers in their first years (and how to avoid them).

- BONUS: Some basic information on how to turn beekeeping into some extra cash!

Enough with the dreaming of one day having your prized colony in your backyard.

It's a great time to get involved in beekeeping, and it will bring you tremendous joy as you give back to Mother Earth and help restore nature to its beauty and balance.

No matter what your current experience level is, with the right network and information, you can establish your very own successful backyard beehive in no time at all and with zero added stress.

Chapter 1:
Prepping for Success

It might seem like the first step you need to take in becoming a beekeeper is to get some bees, but that would be jumping the gun—by a lot. Before you rush off to the store or website to buy a thousand-dollar hive box and hundreds of little bees, it is better to have a base layer of knowledge to fall back on first. If you want to succeed, you first have to prep for success. If you do not, you are working toward disaster.

Good thing that we are going to be covering all bases of preparation. We will first look at something that bees are great at doing—making connections and working together. Before you get started on your own, it is best to make some new friends who are experienced beekeepers.

You can do this by joining a local or online beekeeping club, many of which offer perks beyond socializing. The people in these clubs are just as excited and passionate about bees as you are, and they want to see you succeed in your efforts. There are many different benefits of joining a local club, including training courses, sharing information and tips, gaining a mentor, and eventually allowing you to be a mentee. After all, one of the best ways to test your knowledge is to share it with someone else.

By being a part of a club, you will have a rich resource of knowledge and experience at your fingertips.

But it is good to go into a new group with at least a little knowledge as well. Reading this book, specifically this first chapter, is a great resource for getting some of that initial understanding. The second part of this chapter will go over some of the initial information that you should have before getting too heavily invested in the idea of beekeeping.

Beekeeping Clubs

Have you ever had a subject you were interested in and passionate about? One that you wanted to talk about to everyone all the time, but you were worried that you were boring or pushy? Does your interest in bees fit into those descriptions as well?

Well, if so, do not worry. There is a way to still talk nonstop about bees but not get annoyed looks from those around you. The solution is simple—join a beekeeping club. No more needing to cut yourself off or change the subject because all the people surrounding you will want to talk about bees too!

Like with all clubs or groups, there are numerous reasons to join your local beekeeping club, not the least of which is making new friends. Finding a group to join could be as easy as Googling "beekeeping clubs near me." There are also numerous groups, ranging from local clubs made up of the same ten people to national-level organizations, such as the American Beekeeping Federation and the Canadian Association of Professional Apiarists.

Why join a club? There are numerous benefits of doing so, the main one being that many clubs will offer training courses. These kinds of courses are usually heavily based on theory and so are geared toward beginner beekeepers, but they can also be good refreshers for more experienced apiarists or if it has been a while since you first learned the information. A good way to judge the training offered by your local clubs is to see how they teach—if they immediately go into the more complex aspects of beekeeping, it is probably not the course for you.

You want courses taught by knowledgeable people who teach straightforwardly, starting from the foundation and then building up. Many people who are passionate about the subject may forget that they know things that are not common knowledge and so can use terms that mean nothing to you, which does not make it easy to learn anything. If you can, test out several different local clubs to see which has the best fit for you. If there is only one club in your area, and they teach like this, talk to the teacher and let them know that they are going too fast for any beginner. Hopefully, they will take your feedback in stride and adjust their lessons accordingly.

So, what kind of information should be included in an introduction to beekeeping? The first thing that should be taught is an understanding of the seasons and what needs to be done for your bees in each one. This part of the course should not have too much detail, but it should clearly state what happens in each season, such as the inactive periods that make up most of the year, the high-production time of early spring, and how to prepare your hives for the winter. This information should then be used to help put the rest of the course into the context of a timeframe.

Beekeeping courses should also be teaching you the practical and not just the theoretical parts of hive management. Many newcomers to the practice think that it is as easy as buying a hive and some bees, and then you are rewarded with honey, but that is not the case. For many, when they realize that there is more work involved in keeping a hive than they thought, they give up on their hives which defeats the purpose entirely.

The overview of the practical elements includes being upfront about the time and effort commitment you are making when purchasing a hive. Bees need to be fed nectar during the times of the year when there is not much natural food for them to collect. When preparing for winter, they are going to need even more nectar than normal to help them during the cold months.

Bees also need a lot of room to grow their colony, and their hives need regular inspections for pests, diseases, or if they are preparing for a swarm. Swarming is a very normal action and is the method of the bee colony reproducing or splitting itself into two colonies once it has grown too large for just one queen. Most often, swarming occurs in the spring, but it can happen later in the year as well, and so this is something that beekeepers need to watch out for. If your bees look like they are going to swarm, you will need to act sooner rather than later.

Since you need to be mindful of issues like these and more, it is recommended that inspections happen every week. Any course on beekeeping needs to be upfront about this because otherwise, they are creating a false expectation. As well, it should give you the tools and information that you need to look out for in these inspections. They should also discuss the risks of hive inspections, including getting stung, the heavy-lifting for when your hive is full of honey, the various weather conditions you will be working in, and the unavoidable reality that some bees will be squashed in the process.

These are the basics that should be covered in any beekeeping course you take. Of course, these lessons do not have to happen in person. Online courses are available as well, though the information presented will be more generalized. Going through a class on the basics of bees is a great idea—that way, you start getting an understanding of what beekeeping entails and seeing if it is for you.

It is recommended to take a more in-depth course in person at a local club. That way, the information will be based on the lived experience of the teacher. Another advantage of taking such a course at a local club is that these people know your area and what to expect from it in terms of weather and bee behavior.

Of course, the benefits of joining a club go beyond the training that it offers. A club is made up of more people than just one teacher, so by interacting with the other members, you are almost guaranteed to gain more information as they share their experiences and stories. While listening to everyone can be helpful and entertaining, the best way to take advantage of the expertise at your fingertips is to find a mentor.

Gaining a mentor gives you not only way more knowledge but also a person willing to help you as you set up your hive and guide you through the tricky parts. Having someone willing to come and see your hives and how they are doing gives you greater flexibility in how to care for your bees properly.

To find a mentor, you will first need to get to know everyone at your local club and determine who fits with you best. That fit needs to be not only in personality and temperament but also in project scope and goals. If you are just looking at working with one hive, you would not want someone who has experience with hundreds of hives at a time. By matching scale and end goals, you can also more easily create a collaboration project between the two of you, which sweetens the deal for your mentor. Mentors may also agree because teaching is a great way for them to solidify their knowledge, which you may experience if you stick around long enough.

Of course, beekeeping clubs are not just good for courses and mentorship. Like we said earlier, these organizations are great places to meet like-minded people who are interested in the same things you are. These people may become your new best friends as you work on your hives, and they will encourage your growth and push you to explore different methods of beekeeping you may not have heard of otherwise.

Most clubs do a lot to foster a sense of community, including having frequent meetings and get-togethers for everyone to catch up and share the latest news from their hives. Often these meetings can be themed around something of concern to the members, such as learning about the latest disease affecting hives in the country. Many clubs will also offer special interest events, such as honey tastings and workshops on brewing mead or making beeswax cloths.

So, now that you know the importance of joining a beekeeping club let us take a quick reminder about how to find one. Google is your friend in this search, especially if it takes you to the website of a national organization such as the American Beekeeping Federation of Bee Culture (names to search for both are at the end of the chapter). These web pages are great sources of information, both in figuring out the location of the closest beekeeping club to you and in signing up for additional resources such as monthly newsletters and online forums.

Many of these online groups also have ties to numerous other pages and organizations for you to check out. Additionally, they probably have links to their own and other social media accounts, which allows you to connect to bee lovers all over the world. Joining some of these online groups will let you expand your beekeeper friend group and gain insight from very different kinds of apiarists. This expands on several qualities seen in the local clubs, just on a much larger scale.

What Else Should I Know?

Now that we have looked at the benefits of joining a beekeeping club, we should cover some of the other things you need to consider before buying your first colony.

Something of the utmost importance that you need to know is the regulations around hives and bees in your area. Your beekeeping club can help you here, as well as help keep each other up to date with any new information or potential changes to the regulations.

But it is also important for you to do your due diligence and research to empower yourself and stay up to date on your own. The last thing you want is to have only part of the picture of regulations around honeybees, get your colony thriving and producing delicious honey, only to be shut down due to some rule you did not know.

Regulations and Laws

So, what kinds of regulations do you need to know? Well, the first and biggest one you need to know is whether or not your city even allows beekeeping at all. While some states and provinces have laws stating that beekeeping is legal, laws and regulations will still vary from city to city, so it is important to find your local laws.

The benefits of beekeeping are becoming more well known, and backyard beekeepers are a growing demographic. Because of this, most cities are accepting of this hobby, though they may have limits on the number and placements of your hives. Additionally, you may need to register each of your hives with the city. You can find this information by contacting your municipal bylaw office, looking on their website, or by asking people you know who keep bees. Generally, the requirements that are in place are easily followed and are not time-consuming to follow.

When finding out your cities requirements, you will need to check out the zoning laws, which will state whether or not bees are allowed either as of right (a legal term that means there is no permit required), allowed with a special permit, or not allowed outright. If it is written vaguely or confusingly, talk to your local zoning authority, who should be able to clear up any confusion you might have.

Aside from city regulation, you may also need to find out if there are any rules in place in your homeowner's association (HOA) in your neighborhood, which may differ from city ordinances. It is important when searching these rules to determine whether or not your HOA prohibits livestock (which can sometimes include bees) and what general rules pertain to keeping insects. If you plan to set up your hives as a side hustle, you will also need to check what your HOA states around home-based businesses.

You may be thinking that you need a nice big backyard to house a beehive. Many people could immediately assume that since they are living in an apartment and therefore have no yard, beekeeping is automatically not an option for them. But, there are ways to get around that hiccup. In the last few years, there has been a growing trend toward rooftop hives. If you want to set up one on the roof, you will have to have a chat with your landlord about it, and maybe the promise of sharing some fresh sweet honey will help smooth things over.

Another option is to see if your building has a communal garden or green space or if there are plans to make one. More and more people are looking to grow their food, flowers, or just to get outdoors for a few hours at a time. If you are living in a place with a shared garden, it would be worth it to talk to the other tenants and see if they are open to the idea of having a hive. Sell them on the idea by telling them all about the benefits bees will have on their garden as well as the general environment. Again, bribing with the promise of honey can never go wrong.

No matter where you live, it is a good idea to talk to your neighbors before getting a hive since bees can be intimidating for those unfamiliar with them. It is important to prepare your neighbors for what they can expect living next to a hive and to create a good rapport with them so that if they have questions or concerns, they can talk to you directly.

While you can never guarantee that the bees will not be pests, hopefully, it will just be the odd bee sighting here and there. But if your hive swarms, a large mass of flying bees can be terrifying. Establishing a good relationship with your neighbors before getting a hive means having friendly neighbors who are more likely to talk to you calmly rather than doing something drastic. Make sure you leave a clear channel of communication open with them, whether that be through giving them your email or phone number, so that they feel comfortable contacting you with their queries.

Gear

After figuring out the legalities and logistics of where to house your hive, your next step is figuring out all the gear you will need. Unfortunately, many of these items are very specific to beekeeping, so you cannot reuse items you have found lying around your house. This is where the cost of beekeeping comes in, and for many potential beekeepers, it is what keeps them from engaging with the hobby.

To try and prevent that from happening to you, we are going to go over what is considered the absolute essentials for a beekeeper. These essentials are the hives, the hive frames, bee feeders, a hive tool, a beekeeping suit, and a smoker. Luckily, these things are not ridiculously expensive, so you are not looking at spending tens of thousands of dollars. The price, of course, will vary depending on where you live and how many hives you want to start with. All prices (in US dollars) given in this section are based on what we could find on Amazon at the time of writing.

Hives are the fundamental part of beekeeping since that is where you keep the bees, and it is recommended that you start with at least two. That way, you can compare what is happening in one to the other and potentially use one to help bolster the other if one starts to struggle.

There are two different approaches to buying hives. The first approach is to buy a starter hive, which, while more expensive, comes with the bees and the hive. These kits often include most of the gear you will need, which is where the higher cost comes from. The other option is to buy a bee kit, which only includes a single queen and her worker drones. If you go with this option, you will have to get separate empty hive boxes, which currently cost around $150 for each hive.

When choosing your hive box, there are different style options as well. The three main kinds of hive boxes are the horizontal top bar, the Langstroth, and the Warré box types.

The horizontal top bar design is the oldest hive design in the world, featuring bars laid out across the top of the cradle-looking hive. That enables the bees to build comb down from the frame. Because of this, you do not need to use four-sided frames or a hive foundation. The advantage of this kind of box is the simple and easy access to the combs, which are easy to then remove without any heavy lifting. Though it does require frequent monitoring, those inspections are usually quick and easy.

Both the Langstroth and Warré are vertical boxes, though. As the horizontal top bar uses bars, the Warré uses frames instead. These kinds of hives are good for those searching for low-cost and low-maintenance hives that are lightweight and do not require frequent inspections.

The Langstroth is the most common now, as it has removable frames built into stacked boxes that the honeycomb is built onto. Each style of box has different pros and cons, so deciding on a style is largely a personal choice. If you have the time, tools, and expertise, you can always build a hive box yourself. This allows for even more personalization, but the overall expense will depend on the price of the materials.

The frames are the rectangular pieces that fit inside your hive where the bees make the honey. They can either be bought with your hive or separately, and you can also get them with or without foundations (an underlying base for the honeycomb to be built on) and are around $50. You could also make them yourself, but since they need to be very precise to fit into the hive, you should only do so if you are confident in your carpentry skills.

Bee feeders are used so that your hive does not decide to move when the natural food sources grow scarce. This means that having these is an absolute necessity for a good part of the year when you need to feed your bees sugar water. Feeders are wooden frames with grates over the water to prevent drowning. They are placed near or inside the hive. Placing them within the hive ensures that the food goes to your bees and not to other animals.

The hive tool is pretty cheap (around $10), but it is invaluable for what it does for your hive. Bees line their hives with a substance called propolis, which is essentially a very strong glue that holds everything together. This includes holding the lid of the hive down, as well as holding the frames in place. The hive tool is used to lever the top of the hive off, as well as to scrape along the sides and loosen the frames so you can collect the honey.

After securing the safety and comfort of your bees, you need to make sure that you are keeping yourself safe too. That means getting a beekeeping suit which will help keep you from getting stung. Honeybees are not naturally aggressive, but they do pick up on anxiety, and as a new beekeeper, you are likely to feel pretty anxious.

A good bee suit will cover your entire body and has gatherings around the ankles, wrists, and neck to prevent bees from getting inside. They then have a hat with netting around it to protect your head. You will need to combine the suit with decent and sturdy gloves and boots (tall rubber boots are best).

The best bee suits are ventilated, and though they do cost more than the non-ventilated ones, it is worth it to prevent overheating and sweating. A full suit can cost anywhere between $100 to $200. To save a little money, you could get a beekeeping jacket, which runs around $70. This one only covers the upper body but can be combined with some sturdy overalls, gloves, and boots to give you full-body protection.

The last of the essential items is a smoker ($20-$30), though the use of such devices is somewhat controversial within the community. Smoke introduced into the hive makes the bees docile and masks any pheromones they emit, meaning that they are less likely to sting you as you collect the honey. However, the smoke itself does not sedate them; instead, it puts them into a heightened state of anxiety, which results in them gorging on the honey. They are then calm because they are stuffed full.

Some critics of smokers think that using them stresses the bees out too much to make them worth using. They also say that overuse of them can reduce honey production. Using a smoker will need to be a decision you make after fully researching both sides.

The items mentioned so far are the essential ones. But, of course, there are also other pieces of gear that, while not technically essential, are helpful for first-time beekeepers to have. These include a queen catcher, queen marker, queen excluder, hive scraper, and brushes.

The queen is the most important bee in your hive because there would be no colony working to make honey without her. A queen catcher is a small plastic hair-clip-looking thing though it has rounded edges and forms a container. These are used when you need to separate the queen from the rest of the colony and are generally inexpensive, with a pack of five costing around $10.

But if you need to separate the queen, first you need to know where she is. A queen marker, less than $20, uses a non-toxic bright ink to mark her back legs, making it easy to spot her in the crowd. This is doubly important in case she dies—if you do not replace her soon enough, your entire colony will die as well.

A queen excluder is a metal grate with openings small enough for the worker bees to fit through, but not the queen as she is larger than they are. This grate allows you to control where the queen lays her eggs, which makes it unpopular for those who want to follow a more natural method of beekeeping.

A hive scraper is used to clean the sides and top of the hive. Since these spots need to be cleaned regularly, the scraper can make that job much faster. Additionally, another useful tool is a brush to knock away the bees from the frames you pull. Most often, you can shake the bees off, but a brush can be used to remove the stubborn ones who cling to the frame.

You can get these items, plus others, individually, but they are also often sold together in kits. You will need to do some shopping around to figure out which ones are best and include the tools you want, but it could be a good way to get multiple things together for a lower price. (Small kits start around $430.)

Buying Your Bees

Alright, so now that you have joined a club and bought all your gear, you have built yourself a strong foundation. It is on that foundation that the basis of your experience should rest, and you must have that base before moving onto the next step—setting up the stars of the show and buying your bees!

Buying bees does require some preplanning, but it does not need to be a complicated process. There are three different methods of acquiring your bees; buy packages of bees, buy a nucleus (nuc meaning already established) colony, or catch a swarm of wild bees.

The most common method for first-time beekeepers is to buy a package of bees. These are generally shipped countrywide in screened containers that hold around 10,000 bees and the queen, who is separated from the rest by a piece of sugar candy that the workers can eat through to get to her. You should double-check with the company you are buying from to see if the queen is marked because that will help you identify and place her where you need once the bees arrive.

There are several online stores where you can buy bee packages within the United States, Canada, and other countries. These packages will be sent to you through the mail with special carriers or through the normal mail—you will need to check which shipping method the company uses. It is also probably a good idea to double-check with your local post office to see what their policy is regarding live insects. They may require you to come to the brick and mortar store to pick them up rather than being delivered to your home.

Nuc colonies are more expensive than bee packages, but some advantages go along with the higher cost. With a bee package, you are only getting the bees themselves, but with a nuc, you are getting a few frames of premade honeycomb that were produced over the winter. This means that your new bees will be able to start producing honey much faster, and the queen is already laying eggs. If they have already survived a winter, you know that they are hardy bees. These kinds of colonies can be installed right into the hive and are most suited to the Langstroth style of box.

For both of these options, it is possible to buy the bees from a local merchant rather than from an online source. The advantage of doing so is that if the bees are local, they are already familiar with the area and therefore are better adapted to your unique conditions. When you purchase locally, you can talk to the seller about any difficulties they have had with the bees in the past and what kind of conditions the bees do not like. It can also be an extra guarantee that the species of bee is one suited to your environment.

If you want local bees but want to save a few bucks, you can always try to catch wild bees. During the spring, many existing colonies have grown too large, and they swarm to create a new hive. If you are on the lookout for such swarms, you can catch the queen bee and set her up in your hive—the worker bees will follow their queen. Swarms can look scary, but most of the time, they are very docile as they do not have an active hive to protect, and they have stuffed themselves with honey to sustain the long flights.

This method is better for more experienced beekeepers, so if you are working on your own, you may want to reconsider this method. Joining a beekeeping club can give you the advantage of gaining a mentor or other experienced apiarists who are willing to assist you with catching wild bees. However, there are other things to consider beyond just the cost and physical act of catching the bees. Because they are wild, you will not be able to know anything about their health, what their temperament is like, or any potential genetic issues from the queen.

What to Look for in Your Bees

Now that you know the different ways of getting your bees, we should discuss what you need to look for in them.

First, you will need to decide what breed of bee you want to have. Yes, there are multiple breeds of bees available—it is not just 'honeybee' one and done. The most popular breeds are Italian, Carniolan, Caucasian, Buckfast, and Russian, and each has its good and poor qualities. However, all honeybee breeds can crossbreed, so do not stress about the breed too much. Most packages of bees are a mix of different breeds to help create stronger genetics.

When selecting bees, you are looking at three elements: temperament, their productivity, and how well they will do in your climate.

Italian bees are suitable for many different kinds of environments, but they do not do well in tropical climates. They have a fairly mild temperament, are not prone to swarming, and make white caps on honeycomb, all of which have made them a popular bee for beginner apiarists. However, they are prone to starvation in the winter due to large colony sizes, so if you live in an area with long winters, you will need to make sure you supplement their diet quite a bit.

The Carniolan bees originally come from Yugoslavia and are darker in color than the Italian bee. Carni bees are calm, gentle, and easy to manage, making them a good choice to introduce to more aggressive bees, though they are likely to swarm. They prefer cool, damp climates and will more likely search for food on slightly rainy days.

If your hive has access to lots of natural nectar, a colony of Carni bees will grow quickly, though they are good at self-regulating their numbers. This means that more will be born and work if there is a lot of food, or a hive will be smaller with a lack of food. This equals a smaller colony during the winter, making starvation less of a concern.

Caucasian bees came from near the Caspian Sea and so are better suited for colder climates. They have longer tongues than the other bees, making it easier for them to get nectar from deeper blossoms. Their primary advantage is their calm nature, with many beekeepers considering them the gentlest of all honeybees. Their disadvantage is that they create a lot of propolis, that sticky glue-like substance inside the hive, making inspections take more time and effort. They are also not a common breed of a bee to have, so finding some will be very difficult.

Both the Buckfast and Russian bee are specialty bees bred from several other breeds. Buckfast bees are not as popular as they once were since the offspring of a naturally occurring queen became very aggressive. This trait was negative enough that it overshadowed their ability to produce lots of honey. As a result, in modern beekeeping circles, it is very hard to find Buckfasts for sale.

The Russian honeybee is well suited for cold climates and is somewhat disease resistant, but no bee breed is truly immune to mites and pests. Like with the Carniolan bee, they have smaller numbers in the colony during the winter, but it takes them a little longer in the spring to return to higher numbers. But once they do, watch out! Their population can grow incredibly fast, which means that they are very prone to swarming, so you will need to watch them closely.

But these are just general guidelines—most often, the bees you buy are going to be a mix of different breeds. And this is a good thing! Just look at all the problems any kind of purebred animal has; genetic diversity is a good thing as it makes your bees stronger, more productive, and hardy.

No matter what kind of breed you think is best, there are few tips to make it work the best for you. Firstly, you should ask local beekeepers what kinds of bees they have. You may find that most work with only one particular breed, which likely means that those kinds of bees are best for your local environment. If the local beekeepers are willing, also consider buying your bees from them, because as we stated before, that allows you to know that your bees will thrive in your area.

Secondly, no matter who you buy your bees from, make sure you order early in the year. The later you wait, the fewer options you will have to pick from. As well, many bee companies are slammed during the spring months, so preordering will make sure that your order is scheduled, and you will not miss out on getting your bees.

Depending on the room you have for bees, you may want to consider setting up multiple hives. Having several hives can help you monitor your bees better, as you have something to compare their activity and health to. Additionally, if one hive starts to falter, you can borrow from the other one to boost it back up. If you do not have space, time, or money for more than one hive, ask your mentor if they are willing to use one of their hives to boost yours in times of need.

Final Considerations—Money and Time

Beekeeping is neither a super expensive nor a cheap hobby. Before you commit to creating this change in your life, you need to make sure you have realistic expectations for the time and financial commitment to which you are agreeing. It would not be fair to either you or the bees if you got partway through the process and realized that you could not keep up with the demands. Abandoned hives can end up doing more damage than good, so that is what we want to avoid at all costs.

We did give an estimate of costs with some items of gear, but in this section, we will cover all items more fully. We will also discuss probable events that can occur in your first year as a beekeeper that can create unexpected costs.

The first thing to do is find out the costs of membership to your local beekeeping club. This will vary by location as well as likely by the number of hives you have—the higher number of hives, the higher your membership costs. Most memberships will operate yearly and can range from anywhere from $40 to $500. On top of membership fees, check out how much the club charges for the courses and workshops they run, and build that price into your budget.

After getting a sufficient amount of training and education on the subject, you will want to buy your gear. Here is a breakdown of ranges for it all:

- Hive boxes (depending on size and style): $150 to $300

- Accessory equipment, such as your bee suit, smoker, hive tool, etc.: $100 to $300

- Bees

  - Package of about 10,000 workers, drones, and the queen bee: $100 to $135

  - Nuc colony with premade honeycomb: $125 to $175

  - Catching a swarm: only the cost of treating potential stings

- 10 pounds of sugar from Costco to make supplemental food: $8

Added to these are the unexpected costs. You should have some money set aside as emergency funds, though one thing you can plan for is not so unknown. Mites are a common problem for all and can badly affect novices and seasoned beekeepers alike. Mites can cause a lot of damage to your hive and can spread to others, so you need to monitor and plan for them. Mite treatments cost in the range of $20 to $200, depending on how badly they have spread. So, the earlier you catch them, the better.

So now that we have looked at the financial commitment, the time needed for beekeeping needs to be shown as well. In general, expect to spend 15 to 30 hours caring for your bees in the first year.

After buying all your equipment, you have to set it up. Hives can be made of several pieces that need to be put together Ikea-style. The time needed for that setup will depend on how comfortable you are with assembly. Once the box is set up, placed in the optimal location (covered in Chapter 2), and the bees introduced, next comes the regular work.

The first thing to remember is that beekeeping is seasonal, meaning that certain times of the year will be busier than others. Also, you will likely need to spend more time in the first year on your hives until you are more familiar and comfortable with the process.

Spring is the busiest time of year and is when you will introduce your bees to their new hive. As they settle in and get used to their new home, you will have to feed them for the first few weeks. As the weather warms and they become more active, you will spend less time feeding them unless you are having a poor year for flowers. From here on, you will need to inspect the hive for disease, damage, or signs of swarming once every week. Mostly this can be done on your schedule, but certain situations need precise timing, such as introducing a new queen to the colony.

The weekly inspections continue through the summer. Once the weather starts to cool, and the leaves change color, you know the fun is about to begin. Fall is when your hard work gets rewarded with fresh honey! The time needed for honey extraction will depend on the method that you use (Chapter 6).

After enough honey has been removed, you need to prepare your hives for winter. First, complete a thorough inspection to make sure the queen is strong, the colony is healthy, and no pests have got in or can get in. There needs to be enough honey stored within the hive box to feed your bees as it is their main source of food during the winter—in colder parts of the world, bees will eat up to 90 pounds of honey in one winter (Nickson, 2019a). If there is not enough honey for them, you need to make sure you give them sugar water regularly.

You will want to close most exits to the hive and place an entrance reducer over the few holes left open at the top. The entrance reducer does exactly what it sounds like—it reduces the size of the entrance. This controls airflow and the temperature, and it reduces the chance of other bees or animals getting into the hive and stealing honey.

By mid-October, the hive needs to be wrapped with insulation to keep the bees warm. It is best to use foam insulation. As the bees move around, they generate heat, and you do not want the air inside the hive to get overheated. Wrap foam around the sides and ceiling, making sure to do so in a manner that will not trap water. The entrance hole at the top of the box needs to be left open as you need proper ventilation to prevent mold growth.

* * *

We just covered some of the basics a budding beekeeper needs to know. If any single part of this chapter can be stressed, it is the usefulness and benefits of joining a local apiary club. There you can find courses to supplement what you learn from this book, friends who are interested in the same things you are, and a mentor to help guide you.

With a mentor, some new friends, the right gear, and the desire, money, and time to get after it—nothing is stopping you now!

You can Google these terms to learn more:

- Canadian Association of Professional Apiarists
- American Beekeeping Federation
- Canadian Honey Council
- Bee Culture
- DIY Hive Box Designs
- Top 10 Best Beekeeping Starter Kits

Chapter 2:
Location Is EVERYTHING!

Just as in real estate, the key to bee-ing a good beekeeper is location, location, location.

The previous chapter is a wonderful introduction to the hobby and what to expect, but in this chapter, we will get into the meat of it some more. Figuring out where your hives will go is key and should be the very FIRST thing that you plan out. You have to not only ensure that your yard is a conducive environment to begin with, but you also have to choose the perfect spot for the bees within your yard as they may act differently depending on what interacts with their hive.

So, what should you do if you do not have a lot of space in your backyard or if it is not ideal for bees? Or even worse, what if you do not have a backyard at all?

Well, no need to despair because we will cover that in this chapter as well. After all, if the mountain won't come to Muhammad…

You may not have the proper space or location to house a hive, but that does not mean that you give up on the idea. There could be someone close by who has a large property and would be willing to play host as long as you agree to do the work and cover the cost of upkeep. That way, they see the benefits of having bees on their property, and you still get a brand new hobby to fill your time.

One of the first considerations is food, as bees have to travel to find the nectar they need to feed the colony. While they can travel up to five miles to do so, they will much prefer staying closer to home. So, you will need to consider their food sources and whether or not you can provide that for them or if they have to go elsewhere. And if they travel to find nectar, you will need to be aware of their flight paths—if they regularly fly over where children play in the yard, you may need to consider moving your hive. It is also important to check with your closest neighbors; if one of them is deathly allergic to bees, you should put your hive as far from their property as you can.

Once you have determined the location of your hive, it is time to look at all the other factors as well. This includes the type and intensity of sun they should have, the amount of space between the hives, and how high they should be off the ground. You also need to think about how to access your hives and how to position them so the entrance is easy to get at without being in the way of foot traffic.

Along with all these considerations, you also need to think about your bees' ease of access to water and food. If you do not provide somewhere where they can get nectar and water, they will go to the next best source, even if that is your grouchy neighbor's pool and yard.

You may be feeling a little overwhelmed right now, thinking that there is just too much to consider! Stop. Take a deep breath. It is going to be alright—we are going to walk through it all together. By the end of this chapter, you will know how to pick the perfect location and what you can do to make it optimal for bees to thrive for ultimate honey production.

The First Steps

Now that you are a card-carrying member of a beekeeping club, you are building up the knowledge to get you through your first year, and you have bought and assembled your hives and gear. It is time for the next step. Before you buy your bees, you need to create the perfect spot for your hive—it is vital to do this before your bees arrive because it is incredibly difficult and backbreaking work to do afterward.

This means creating your yard into the perfect environment for bees and choosing the right spot for the hives.

First, wherever you place them needs to be perfectly level side to side, with the front of the hive box just slightly (one inch or less) lower than the back. You put hives this way because bees build comb perpendicular to the ground. If you are on a slant, that means the comb will be as well, making it harder to work with. Also, uneven leveling makes it easier for your hive to tip over.

Have the front lower than the back. This way, if any rainwater ends up in the hive, it drains out of the box rather than staying inside. Standing water in the hive creates a drowning hazard for your bees and promotes mold growth, which can be fatal for the little guys.

To help the water drain even more and to get a perfect balance, you may want to consider getting a hive stand. When the box is off the ground, it prevents water from leaching from the soil, adds an extra boost of gravity to drain water out of the hive, and makes ventilation and temperature regulation a little easier. It can also save your back from bending and lifting the heavy frames from lower on the ground.

Certain kinds of pests and parasites thrive in damp ground, so keeping the box above ground makes it harder for pests and any predators to get in. There is a huge range in type and threat level of predators, which include bears, skunks, mice, raccoons, and wax moths. (We'll cover more on dealing with predators in Chapter 5.) There are several options for store-bought stands, but a do-it-yourself solution should be fairly simple as well.

Speaking of ventilation, make sure that wherever you put your hive, it has good airflow. You do not want it located somewhere where the air stills and gets heavy or at the top of a hill where it is open to wind and the full fury of summer and winter storms.

Having a windbreak (either a fence or hedge) is also very useful. Some areas get very little wind, while others have such strong wind that it is part of the city's identity. If you live somewhere where there are strong winds, consider placing your beehive in a location that protects the bees from strong winds, especially as they enter and exit the hive. A large fence or shrubbery will act as a windbreak as well as having the benefit of making the bees fly high above people's heads.

It is best to have the entrance of your hive facing southeast. The early morning rays will wake your bees, getting them foraging earlier in the day and therefore productive for longer. But you do not have to have the hive in direct sunlight—dappled light, such as the limited amount through the leaves of a tree, is best because too much sunshine means that the bees have to spend a lot of time regulating the temperature of the hive instead of making honey. At the same time, do not put them in the deep shade either, as that can help dampness grow and make your bees listless, which slows down honey production as well.

Speaking of honey, the final thing you need to be thinking about when you place your hives is the ease of access when you are ready to harvest the honey. You need to make sure it is in a spot that is not too far from where you want to process the honey since it would suck to be lugging dozens of pounds of honey in the hot sun as you go up and down hills or over obstacles.

These tips are great to help you put and make your bees productive, but you need to consider their quality of life as well. Bees forage for food, meaning that they fly around and collect pollen from flowers and plants, even those that do not produce nectar. This means that they often collect pollen from plants that may have been sprayed with pesticides, which can harm them in the long run. You do not need to have a lot of flowers or plants in your yard to provide food, but it can be a way to help make sure that they are staying safe, especially if you live near places that use a lot of sprays.

Additionally, you also need a good source of water for them; as a good rule of thumb, that water needs to be less than 50 feet away from the hive. We will talk more about water needs later in the chapter.

If you are in an urban area without a backyard, there are still options for you as a beekeeper. As we said in Chapter 1, placing a hive in a communal garden can be a great idea, both for the gardeners and you. If you go with that method, keep the same information in mind when you decide where to put the hive.

The other option we mentioned was to make a rooftop hive, which has many of the same considerations. However, there is more to consider about staying safe on a roof.

Firstly, if the only way to get to your roof is through a fire escape, climbing a ladder, or going through a rooftop hatch, it is not a good location for a hive. Trying to travel in these methods while decked out in a full bee suit or when removing heavy loads of honey is dangerous. If that is your situation, you need to have an alternative location for your hives.

If you can get to the roof safely, do not put your hives near the edges of it. This seems like pretty standard information since going near the sides of a tall building is never a good idea. Also, make sure you tie your hives down with strong straps or cords. Winds get much stronger on top of buildings, and it would not be good for a strong wind to come along and rip your hives apart or blow them off the side. Forget a piano falling on your head! We think a box full of bees would be way worse.

But what should you do if you do not have that kind of setup in a yard, or you can't have a rooftop or communal garden hive? Can you still be a beekeeper?

The answer is yes—if you are willing to have a commute. If you know someone in the area who has a larger yard, or a farmer not too far from you, talk to them about hosting a hive. If they are willing, you can set up your hive on their property and come out and check it regularly, just as you would if it was in your yard. That way, they get the benefits of bees, but little to none of the work required.

If all else fails, look into wooded or forested spaces around. You need to check with the city and state (or province) to see what rules are in place about beekeeping on public land, but other than that, the same principles stated above apply. Another consideration with forested areas is the increased likelihood of more significant predators, like skunks, who love to eat bees as a tasty treat. A hive stand is a really good idea to help keep the hive away from critters like that, to get it further away from their paws.

Now that you have the physical location figured out, you still need to keep in mind a good number of things. Ensuring that you are working with the best possible situation will keep your bees happy and productive, meaning that you can manage a successful hive.

Sun

When you drive through the country and see hives out in the fields, they are often in open areas without any shade. It can be easy to think that means that direct sun is the best for bees, but it is not necessarily true. Those hives are often placed in locations with full sun because there is no other option—many fields are wide open with no trees or natural objects to provide a break from the sun.

When observing wild colonies of bees, they tend to create their hives in shady areas, which makes some wonder if that is the better way to go. So, which is it; sun or shade?

We said earlier that south-facing, dappled sunlight is best for bees, but you can make a different choice. There are pros and cons for both full sun and shade, so we will do our best to outline them fully here.

Full Sun

As we said earlier in the chapter, direct sun and southward-facing hives benefit from warming up faster. Bees rise with the sun, so during those long summer days, they will have an earlier start and longer working days if they are in direct sunlight. Having the sun on the hive all day can also help keep any water that found its way into the hive box from sitting there too long.

There are also seasonal advantages to direct sun as well. During the winter, direct sun can have the benefit of keeping your hive warmer. It may feel cold outside, but with the sun warming the insulated foam around the hive, the bees stay nice and toasty. That helps you stay secure in the knowledge that your little friends are not going to freeze. And when winter gives way to spring, the warmth from the sun reaches the hive much faster, meaning that the bees can get out and about earlier in the year than those in shaded hives.

However, there are downsides to full sun as well. The first is the temperature inside the hive. Bees, just like us, do not like getting too hot—they like to stay at a nice 95 degrees Fahrenheit. To stay cool, they gather water and spread it in a thin layer over the brood comb (where the queen lays the eggs). Once the water is spread out, they stand on the comb and vibrate their wings at high speeds resulting in evaporite cooling. Essentially, they vibrate their wings so fast that air currents are created, traveling over the water layer and evaporating, just like air conditioning.

The hotter it gets inside the hive, the harder the bees have to work to create the evaporite cooling, so there are fewer bees out collecting pollen and making honey. Additionally, the more bodies there are in the hive at any one time also increases the heat since they are all moving around so much and generating their own heat. A sign of a hot hive is when the bees hang out in clumps outside of the hive—called bearding.

If the hive gets unbearably hot, the colony can swarm and try to find somewhere cooler to live. In extreme cases, when it is too hot, and the hive is not properly ventilated, the wax bombs can melt and drown the bees. To avoid this, if you have to place your hive in direct sun, make sure that there is a lot of water nearby and that the bottom of the hive is a screen, as that promotes airflow.

Shade

If you were to base your hive location on the behavior of wild bees, you would want to place your hive in an area of deep shade. Most wild bees like to nest in shaded areas that are still close to open areas, such as at the edge of a forest. This protects them from the worst of the sun in summer and gives them clear flight paths for foraging.

Some will say that leaving the hive in direct sun benefits the beekeeper more than it does the bees since there are risks associated with direct sunlight, as we stated above. However, by staying in the shade, the bees do not have such a high risk of overheating, though they will have less productive hours in the day.

There are downsides to too much shade, aside from less honey production. If you live in an environment that gets a lot of rain or has a humid and cool climate, placing your hive in the shade may make it harder for it to stay dry. Additionally, some beekeepers feel that shade encourages hive beetle infestations, though others strongly disagree with that idea.

So, What's Best?

Like so many parts of being a beekeeper, deciding how much sun or shade is a personal decision. You need to weigh the pros and cons as well as consider your environment.

If you can, it is generally considered the best approach to place your hive where there is a good mix of sun and shade. Ideally, you want your bees to be woken by the early sunlight, have a place to stay cool during the hottest part of the day, and then have some extra sunlight in the evening. That way, you (hopefully) get the benefits of both without straying into the negatives of either.

If you have a nice deciduous tree, putting your hive in its shadow is a great idea—that way, the hive gets shade in the summer, and the winter sun can warm it once the leaves have fallen.

Also, you get the benefit from working in the shade when wearing a bee suit, which can get very hot quickly. Even a little extra shade could be a godsend on a hot summer day.

Space

Another thing you need to consider when setting up your hive is the issue of space—space for yourself, your neighbors, and the bees if you are going with multiple hives.

The first concern of space is safety; are your bees somewhere where they and others will be safe? You will want to keep the hive away from areas of heavy foot traffic or frequent use. If bees have to fly through such areas, there is a greater chance of someone being stung or your bees getting squashed.

It is also a good idea to have the entrance of the hive facing toward a tall barrier, which can help direct the bees to go where you want. It also acts as another safety measure, as it can keep them out of easy visibility of your neighbors, friends, or family that are nervous around bees. Honeybees are gentle little creatures, but they pick up on anxiety easily, and they will notice if someone gets nervous just by looking at them. This could result in them becoming agitated and defensive, increasing the likelihood of stinging, so it's better to keep them somewhere out of sight. After all, out of sight, out of mind, right?

When thinking about space with multiple hives, you need to make sure that you are giving yourself good ease of access. You will need to complete regular inspections, maintenance, and eventually harvest honey, so do not put your hives so close together that you can barely move around between them. At the same time, do not put them so far apart that you have extra walking to do to get to each. When placing multiple hives, it is a good rule of thumb to have between two and three feet of open space around each hive.

Aside from making it easier on yourself, having hives too close together can create problems for the bees as well. When placed too near each other, bees tend to drift (go back into a hive that is not their own).

Bees mostly navigate by the sense of smell, and each colony has a unique smell based on the scent of their queen. They do not rely just on scent, but landmarks as well. So, if there is not enough variety between hive boxes for them to focus on, they can end up going into the wrong home. This is a problem because the established colony will view them as intruders and will often kill the new bee. To avoid drift, place your hives far enough away from each other so that the bees can distinguish between them. Painting each hive a different color will also help create unique markers on the landscape.

Having hives close together can also make the spread of pests and diseases easier. Another concern is having the bees of one colony pick up the distressed pheromones of another, making them unnecessarily agitated and aggressive. Because of all these reasons, placing hives two to three feet apart is the best method.

Height

Earlier in the chapter, we talked a little about the uses and benefits of hive stands, but we should probably look a little more into the height of hives.

As we said before, stands are a great way to get some extra height for your hive, which prevents water buildup, promotes water drainage, and makes it harder for predators to access the hive. Additionally, they are really helpful in saving your back—a stand makes the hive the right height for you to be reaching and lifting things from with as little strain as possible.

Height is very important to get just right—too low, and it makes it easier for predators and pests to bother the hive, too high, and you cannot get into them easily or safely. Ideally, the base of the hive should sit around 18 inches off the ground, though some adjustment will need to be done based on your height.

Water

Like all living things, bees need water to drink and cool themselves down (evaporative cooling). They will get that water anywhere they can, even if it comes from a bad source. And unfortunately, in most urban centers, the available water is going to be filled with pollutants. You also need to consider the potential of harm. If the nearest water source is a neighbor's pool, the bees will drink from it—and then you are worried about them drinking the cleaning chemicals, not just stinging people or getting swatted.

If you live in a more rural setting, you might think that you are alright, but even then, water contaminants get into everything. Rivers and ponds could be filled with the run-off of pesticides and refuse from who-knows-where or who-knows-what. It is better to make a water source for them yourself.

There are so many possible ways to provide water for your bees that we won't bother listing them. It can be as simple as a bucket refilled with fresh water every few days or as complicated as a water fountain feature. It is your choice, though whatever you do, that water should be less than 50 feet away from the hives and needs to include a shallow place for the bees to stand and collect the water since they can't swim.

* * *

As you have now seen, the location of the hives is everything, and there is a lot to consider when making that decision.

You need to make sure that you set up your hives for success and set up a good workspace for yourself. This means setting your hive on level, solid ground, deciding how much sun and shade they are going to get, and providing a nearby water source for them.

Any hive should be off the ground by at least 18 inches to prevent the growth of mold and dampness, as well as to protect from nosy predators. Having the hives off the ground can also save you from future backache. If you have multiple hives, there should be between two and three feet of distance between them.

You should face the entrances in the opposite direction of foot traffic. The bees won't mind, and this helps to prevent the bees from perceiving people and pets that walk in front of the hive entrances as potential threats, making it far less likely for anyone to be stung. You can place fences around your hive or your entire yard as another great way to direct the flight path of your bees away from neighbors or high-traffic areas.

And with these considerations, make sure that you are setting up your backyard hive in a way that works for you as well. Do not put the hive in a spot that is difficult or dangerous to get to or that would require lots of extra walking while carrying heavy containers of honey.

This is a new hobby, and it should be a fun one. Poor location planning can quickly remove the joy from the work, which is the last thing that we want. So, when planning for your bees, remember the title of this chapter; location is EVERYTHING!

You can Google these terms to learn more:

- DIY Hive Stands
- DIY Bee Fountains

Chapter 3:
Preparing the Hive and Your Chosen Location

Now that you know everything about picking the proper location for your hive, it is time to look at the practical guide of setting one up. While the last chapter covered the whys behind choosing your hive location, this one will look at the how of setting up. This will need to be done before your bees arrive because, as we mentioned in the previous chapter, trying to change things once the bees are in the hive and working away is much more difficult.

So, what does hive setup require? Firstly we will cover some of the necessary time constraints and commitments, such as when to order your bees and making sure that you have enough time between ordering and arrival to set up your chosen location. With the amount of time in mind, we will look over the specifics of your hive, such as the pros and cons of different hive material choices and whether or not to buy a premade hive or make one yourself. We will also consider the hive's bottom board. The options are to have either a screened or solid bottom—we will outline the pros and cons of each choice so you can pick what is best for you.

The final section of the chapter will outline how to install your bees in their new home. This will cover what to do with both packaged bees and nucleus (nuc) colonies.

These are suggestions only, so feel free to play around with the different options to figure out what is best for you and your bees.

Time and Setup

After reading Chapter 2 and applying that information to your situation, it is time to move on to the more practical part of beekeeping. This is the time for you to ensure that you have everything you need—the gear, items, and space needed for your bees. At this stage, the only things that you shouldn't have yet are the bees themselves. That is because this is the stage where you need to be considering timing—timing for ordering your bees and the timing required to prepare for their arrival.

As we have said before, the duties of a beekeeper are closely linked to the seasons and time of year. You need to prepare your hives for temperature and weather changes before they happen, and that includes the initial setup. What follows is a basic rundown of the beekeeper's year and what needs to be done each month—variability exists based on your location.

The best time to start preparing for the bee year is actually near the end of the calendar year, in November. During this month, as the temperatures drop, bees become less active and are preparing for winter. Experienced beekeepers will be preparing their hives for winter, but for beginners, it is the perfect time to get into the hobby.

To properly prepare yourself for the next spring, you should attend a beekeeping course and buy your tools and gear during the winter (November to January). This includes buying hive boxes and preordering your bees to make sure that you do not deal with shortages or backorders in the spring. Ordering bees at the start of the new year is standard practice for experienced apiarists since it will help avoid lengthy delays in the productive season.

For most areas in the northern hemisphere, April means the start of spring and the bee season. But, that will be different in certain parts of the world, and with climate change, the warmer seasons are being pushed earlier. April has always been the month when the temperature consistently reaches 50+ degrees Fahrenheit, and new growth begins, providing pollen for the bees.

This means that you need to have your hives and locations properly set and prepared for that change in the weather, whenever it may come for you. Make sure that you have a good understanding of local weather and climate patterns so that you can give yourself the correct amount of time to set up. There is nothing worse than getting all excited and finding out that you needed more time than you gave yourself, and you have bees sitting and waiting for their new home.

The rest of the beekeeper's year is related more to care and upkeep, with May to August being mostly concerned with inspections for diseases, signs of swarming, or other potential pitfalls. September sees the harvesting of honey before the bees begin to slow down and prepare for winter in October. We will go into further details about these ongoing beekeeper duties in later chapters.

Setting Up the Hives

Now for the setup. The first thing you need to do after making all the location decisions is to set up your hives. But first, you need to decide on the kind of hive you are going to get and how much work you want to do in the assembly of them.

Chapter 2 gave a rundown of the three main kinds of hives; the horizontal top bar hive and the Langstroth and Warré hive boxes. Once you have decided which style you prefer, you also need to figure out if you want one preassembled or not. Likely it is much easier to buy one that is already ready to go and simply install it in your yard hassle-free. If you want to assemble the hive yourself, be sure to account for the time and tedious nature of this option.

The third option is to build your hive box. This should only be considered if you already have the tools and experience required for carpentry, as hives need to be fairly precise in their layouts.

But, if you do want to make your hive, aside from the style, the other major consideration is what kind of material to make it from.

Of course, with the hundreds of lumber options out there, you could have a hive made out of pretty much any kind of wood on the planet. But it is best to go with the more easily accessible, cheaper, and environmentally sound options.

Commonly, hive boxes are made out of pine, cypress, or cedar. Hives can be made out of more exotic woods as well, but with those, you need to consider the costs (a mahogany hive can be upwards of $1,500) and the potential downsides, such as negative health effects of the wood on bees. The only kind of wood that you definitely need to stay away from is pressure-treated boards, since having your bees' home made out of chemical-laced wood does not sound like a good idea.

Pine is the most commonly used kind of wood due to its versatility, wide availability, and lower price point. There are different grades (visual characteristics that can impact manufacture) of pine. The two that you are most likely to run into are knotty or clear.

Knotty pine is visually more rustic as it has the knots and imperfections of the tree present in the boards. Usually, these features are mainly cosmetic, but they can make working with the wood a little more difficult if you need to cut around a particularly stubborn knot. This grade is the least expensive. Clear pine just means that it is free from any defects or cosmetic imperfections, resulting in a cleaner and more straightforward aesthetic. This grade will be more expensive than knotty pine.

Something to keep in mind if working with pine is that it is not the best kind of wood for the outdoors. It weathers quickly, so you may need to protect it with outdoor bee-safe paint, varnish, or stain.

Cypress is a wood that is naturally good for beekeeping and outdoor uses since it produces a sap that naturally repels mold and insects and preserves the wood. But, it is less widely available than other kinds, with it found more easily in the southern United States than elsewhere in the northern hemisphere. This will make it more pricey, but the results will be well worth it if you can spend the money.

The second most popular choice after pine is cedar. The natural oils in cedar (the most common of which is Western Red) make it more resistant to rot, warping, and bug invasions than other woods. It also has a beautiful look and smell to it, making working with this kind of wood a real pleasure. Though nowhere near as expensive as cypress, cedar will still have a higher price than pine, which makes it less commonly used.

But just because you are making your own hive does not mean that you need to restrict yourself to wood. There is a growing emergence of reasonably priced, environmentally friendly, synthetic wood made from recycled plastics and wood fibers. The advantage of this material is its ability to last through all kinds of weather and that there is a low level of maintenance required (mainly just washing).

Bottom Board Concerns

No matter the style or level of work involved with getting your hive, you will need to decide what kind of bottom it will have, whether screened or solid. As with all options, each has different strengths and weaknesses.

The first advantage of a solid board is that it will keep your hive warmer, which is good for winter and early spring since the bees will start to be active earlier. A solid bottom is also meant to deter some pests, such as fire ants, from getting into the hive while also making it easier to treat mites as they do not have anywhere to escape.

The downside of a solid board is that you will need to clean it, and it can get very messy very quickly. Additionally, by having less airflow, a solid board could cause heat concerns for your bees if you experience very hot summers. Without the airflow offered by a screened bottom, your bees will need to work harder on staying cool.

That is probably the biggest advantage of a screened bottom—it is easier for air to flow through the hive, making temperature regulation easier. Along with this, a screen makes it easier to see what is happening inside the hive and allows mites to fall straight out of the box rather than needing to be cleaned up.

The disadvantages of a screen bottom are the flip side of their positives. In winter, more cold air will get in—meaning that more intervention will be needed to make sure the hive stays warm. And while pests can fall out the bottom of the hive, they can also climb into it through the screen.

The best way to figure out which will suit you better will be to talk to others in your club and see which kind they have the most success with. That way, you can use their experience to figure out what works for your area.

Housing the Bees

After picking and preparing the location and setting up your hive, it is time to install the bees when you have them. As we said in Chapter 1, you can buy either a package of bees or a nucleus (nuc) colony. Each will have different methods of installing into the hive, which may influence your decision of which to buy. Either way, the very first thing that you need to do with them is to see how they have dealt with shipping. Some dead bees are normal, but if there is a whole lot, you will need to be in contact with the seller.

Keep them in a cool place away from direct sunlight until you are ready to put them in the hive. If you need to keep them in their shipping packages for a while, make sure to give them some sugar water (1:1 ratio) to eat—misting the mixture from a spray bottle should work out well. Installation of the bees into the new hive needs to happen no more than 48 hours after getting them, which is why it is so important to have everything set and ready beforehand.

You can install a package of bees in two ways; either let them migrate in on their own or gently shake the bees inside. Both should be done only after the queen has been carefully removed and placed in the hive, with the candy barrier between her and the others pierced so they can eat through it faster. In either case, make sure you have a good nearby supply of sugar water for them to eat as they get settled in.

Since a nuc is its own little hive box, getting the bees into your larger hive is a little easier. First, you want to place the entrance of the nuc next to the entrance of the hive, remove the screens from each, and then wait 24 to 48 hours. The bees will circle above the hive at first, but that is their way of getting situated in the landscape—eventually, they will move into the bigger space.

If they do not migrate naturally, you will need to intervene a little more. Suited up with the proper gear and tools, open up the nuc and remove a few of the frames, which you will place into your hive. Doing this is a good idea, even if they are migrating on their own. This way, they get to keep the combs (and potentially larvae) that they have already created. It also allows you to inspect them for disease or damage.

After moving the bees into the new hive, you can leave them alone for five to nine days, aside from regular feeding of sugar water. After that initial nine days, you will need to do a more in-depth inspection to make sure that the bees are doing well and that the queen is out and about doing her duty of laying tons of eggs. If you use a package of bees, make sure that the candy has been broken through, and the queen is free to move around as you want her to.

* * *

This chapter was pretty short and sweet. The main thing to remember is proper time management. Order your bees early in the year so you do not deal with any delays, and make sure that you are 100% set up and ready before the bees arrive. Doing this will ensure that you do not deal with an overabundance of stress, frustration, or feelings of defeat.

After choosing and prepping the hive location, make sure that your next step is picking the hives themselves. There are several different options for style, as well as options to buy them premade or with assembly required. If you are ambitious, you can even build a hive from scratch. With your hive, you need to decide whether you want a solid or screened bottom, though figuring that out may require asking advice from the members of your club.

Once the location and hives are set up properly, and your bees have arrived, it is time to get them settled in their new home. How you do so will depend on whether you bought a package of bees or a nuc colony, but either way, after 24 to 48 hours, you need to do a quick check to make sure the queen and other bees are free and working.

There is quite a bit of variation and experimentation that can be done with all this information. The main thing is to give yourself the proper time needed, but other than that, make sure that you are relaxed with it all. It is a new hobby, and it is meant to be fun still. The things above are just some considerations—feel free to experiment with what works for you and your bees.

You can Google this term to learn more:

- 38 DIY Hive Plans

Chapter 4:
Look After Your Bees!

Your yard, hives, and bees are now all prepped and ready for the next step, and so are you! It is time to learn about the proper care for your bees and what that looks like.

You want to ensure that you continue to look after your bees and make adjustments to the hive as necessary while you learn, adapt, and your knowledge continues to grow. You are starting a long-term relationship with these bees, and just as you would with a romantic partner, your bees require your tender love and care to thrive.

This chapter is all about proper maintenance, showing you what you need to be aware of and what you need to focus on the most to fully succeed as a beekeeper.

The first section in this chapter is going to be a detailed overview of how to fill your hives with bees—this part will go into more depth than what was covered in Chapter 3, which mostly discussed methods. So, while it is likely there will be some repeated information, it'll be handy because this way, it can help stick in your mind more!

An important part of re-homing your bees includes the successful installment of the queen bee. If you goof up on this section, it will cause both you and the bees stress, so you want to make sure that you are doing the best method the first time. It is the queen who attracts and keeps the rest of the colony in place, so getting her settled in first is the top priority.

Once we have gone through the details of settling your queen and bees into the hive, it is time to look at what else is needed to keep them alive and happy. This includes more short-term, immediate needs, such as feeding them while they get settled in, and long-term concerns like setting up your yard for pollination.

The final part of this chapter is all about hive inspections—how often you should be checking them and what you need to be looking for as you do so. It will also cover what you will need to do when encountering any issues, such as how to repair or replace damaged parts of the hive and how to replace and clean up lost beeswax. Issues of ventilation, shade, and rain will also be discussed in this part, though briefly.

With all this knowledge, you will be well on your way to becoming a happy and successful beekeeper! If you look after your bees properly, it will save you time and heartache (and likely backache) in the future, as you will be more than prepared to deal with any potential pitfalls.

Filling the Hive

We may have mentioned it before, and we will say it again right now— filling your hive with bees is a crucial step in bee-ing a beekeeper, if not the most crucial. After all, can you even call yourself a beekeeper if you do not have any bees?

So, with it being an incredibly important step, that means that there needs to be a solid foundation of knowledge to draw on. That can be achieved through reading this chapter and additional written sources about it, but if your beekeeping club offers courses on this subject, make sure to take them! That will let you practice the installation with someone who has done it before, who can give tips or advice on the best methods.

We should first lay out the things that you are going to need for installation.

- **An Assistant**: You are about to be handling thousands of bees, so it is best to have an extra set of hands to help out. This job would be an excellent use of your mentor, as they can then help out with their experience as well as their hands.

- **The Bees and the Queen**: If you bought a marked queen, that is all the better to get started with. If she is not marked, doing so now will save you hassle in the future of trying to find her.

- **The Hives and Frame**s: At this stage, your hives need to be completely set up and ready to go, no matter the style. Additionally, if you have a hive divided into different box sizes, the largest needs to be the one where the queen will lay the eggs, while the smaller ones are perfect for honey collection.

- **Tools and Gear**: This is your first opportunity to wear and use all the fancy gear (Chapter 1) that you bought! You should be outfitted in your beekeeper suit or jacket to protect yourself. If, for whatever reason, you do not yet have a suit, just wearing a veil can work, but make sure that you wear all white. (Bees' natural predators are dark in color, and so they do not see white as a threat.) Along with the protection, have your hive tool handy for any lifting or prying that may be needed as you open the package or nuc of bees.

- **An Entrance Reducer**: An entrance reducer is simply a barrier of some kind (wood, metal, etc.) that is placed in front of the hive entrance to stop the bees from leaving in large numbers. It can also act as a barrier against invading pests, so it could be something left at the hive full-time. When you are introducing the bees to the hive, the entrance reducer helps stop them from leaving while you are trying to get them set up, which is unlikely but still a possibility.

- **Food**: The bees will need some initial food to eat as they get settled into their hive. This includes having a spray bottle of sugar water to put a thin layer of the solution over the frames. For longer-term feeding, place a container (like a simple mason jar) or sugar water near the hive entrance or a pollen cake on top of the hive. Most packaged bees are fairly young and so are not yet skilled in foraging. Placing sources of food nearby keeps them fed while also getting them more familiar with their hive as a landmark.

Now that everything is organized and set up, it is time to get started! In total, the process of installing your bees takes around two hours—make sure that you have given yourself enough time to get the job done in one go.

The first step is to lightly spray your bees down with the sugar water (a 1:1 ratio for the spray water). It is important to make sure that you use a new spray bottle so that there are no leftover chemicals or harmful substances that can get on the bees. Spraying them with the sugar water gets them eating, and bees that are full are more docile and easy to handle. Additionally, the lack of an established queen or honey will make them easier to handle.

Once you have sprayed the bees down, take some time while they eat to get all the frames out of the hive so you can spray down the walls next. This gives the bees an even better boost of food, but this time they have to travel along their new hive to get it, meaning that they are familiarizing themselves with the space at the same time. Make sure to give the frames themselves a quick spray before replacing them in the hive.

The next steps are about working directly with the bees. First, if your package of bees included a sugar-water feeder (which it should have), you need to carefully remove it and brush the few bees who may be hanging on. This is your first physical interaction with your bees, so you need to be calm and relaxed, which helps them feel relaxed as well. If it has been a while since you fed them, give them a quick top-up to fill their bellies.

Once you have the sugar-water feeder removed, it is time to remove the queen from your package. Different companies will have different methods of transporting the queen. If you have one that had the queen in a separate container blocked off with sugar candy or paste, remove a little bit of the block and then put that into the part of the hive planned for the queen.

It is important to keep the queen in her container or separate cage for a few days before she is free to roam around, so you do not want to remove all of the candy or paste. Leaving it in place means that the bees have to eat their way through it, ensuring that the queen permeates the inside of the hive with the pheromones that keep the rest of the bees in place. If she gets loose too soon, you run the risk of her leaving the hive or being killed by the other bees. If you have a nuc, this is less of a concern.

When you are putting your queen into the hive, make sure that the cage is somewhere accessible so you can remove it in a few days. One trick to make this easier is to loop some wire into an opening of the container and then hook that over the edge of the hive, making it easier to find and remove when the time is right. After three days, check the container and make sure that the queen is now free.

If you have bought a package of bees that does not have the sugar candy blockage, then you will need to create that barrier. This is easily done by placing some sugar-candy material in the exit area. You can make your own kind of blockage, but you need to make sure that it is the right kind of food for your bees and also something that will not take them long to get through. To make it easier on yourself, you can just put a marshmallow into the exit as a block instead.

After getting the queen and her container into the hive, it is time for the rest of the bees to get in as well. You can do this by leaving the package or nuc close to the entrance of your hive and let them migrate naturally, but this will take more time and include some additional risks (such as them flying away or attracting pests and predators who want to eat them).

The faster method is to open up the hive, hold the package of bees over it, and gently shake until they all drop inside. If you have some bees that are stubbornly clinging to the sides, you can give them a little extra firm shake to dislodge them. Keep shaking until most of the bees are in the hive—any stragglers can be left in the package, angled toward the hive entrance, so they know where to go to rejoin their friends.

Once all the bees have successfully U-Hauled into the hive (around an hour or so), it is time to close up shop. Place some sugar water close to or on the entrance reducer, close the top lid, and place a pollen cake or other source of food on top of the hive.

After three days have gone by, remove the queen container from the hive. This is where the wire hook comes in handy—dropping the container into a hive full of active bees would not be a fun experience. Ten days after installing the hive is the time for the first in-depth inspection to make sure that your queen is laying eggs and if the comb is starting to form.

Other than the queen cage removal and inspections on days three and ten, there is very little to do for the first stretch of time as a new beekeeper. However, one significant thing that you need to do is monitor their sugar water levels to make sure that they always have enough. You should continue to give them reasonable amounts of sugar water for a month or until you can see that they are gathering enough pollen on their own.

If you are concerned about amounts, it is better to have lots available than too little. Of course, it is a personal choice whether to reduce the sugar water right away or keep it going longer, but there are some benefits for the longer feed.

If you bought a package of bees, keeping sugar water available for the bees will help promote the faster creation of the combs. The combs, made of beeswax, give the bees a place to live, work, store food, lay eggs, and raise the hatched eggs. In short, the comb is essential to the hive, and to make it, your bees need food.

Talk to your mentor and beekeeping club friends about the length of time to feed your bees sugar water. Like we just said, it is a personal choice, but they may have some good insight into what your area needs. Options for the length of time include waiting until a few frames of the comb are made, for the brood boxes to be full of comb, or just to keep feeding all-season or until the bees get bored of the sugar water. So, there are plenty of options, and leaving the sugar water available a little longer is not going to hurt your bees.

And there you go! Your bees are all set up in their new homes.

Keeping the Bees Happy

Now that you have a hive full of buzzing bees, it is vital to keep them safe, productive, and happy. There are many different ways to do this, including setting up your yard for optimal pollination (if you can), staying on top of hive inspections (and knowing what to look for), and managing any damage your hives may sustain. It is also important to keep an eye out on the comb and know how to clean up any lost comb and what to do if many have broken. And as the year travels into the hotter summer months, make sure that your hives have the proper ventilation and shade to keep your bees working on honey-making instead of air conditioning.

A Pollinating Yard

As we have mentioned, it is crucial to keep your bees fed since that will directly translate into how productively they work. Sugar water is a great first step, but getting back to natural options is even better. If you have a yard, here are some tips and tricks to make it into a pollinator's paradise. Pollinator plants will attract more than just your honeybees as well. Red plants and flowers attract hummingbirds, and fallen foliage is perfect for butterfly nests in the fall.

It may seem counterintuitive to common practice and possibly a hassle with a homeowners association, but keep your yard messy. In the spring, leave some leaves and twigs around in a dedicated messy spot. Additionally, do not get overzealous in weeding your lawn or garden—most times, the common types of weeds produce lots of pollen that your bees can collect.

If you want to plant some plants specifically for pollinators, make sure that you are choosing the right kinds. These plants need to have continuous flowers throughout summer, with single flowering plants being the best since they lack extra spaces or parts that make the pollen harder to get. For information on the best kinds of plants to grow, talk to your club and do some research into what grows well in your area.

Another way to attract more kinds of pollinators is to build or buy a bee hotel. These tiny structures are full of tubes (made of bamboo or drilled holes in a piece of wood) that are the perfect nooks and crannies for other species of bees or insects to rest. Most often, the bees that use these hotels are species that are solitary rather than hived, and they may even lay some larvae in the hotel. To make it extra hospitable, have a small container of sugar water near to the hive or scattered around the yard so that any tired bee can get a boost of energy and keep buzzing on its way.

In the fall, you can also make a bumblebee nest out of a pot, some moss, and hay. Wild bumblebee queens will seek out a safe, warm, and dry spot to hibernate over the winter, so creating a little nest for them is an extra method to keep them safe.

Use all these ideas, and you will see so many different kinds of pollinators using your yard, from bees and butterflies to hummingbirds, if you are lucky.

Hive Inspections

In this section of the chapter, we will outline the steps for the more time-consuming kind of hive inspection, which is done once at least every ten days. But, those are not the only kinds of inspections and times you should be checking on the hive. Daily visual inspections of the hive, specifically around the entrance, help to head off any issues that could become threatening if not treated right away. These kinds of issues include pest interaction or robbing activity, such as what is done by yellow jacket wasps or skunks. If not dealt with right away, these invaders could potentially kill your hive within a week, putting the danger within the free time between full hive inspections. How to watch out for these pests is covered in Chapter 5.

It is important to continue to check in with your hive and the structure within which the bees are now living, and doing these inspections will be your main duty as a beekeeper. Because this is needed for success, it is important to stay on top of daily look-throughs and do an in-depth inspection every seven to ten days. For this section, the inspection instructions will be covering box-style hives, such as the Langstroth or Warré types.

To complete an inspection, you will need to smoke or otherwise calm your bees. Then you will need to remove each box, look at it and the frames inside over for damage or danger until you reach the bottom layer of the hive. An inspection needs to happen every seven to ten days, with your first few occurring closer to the former than the latter, but not more frequently. Too many inspections will bug your bees, making them more anxious and prone to stinging.

You will want to pick your inspection days carefully, as you want to do so on a warm, dry day. Only inspect on a wet or cool day as a last resort, as that will bring extra water into the hive, which is not good. Try to time the inspection during a part of the day when most of the bees are out foraging so that you have fewer on hand to work around.

To complete an inspection, make sure that you are wearing your bee suit or jacket, use a smoker (if you so choose), and have your hive tool on hand. It is also a good idea to have a notepad and pen available to take notes of anything you see during the inspection. If you have any sugar-water feeders for the bees, now is the best time to refill them.

So, first, even before putting on your suit, make sure that you have a solid plan in mind for your inspections. The purpose of this deep-dive inspection is to make sure that your bees are healthy and doing what they are supposed to—

namely, the queen laying eggs, those eggs hatching into larvae, and the worker bees taking care of the larvae, making comb, and producing honey.

When you put on your suit, make sure that it is comfortable and secure against any bees getting inside. Make sure that you pick where you stand carefully. Do not stand directly in the bees' normal flight path as they may fly out en masse to escape the disturbance you are causing. If there is any wind, try to position yourself so that it is blowing over your shoulder; otherwise, the smoke could end up in your face rather than on the bees. For the last tip of positioning, try to make sure that the sun is shining over your shoulder so that you provide shade—the hive is normally dark inside, so having a sudden bright light there could cause your bees some worry.

Once you are snug in your suit and have picked your work location correctly, get the smoker activated and pump cool smoke directly into the entrance to subdue the guard bees. Once they are smoked, open the lid of the hive just a little, and get some smoke into the hive that way. Quickly close the lid and wait for a minute or two for the smoke to start calming the rest of the bees.

Make sure not to put too much smoke into the hive. Smoking makes the bees think there is a fire, so they produce pheromones to let the rest know that they need to start gorging on the honey in preparation, which makes them lethargic. Too much smoke covers all of the communication pheromones they emit, meaning that they get scared and confused, making them more likely to sting.

Once enough time has passed with the smoke inside the hive, remove the outer cover and place it upside down on the ground, far enough away that you do not worry about stepping on it by accident. If your hive has an inner cover, pump some more smoke into that section and wait another few minutes. The next step is to gently pry the inner cover off, using the hive tools to break through the propolis or beeswax. Once the inner cover is off, place it on top of the outer cover—be careful, as this may have some bees hanging on, so do your best not to squish them. Make sure to move slowly and methodically—fast and abrupt movements are certain to agitate your bees.

The next step is to remove the top box of the hive—this is usually called the honey super since it is the part of the hive where honey is collected. You will most likely need to use your hive tool to pry the top box off the lower box where the brood lives (often called the brood box). You need to repeat these steps—smoke, wait, remove—for all the boxes all the way to the lowest box.

Once you have smoked the bottom box, you then remove the frames one at a time and carefully inspect them. It is a good idea to inspect them the same way each time so that you form a habit that will help you get through them faster.

You are looking for the queen to ensure that she is still alive and that you do not accidentally kill her during the inspection process, parasites or pests, and how many frames have been filled with a comb that is ready for honey (drawn out). When you first start out keeping bees, your hive may not have the honey super or additional boxes. Once seven out of ten frames are full of comb, you can add the additional boxes.

Looking for the queen is easier if she is marked, but still possible if she is not. The queen looks different from the other bees. She will have a long and slender abdomen that is not striped, and she will be surrounded by a circle of worker bees. If you still cannot find her that way, look for where the eggs and larvae are since she will not be very far from them.

The eggs themselves can be difficult to spot for new beekeepers since they are very small and look more like grains of rice than an egg. They will be found on the comb, one in the center of each cell. To see the eggs more easily, hold the frame up to the sky, sun shining over your shoulder and into the frame. The larvae will be easier to spot if the comb is uncapped (second stage of growth). Instead of a small grain-sized item, there will be a wriggling little brilliant white bug! There will also be larvae that are capped or sealed into the comb cells (the last stage before they become adults). Ideally, there should be a ratio of 1:2:4 for the eggs, larvae, and sealed brood since they are eggs for three days, larvae for six days, and sealed for twelve days.

Once you are done inspecting each frame, replace them in the hive box in the same order that you removed them. Once all the frames have been inspected in the bottom box, move onto the middle box and do the same, replacing the entire box once you are done. Repeat these steps for every box on your hive until there are none left on the side, then put the inner and outer covers back in place. If you have any notes, write them down now right away, so you do not forget anything.

Repeat all these actions for every hive that you have, and when you are done, leave the smoker to burn out and cool on its own. If you need to, make sure that you clean your bee suit, so it is ready for the next inspection in seven to ten days.

Dealing With Hive Damage

During your inspections, make sure that aside from checking over the bees, you are also making sure the hive boxes themselves are still in good condition. The hive is outside year-round and is subject to all the weather that mother nature throws its way. No matter what, repairs and replacements are going to be required at some point. You may even need to repair the damage that you accidentally caused when taking them apart or scraping the propolis off with the hive tool!

These kinds of interventions can include full replacements or just minor repairs. If you have a small spot of rot on one of your boxes, see if you can cut it out before buying or making a whole new hive. This could include gouging out a small spot or cutting off a larger section of an entire wall. Whatever it needs, make sure to get it done quickly—once the rot starts, you cannot stop it, and it will spread to the rest of the hive if not dealt with.

Once the rotten section has been removed, you need to replace it with some fresh wood. Make sure that you use the same kind of materials as the rest of the hive; otherwise, you will be looking at different rates of breakdown. With the new piece in place, give it a quick paint (water-based or latex) or varnish to help protect it from the elements. It is up to you whether or not the new paint or varnish matches the old, but if you go with a different color, it is best to go with a light one that will not soak up as much sun.

If you can, work repairs and replacements of regular wear and tear into your yearly schedule. During the winter, move the bees between hive boxes so that you can bring in the older hive and give it a complete makeover while not having to worry about the bees. If you do this, give the inside of the hive a quick scrub as well, going as far as to scorch it lightly with a torch—and then scrape the burned part away since this will help remove any mites or parasites that may be burrowed into the wood.

Keeping an eye out for any damage and stopping it right away is the best method of extending the life of your hive. Scheduling a full hive overhaul and repair session during the off months and rotating your bees between new and older hives is another great way to prevent any major issues during the months when you want your bees to make as much honey as possible.

Beeswax

As the season progresses and your bees stay hard at work, there is inevitably a buildup of beeswax, from which they make all the comb. This can be seen in old comb that is no longer being used, oddly shaped comb that is 'growing' in the wrong way or just located in the wrong place so that inspection is extra hard. When that is the case, you need to remove that wax buildup—but be careful. Remove too much, and the bees will start eating even more honey to rebuild them.

You can remove the beeswax with your hive tool since it is perfect for scraping away the excess. But what do you do with it once it is removed? Well, store it and build up your collection first. There are hundreds of uses for beeswax— maybe you can even include a nice sideline of beeswax products that you sell alongside the honey. If you want to do that, you will need to safely melt it and reclaim the cleaned wax.

Temperature Control

We discussed issues around keeping your hive cool and warm before (Chapter 2), but it is important information, so we will briefly go through it again and add some additional tips and tricks that are good to know.

So, as has been established, bees are pretty good at regulating their temperature, but that does not mean that you should not be doing anything to help them. The less time and effort they put into keeping cool or warm, the more time they spend making the honey!

There needs to be the proper temperature, condensation, and humidity inside the hive for your bees to be comfortable, but too much (or too little) of any of those can have nasty side effects. You need to remember this because it is easy to take ventilation or temperature control too far, making it, so that the bees then work harder on getting it back to normal. A certain level of warmth inside the hive is normal, as is a little bit of condensation dripping from it since they can use that water for their cooling systems.

So, what can and should be done then? First, to help your bees, they need good airflow through the hive. Having them off the ground helps with this, as it opens it up more, gets them away from the wet ground, and can increase airflow through the bottom if you have a screen there.

Some beekeepers will also prop open the top of the hive or make large openings for extra airflow, but too much of this is not a good thing. When left alone, bees will naturally try to close those large gaps since they like a few small entrances and exits. Besides, permanently open sources are going to cause problems, depending on the weather you are experiencing.

Instead of making permanent holes or leaving the top open, drill some holes into the outside of the hive that you can block off with a cork. That way, you can pull them out if your hive needs a little more air and close them back up if the conditions are perfect for them.

As we mentioned in Chapter 2, a mixed area of shade and sun is perfect for your bees. That way, they can be warmed up in the morning, protected from the hottest part of the day, and then be a little warmer into the evening with the last rays of light. If you have them under a deciduous tree, that has the added benefit of letting more sunlight in during the winter and acting as a barrier for rainstorms during the summer.

Speaking of winter, we should talk a bit about preparing your hive for the colder months. The first thing that you need to do is take away the top box of your hive (the honey super) and store it somewhere inside—if left out in the elements, not only is it more susceptible to damage, but they often get infested with moths which ruin the comb and honey.

During the final inspection of the season, remove any excess propolis or beeswax present so that you can wrap or insulate (they are different) your hives. There are some differing opinions about these practices, with some beekeepers seeing them as unnecessary or even bad, but doing so can be an extra way to secure the lives of your bees during the cold.

Wrapping involves taking roofing felt or tar paper and wrapping it securely around the hive, leaving the entrance and ventilation holes open. It does not do much in the way of preventing heat loss, but it sure does add a lot of heat into the hive during sunny days and protects the wood. On the other hand, insulation adds materials around the hive, such as a foam board, which allows not too much heat to be lost.

Either option is available, or you can choose neither. It is up to you. That choice comes down to preference, what your winters are like, and what advice you can get from other local beekeepers. Whatever you choose, make sure that you research the reasons for doing so enough that you feel confident in your decision.

* * *

Looking after your bees is the most important part of being a beekeeper. First, of course, you need to make sure that they are safe, happy, and productive. But that does not mean that you have to spend a significant amount of time or labor working on upkeep. By careful planning and regular inspection, you will be sure to catch any problem before it can become destructive.

Planning and preparation are crucial for all steps of bee care, from the introduction to the hive to the weekly inspections, regular maintenance, and keeping the bees comfortable as the weather changes. The amount of work necessary to maintain a positive and productive beehive is minimal so long as you stay aware and in front of any potential downfall or "bumps in the road." What might those bumps be? Read on to Chapter 5 to find out!

You can Google these terms to learn more:

- Build a Bug Hotel
- Make a Bumblebee Pot
- How to Clean Beeswax: Easy Tips for Success

Chapter 5:
Bypassing Potential Pitfalls

You are well on your way now! With your hives and bees set up and cozy, and regular inspections taking place, it is easy to get into a good routine of care and concern. But, there are always unexpected problems that you can run into that set you back if you have not properly prepared for them. And while you can't prepare for every eventuality, you can be forewarned on some of the more common pitfalls that plague beekeepers.

That is what this chapter will be going over—how to stay ahead of the curve and avoid any potential roadblocks or prevent negative events when managing your new hive. These are some of the most common mistakes that new beekeepers make, so being aware of them beforehand is your best bet in avoiding making them.

The first section of the chapter will look at issues that can spring up from your style of beekeeping rather than outside threats. The first pitfall revolves around the queen, or more accurately, the potential problems of not having a queen anymore. Becoming queenless is a huge dilemma that you want to avoid at all costs since the hive is based around her. We will look at the signs of the lack of a queen, the possible reasons why you have lost the queen, and what to do next before you lose the rest of your bees.

The next few topics in this section will cover technical mistakes you might make. These include harvesting too much or too little honey, not feeding new colonies enough, improper wear of a bee suit, and incorrect use of a smoker. A common reason these problems pop up is if you have limited knowledge of beekeeping before starting and thinking that it is enough. It is always better to be over-prepared than under-prepared, especially when it comes to your bees. Also, never be satisfied with what you already know! There are numerous opportunities to keep learning and grow your knowledge base—doing so will only serve to make you a better beekeeper.

The second section will look at outside threats and pitfalls and how to deal with them if they arise. Keeping an eye on what mother nature is doing to your hives is paramount. You need to know how to look out for condensation and dew buildup and avoid it at all costs.

Pests of all shapes and sizes can also create a headache for you, so we will also cover how to control small pests such as ants, beetles, and mites. Bigger predator concerns include, among other things, bears, raccoons, and, potentially, the most damaging of all—children. Kids may be curious about the hive, and in poking around it, accidentally destroy it or get stung for their curiosity. The final part of this chapter will look at keeping your bees and kids safe by child-proofing the area.

There are innumerable things that can go wrong or negatively affect your hive, and you can never be fully prepared for them all. But these are the most common pitfalls, and being forewarned is being prepared, right?

Beekeeper Pitfalls

As a brand new beekeeper, it is easy to make mistakes. This may happen because of your inexperience, like forgetting something important or not knowing what to begin doing. The first two are bound to happen until you get the hang of things, but the last is something that you should do your best to avoid at all costs. There is nothing worse than having something bad happen with your hive and then realizing afterward that it could have been avoided if you had had just a bit more information to draw on. This section is designed to be that extra information in your hat—something that you can draw on to avoid making massive mistakes that could hurt you or your bees.

Queenlessness

Queen bees are the most crucial part of your hive, so losing her is a quick recipe for disaster. Or, it will be unless you take the proper steps to remedy her loss as soon as possible. But losing a queen can be a subtle thing without much change to the hive—at least at first. Given enough time, the changes are very dramatic, and the problem is that when those dramatic changes start happening, it becomes harder to stop the damage that has already been done.

So, it is best to stop those changes before they happen. The changes will be slow. At first, everything will look normal, with bees flying in and out of the hive and building comb. Then the number of bees starts to fall, and they become more aggressive. On a closer look, you will see that only comb and honey are being made—there are no new eggs or larvae. Checking for both stages is important in the hive inspection since a dearth of either or both can indicate that the queen is missing or not laying as much as she should be, which is around 2,000 eggs a day.

Aside from the lack of eggs and a brood of larvae, a queenless hive can be seen in the increase of honey and pollen. The bees that had previously been caring for the baby bees will now have switched to foraging and honey production, meaning that there will be a short period of dramatically more production occurring. An excellent way to see that this is happening is by knowing what activity usually happens on which frame—if a brood frame is now being filled with nectar and honey, that is a sign that no queen is laying enough new eggs.

Another indicator of the lack of a queen can be the presence of a queen cell or cap. These cells are different from regular egg cells since they are designed for the sole purpose of growing a new queen bee. The presence of these on their own does not mean that you lack a current queen, but if they show up around the same time that there is a decline in the brood, it is a pretty good indicator that your bees are working hard on getting a new queen in place. A colony that has recently made a new queen will appear queenless for a short amount of time until she gets used to her new role.

To test whether or not you have lost your queen, put a frame of a young brood from another hive into yours. If the bees begin to build queen cells on that frame, it is pretty hard evidence that there is no queen in your hive. Your options then are to let your bees finish making their new queen or buy a new queen that you can install yourself.

But timing is critical in this—if you wait too long, the worker bees will start laying eggs themselves. Those eggs will not be fertilized and result in more drone bees (male bees that are only there to fertilize eggs). Fewer workers will be going out and foraging for food. The increase of drones also means that the bees' instincts will be to kill any new bee—trying to introduce a queen at this stage will likely result in her murder. Upon seeing the signs of laying workers (multiple eggs per cell, spotty brood pattern, lack of worker bees, and increased drones), many beekeepers will write off the hive as a total loss since it is so hard to bring back.

So, if you think you have lost your queen, do not despair. Depending on how long she has been missing, there is still hope. Worker bees do not start laying eggs until two to four weeks have passed without a queen—if you are inspecting your hives regularly, you should be able to catch this much sooner.

Inspecting the brood is your best bet for figuring out how long a queen has been missing. If you see eggs (that were not laid by worker bees), your queen has only been gone for three days, which allows you plenty of time to get a new one in place. If there are no eggs, but you still have uncapped larvae, there is a little less time, but you'll still have room to work. But if there are only capped larvae, then that is your last chance to get a new queen in place since they will be the last generation to reach adulthood.

If you still have time to manage the situation, you have two choices—either let the bees naturally create a new queen or buy one and install her in the hive. Time is a crucial consideration for both. It takes 15 days for a new queen to be raised, and then it takes another five days for her to mate and start laying fertilized eggs.

Aside from these time constraints, your bees also have a narrow time window to start the process of raising a new queen. The new queen must come from a fertilized egg so that only gives them three days to realize that they have lost the old queen and to start feeding the egg royal jelly (a secretion that is fed to all larvae for the first three days, but only the new queen after that). If you have multiple hives, you can take a brood from a colony that has a queen, which will be fertilized, and introduce that into the struggling hive.

The other option is to introduce a new queen, one that is already mated. Similar to the process of installing your hive in the first place, the queen needs to be in a separate cage that is blocked by a sugar candy barrier. It takes time for the bees to eat through the candy to get to her, giving them time to get used to her scent and pheromones. This creates a better chance of them accepting her rather than seeing her as an invader to be killed. To prevent her death, watch what happens when you introduce the cage. If it gets attacked by workers, take the cage out and try again in a few days.

However, most often, if you introduce the queen early enough, the hive will want the new queen and readily welcome her into the colony. That is why timing is critical. Carefully search for eggs and broods while completing your regular inspections, and you can avoid the problems that would come with waiting too late to get a new queen.

Honey and Food

Another common mistake that new beekeepers make that can have dramatic effects on their hive is harvesting too much honey or taking it too early. Bees need honey to help them get through winter (and other periods of low natural pollen), as it is their main source of food—they then turn that food into energy to keep themselves warm and active. So, when you are harvesting your honey (Chapter 6), make sure you are not taking too much.

The amount of honey that they need for the winter depends on numerous factors: the climate where you live, ventilation, size and shape of the hive, number of bees, how much intervention you plan for, and so much more. Because of all these factors, it can be impossible to plan the exact amount needed, so it is better to leave more honey than you think is needed rather than less.

When preparing the hive for winter, make sure that you check all frames and boxes for honey. It can be easy to assume that the lower boxes are full of honey because of their weight, but it is best to check for sure before you take away the honey super.

On average, there should be between 80 to 90 pounds (36 to 41 kilograms) of honey per hive for the winter. If you live in a warmer climate, you can do with less. A colder environment needs that amount or a little more depending on just how cold it gets. To calculate the amount of honey in a hive, figure out how much a full frame of honey is supposed to weigh, which should also have been included information when you bought the hive. Then, multiply that by how many frames are in your hive. Sorry about the math—it is a necessary evil.

For a quick tip, generally, a large frame holds eight pounds (four kilograms), and a medium-sized frame holds six pounds (three kilograms). But it is always best to double-check the specifications of your hive.

Even after knowing how much honey should be in the hive, it is important to check in periodically to make sure that the bees still have enough left. When checking on the hive in winter, choose a warmer day, and keep the inspection as brief as possible so that not too much heat is lost in the process. If you have found that there is not enough honey left for them to eat, you need to be giving them either sugar water, syrup, or more honey to eat instead. If you give them additional honey, make sure that it has come from your hives so that you can guarantee that it is disease-free.

If you need to feed your bees, make sure that you are putting the food, either honey or sugar water, inside the hives. This way, it reduces the chances of the food being robbed by other insects or pests.

Dry white sugar can also be used as a food supplement for stronger (i.e., more established) hives. With this method, make sure that the bees have access to sufficient water, as they will need that to liquefy the crystals for their use. So, it is possible to use it dry, but many beekeepers prefer either wetting the sugar a little or just going with a sugar water (1:1 ratio) or syrup (2:1 ratio) system. Since it is thicker and has more sugar, Syrup should only be used when the stored honey is low—such as when first introducing the bees or preventing them from starvation in the winter.

Whatever method you choose, it is vital to make sure that your bees have enough food to survive through lean times. If you are uncertain about how much to feed them or how often, it is better to overfeed your bees. This prevents starvation and the potential death of your colony.

Proper Suit Wearing

To quote a popular character from a show supposedly telling a story about parents meeting—suit up! Another common mistake first-time beekeepers make is to either not wear a bee suit or to wear it improperly. Bee stings hurt, and in the case of allergy, can be very dangerous. You need to wear the suit properly to prevent any harm coming to you—no matter how friendly bees are, you are messing with their home, and that will get them riled up.

Make sure that you wear a hat and veil. You will need both because stings in the neck or the face are incredibly painful, and the stingers are difficult to remove. This part can either be attached or separate from the main body of the suit, but either way, make sure that it is sealed correctly and has absolutely no open spaces that a bee can fly through. If the hat and veil are separate, it is best to get the kind that zips together.

The main body of your suit needs to be white for two reasons. The first is that bees do not have white-colored enemies, so they are calmer with that color. The second reason is that white is much cooler in summer than other colors, and since the suit is usually made out of thick and durable material, you want any help you can get with keeping cool.

Back in Chapter 1, when we outlined bee suits, we stated that the option is to get either a full suit or just a jacket. The advantage of a suit is that it will have gatherings at the arms and legs that keep you protected from bees getting at your skin, but if you get separate pieces, just make sure that any loose ends are tucked into each other to make it extra secure. The jacket sleeves should be put into the gloves, and your pants should be covered by the tops of your boots. Tall boots, like rain boots, are best since as you move frames around, bees can fall to the ground and then crawl up your legs—with the boots on, they cannot get to your skin.

Smoker

A smoker is an absolutely valuable tool, but it does need some knowledge on how to use it properly. As we have stated before, smoke makes your bees more docile because it makes them believe that a fire is nearby, so they gorge on honey, which makes them slow and less likely to attack.

But how does the smoker itself work? The main body of the smoker is taken up by a fire chamber or firebox, where you burn fuel that produces the smoke that escapes through the nozzle. A bellows is attached to the fire chamber and allows you to pump in fresh air to get the fire burning stronger.

It is best to use three parts of fuel to get the fire burning: some tinder that has a short burning time, kindling that burns slightly longer than the tinder, and the main fuel, which will burn the longest. There are numerous options for these, ranging from natural and everyday products (newspaper, pine needles, and wood chips) to specially bought products.

Whatever fuel you decide on, make sure that you are lighting it the proper way. You want your fire to burn for more than ten minutes without needing to use the bellows when you are using it in your hives, so it is necessary to get a strong burn going before opening the hive. The steps you need to take are to:

1. Make sure you have all three parts of the fuel at hand.

2. Light the tinder and then put it into the fire chamber, placing it into the bottom with your hive tool. Make sure you leave lots of open space around the tinder—give the bellows a couple of pumps to get some extra air on the fire.

3. Add the kindling to the fire, carefully pumping the bellows. Once the first amount of kindling has lit, carefully add some more, making sure that you are giving the fire plenty of room to breathe.

4. Keep adding kindling until you no longer need to pump the bellows— at this point, push the fuel down more compactly, filling up half of the fire chamber, then add your main fuel.

5. Continue using the bellows until a steady fire is burning and smoke is constantly coming out. Once the fire is burning well, leave it for a minute to make sure that it will stay burning, and then you are good to use the smoker in the hives. Make sure that the smoke is cool to the touch.

Once you are ready for the inspection, make sure that you first smoke the entrance of the hive and then leave it for a few moments before lifting the lid and smoking the inside. As you move through the different boxes, you can give a quick puff of smoke, but make sure that you do not use too much, as that can leave soot buildup on the comb. If sparks start coming out of the top of the smoker, it means that the fuel is running low, and you need to add in some more. Once done, let the fire burn through all the fuel, let the embers cool, and then dispose of them.

Smoker tip! If you get stung, direct some smoke onto the area, as that helps mask the pheromones the angry bee left behind, making it less likely that others will attack.

Outside Threats

Now that you know some beekeeper mistakes to avoid, it is time to look at common external threats to your hive. These problems are harder to plan for, but knowing what to do in case they strike will save you time and stress if they do happen.

Excess Moisture

If there is too much moisture in your hive, condensation can form, which is not good for your bees. They do need some water for proper maintenance, but too much forms cold drops that cling to all the surfaces in the hive. This excess water then cools the hive down more than what your bees want, and the bees themselves get wet, which makes it harder for them to survive.

The seasons where you need to watch out for condensation are winter and spring. Dealing with excess moisture in winter is a little easier since you can just open the top lid or your ventilation holes for a short period to help get some more airflow through the hive.

Spring is a little harder since the water buildup is likely a result of the wet weather and water clinging to foraged pollen. If you are seeing lots of water buildup during the rainy months, consider installing moisture control items, such as a moisture board or an empty hive box filled with absorbent material.

Pest Control

Probably one of your main concerns is how to deal with all the different kinds of pests that can plague your hive. One common way to help deal with all pests is to put your hive on a stand so that it is off the ground. That helps to make it harder for them to crawl into the hive. Another tip is to properly discard the comb as you remove it from the hive and not let it fall to the ground. Try to keep as much honey off the ground as well, since that sugary sweetness will attract pests, who will then try to get into the hive for more.

Some chemical methods can be used to deal with pests, but make sure that you do your research first. Many insect killers will work against the invaders, but will also kill your bees, so use sparingly and only the kinds that are least harmful to your bees (and yourself). Always wear proper protection when spraying chemicals.

Ants

Depending on the area you live in, ants can either be a major or minor concern. Luckily, if your colony is well established and strong, they will have an easier time driving the ants away. It is with new hives or ones that have gone through some hardship that you need to be most vigilant. Not only will they steal honey, but also larvae, which will further weaken the hive.

There are a few steps to take to prevent ants from becoming an issue. First, know what ants are in your area and during what season they are most active. This will help you know when you need to be observing more closely. Second, keep the areas around your hives free from tall weeds, as that gives fewer places for the ants to hide, so you can see them easily as they try to get into the hive.

Observing how they get into the hive is important because ants, like bees, are pheromone-driven. This means that they leave a lovely trail to follow, so finding that trail and disrupting it can stop their procession into the hive.

The unfortunate thing is that similarities between bees and ants do not end there—if you try chemical methods of killing the ants, it is just as likely to kill your bees. So, if the ants are already in your hive, the best option is to physically scrape them out. Of course, this is hard to do since they are so small.

It is better to prevent them from getting inside at all. A common method that beekeepers use is to create moats around the legs of hive stands. Ants cannot swim, so putting some water (mixed with a little oil) around the stand means that they cannot climb them. This can be as simple as putting cans of water (made slick by some means) under the hive stand legs, covered by disposable cups so that the bees do not fly into the moats.

Other options would be to slick up the hive legs with motor oil or grease so that the ants cannot climb them, though this can get messy and needs to be reapplied after a few months. Another option to put directly onto the legs is Tanglefoot, a natural glue product often used on fruit trees that traps the ants in place. Like the motor oil, this can be messy to work with and needs to be reapplied. A more natural approach is to create barriers of ground cinnamon around the hive legs, which deters the ants but needs to be reapplied more frequently since it is easily blown away.

Beetles

Hive beetles (small and large beetles) are pests that can do a lot of damage to your hive and bees. Detecting and getting rid of them early is crucial.

Small hive beetles are dark brown or black and are only five millimeters long! Despite their small size, they can cause a lot of destruction—they burrow through the comb, defecating as they go, which ferments and discolors the honey. They also have a taste for bee larvae.

Once in a hive, they are everywhere! The bees will try to fight back and drive the small beetles into crevices that they then seal off with wax. Unfortunately, the beetles then lay their eggs in these sealed areas, which then hatch and start eating through the comb.

Large hive beetles are also black but much larger, around 20 to 23 millimeters. Unlike small beetles, these do not lay their eggs in the hive but in the ground under and around it. However, they cause damage by getting it as adults and eating through your brood. To keep large beetles out of your hive, make sure that your entrance is small enough that they cannot get through.

Treatment for beetles includes the use of different kinds of bee-safe chemicals to be put on the ground or around the hive legs. Other options are to shine a light near the larvae-infested area, which gathers them together so you can collect them all. You can also take infested frames out of the hive and hang them near chickens if you have them. The beetle larvae will drop out of the frames and get gobbled up by the chickens. Another option is to freeze the frames for four days, which will kill the larvae.

Mites

The most damaging pests a beekeeper has to deal with are these mites, as they threaten the survival of a hive once they become established. They attach themselves to adult bees and suck their blood and lay their eggs in brood cells, where their larvae feed off bee babies, infecting them with viruses and weakening and even killing them.

Mites are difficult to detect and require regular testing to find them—waiting too long lets the mites get stronger as they slowly kill your hive. There are several methods of detecting and dealing with mites, but all take time and effort and have pros and cons. When picking one, make sure that it is a method that you can use as quickly and least invasively as possible.

Sugar Dusting

Have some powdered sugar in a container, and during an inspection, take a group of adult bees from at least three frames. Quickly place those bees into the container, sealing it with air holes, so they cannot escape. Then, gently shake or roll a couple of times—this coats the bees in the sugar, which does not hurt them.

Have a mesh screen or strainer on hand. After a few minutes and several coatings, since the more sugar on the bees, the more effective it is, sift the sugar through the mesh into another container filled halfway with water. Then leave the bees near the hive entrance so they can fly home.

In the water container, the sugar will dissolve, but it may need a stir. The mites will then be revealed. You may need to look very closely, as the mites are very small.

Drone Uncapping & Mite Trapping

Mites prefer to suck the blood of drones—no one knows why exactly, but it makes knowing where they might be a little easier. By examining the drone brood or having a specialty drone-trapping frame, you can find and get rid of some of the mites.

During an inspection, remove the frames that house the drone brood. This is when the special drone frame comes in handy. You need to make sure to wait for the brood to be capped for this to work. With the capped brood frame out of the hive, scrape away sections of the cap, examining the exposed pupae for the reddish-brown mites.

Once you have determined that they are present, either freeze the frame or scrape it clean. Both of these do kill the brood as well as the mites, but it is a better option than raising a batch of mites along with your drones. Make sure to clean it thoroughly before placing it back into the hive.

Having dedicated mite traps comes in handy here—with one or two frames, the majority of the mite population will be in these broods. Monthly cleaning of these frames then removes most of the mites before they start affecting the rest of the hive.

Medical Intervention

If all else fails, there are medical or chemical methods (miticides) that you can use against the mites. This should be your last choice since there has been growing evidence that using medicines as a preventative measure makes the mites more resistant (Blakiston, n.d.). It is also important to note that if you use medications when there is honey present, that honey cannot be consumed by humans, though it is safe to feed that honey back to your bees.

Apistan® strips are laced with the miticide fluvalinate. Place multiple strips throughout the hive, and the bees will brush against them, transferring the chemical throughout the hive. It will not harm the bees but will kill the mites.

Formic acid gel packs can also be used, though they are caustic and can be hard to handle. Instead, try Apiguard—a natural product that contains *thymol* (a substance from thyme). Apiguard is also in gel packets that you place on top of the hive frames, though these are time-released to ensure that the correct amount of miticide ends up in the hive.

Large Pests

Along with the smaller pests, you also need to think about the possibility of larger pests and predators giving you trouble. The threat of most of these creatures depends largely on where you live, but even in a city center, they have a habit of creating problems.

Of these largest pests, bears are the most worrisome. These are not Winnie the Pooh looking for honey pots—they are large wild animals that will tear apart your hive to get at the honey and larvae inside. If you are visited by bears, you will most likely need to fully replace your hives and bees and also contact local conservation officers. Once they know where a hive is, the bear will likely come back again for another snack. Unfortunately, the only guaranteed way to keep bears away from your bees is to install an electric fence as protection. This is not the cheapest or easiest option, but much better than having bears visit and wreck things.

In an urban setting, it is more likely that you need to worry about skunks and raccoons. Skunks love to snack on insects, so when they target a hive, they will be going after the bees and not the honey. Active at night, they will scratch at the hive until the bees come out so they can eat them. Having your hive on a stand prevents the smelly buggers from eating your bees since they have to stand up to get at the hive, which then exposes their soft underbellies. The guard bees then target that area, making the skunks think twice about whether the snack is worth the pain. Other options for keeping them away are:

- Poultry fencing (since skunks do not climb)
- Live traps
- Hammering some nails into a board and laying it on the ground as a barrier

Just make sure that you do not step on it yourself!

Raccoons will climb over any fencing in place to get on top of your hive. Once there, they can open the lid and scoop out the honey and bees, so the best bet to keep these bandits away is placing heavy rocks on top of the hive. Simple and inexpensive!

Another concern is mice—these horrid little things will not hurt your bees, but if they get into the hive, they will damage the comb. In the winter, they will make nests inside the hive, and in doing so, they will chew through the comb and possibly the frames as well. To avoid mice, once it starts cooling down, install a metal grate entrance reducer or mouse guard that has spaces large enough for your bees to get through but too small for mice.

The last 'pest' that you need to worry about is—children. Kids are very curious, and if you do not take the proper precautions to keep them away from your hives, it is likely to result in stings or even hive damage. It is best to keep your bees and children safe by child-proofing the apiary area as much as possible. To do this:

- Teach children how to act around bees—i.e., try not to get scared or swat them.
    - Also, teach them to stay calm and get the help of an adult in removing the stinger if they get stung.
    - Have rules for when they can and can't go to the hive—if their activity near the hives is monitored, there is less chance of any accidental destruction taking place.
- Warn neighbor families that bees will be around—you do not want to take the chance that a local child who is allergic to bees will get stung.
- Keep children away from the hive in late summer when the bees are most active and protective of their honey.
- If they are helping you with the hive, make sure that they are wearing the proper protection just the same as you are.
    - Only give them age-appropriate tasks.
- Have a good amount of distance between your hives and the areas where children play.

All of these will help to protect the children and the bees as well. They can co-exist—it just needs to be done carefully.

* * *

While not an extensive list of all the potential roadblocks and hardships you may face as a beekeeper, at least now you have an idea of some of the most common ones. Being forewarned is forearmed, after all.

But to stay truly ahead of any pitfall, you need to continue growing your knowledge. You need to always keep learning and expanding your knowledge base—if you stagnate, so will your hive, and eventually, it will all taper off into nothingness.

You can Google this term to learn more:

- Getting Rid of Hive Beetles

Chapter 6:
A Growing Operation

All of the information presented in this book has come down to this point. Following what has been written, you should be progressing from a beginner to an expert beekeeper. This chapter is all about expanding your operation and possibly turning it into a profit as well!

It does not matter when, or if, you move on to this stage—you can do this after the first year, after your first hive is fully established, or whenever. The only important time constraint is making sure that you are comfortable dealing with the changes.

From here, we will cover taking it all to the next level—how to be prepared for adding additional hives and how to deal with the expansion that needs to happen within the hives. As a bonus, the final part of this chapter outlines how to begin making beekeeping a profitable endeavor!

Hive Growth

As your colony gets more established, its numbers grow. This means that the space they need also grows, and as a dedicated beekeeper, you need to provide that space unless you want your bees to swarm away.

Starting from the very beginning of installing your bees, you probably have only a few boxes in your hive. This is good since the smaller colony will be able to stay warm in a smaller space better than a large one. This is good to start with, but as they begin to be more productive, you need to add specific spaces for the queen and brood and honey production. This results in having separate boxes, such as the honey super box, or maybe even multiple honey super boxes! After all, you do not need to limit yourself to just one of any kind.

The number of boxes you need in your hive depends on the size of your colony. As the number of workers increases, that means that the working space increases as well. Keep a close eye on your frames and see how many are currently being used by the bees.

No matter the number of frames you have within the hive, when there are only three or four empty frames left, it is time to consider adding another box with additional frames. This will give the bees room to keep building comb on the older frame as well as expand upwards.

Keep adding extra boxes as needed, stopping when it reaches the point where inspections and management are no longer easy or possible. At that point, you are going to have to introduce the bees into a new hive altogether or risk them either dying or swarming to locations unknown.

Honey Extraction

No matter the end goal you want with your honey, whether that's a delicious personal snack or a jar to sell, you still have to harvest it from the hives. Before going into the steps needed, make sure that you know how much honey you need to leave for your bees and that you have a honey extractor that you can use. You can work without the extractor, but it is much messier and harder to do—if you do not have a personal one, see if anyone in your club has one you can borrow.

Also, to prepare for honey harvesting, you can put a bee escape in the access hole between the brood and honey boxes. These pieces make it so the bees can only travel in one direction—placing the escape 24 hours before harvest will make it so that there will be fewer bees in the honey super that you will need to deal with. If you do not have that much time, you can use a product like Bee-Quick, which releases a smell that bees do not like, driving them away.

Once everything is planned and prepped, you start the process the same way you would an inspection—with your suit on and the hive smoked. Once that is done, and you have gotten into the honey super, remove the frames that you want to harvest, at least three-quarters capped. These frames then get fully removed from the hive and taken away. Store them in at least a room temperature area to begin softening them up.

Choose your harvesting location carefully—no matter what, it will get at least a little messy, so it is best to have that all sorted and set up before working with the honey. Honey extraction (when using an extractor) then happens in these steps:

1. Remove wax caps off the comb. This is easily done with a heated electric knife. Starting from the top, carefully cut away the wax, leaving as much honey and comb behind as possible.

   a. These wax caps are your stored beeswax, which can be used and sold as well.

2. Place the cleaned frames into the extractor, trying to balance out the weight of frames on either side. Start the extractor spinning with a bucket to collect the honey underneath the spout.

   a. Most extractors only remove honey from one side at a time, so you will need to flip the frames to make sure both sides are emptied.

   b. How fast the honey flows depends on the machine and the temperature of the honey—the warmer it is, the faster it moves.

3. Once all the honey is off the frames, return them to the hive. The bees will then clean them the rest of the way.

4. For the honey, leave it for a while in the buckets or jars so that all air rises to the top and escapes. After that, it is good to be bottled and stored.

And that is it! It is a pretty simple process and only requires a few different steps from a normal inspection. If you can't get access to a honey extractor, you can also hang the frames in a warm space (not direct sun) and let the honey drip into some buckets, but that will take longer.

There are two other methods of honey harvest—comb honey and the crush-and-strain method. Comb honey is perhaps the simplest since instead of cutting the caps off, you just cut the comb up altogether and package it with the honey. This may not sound good, but apparently, it is very tasty and the desired bonus by some people. The crush-and-strain method is very similar to comb honey, though after cutting the comb into pieces, it is squeezed or strained to remove as much of the honey from the wax as possible. The leftover wax then gets discarded.

BONUS—Turning Beekeeping Into a Business

Whether you have arrived at this stage because it was your intended purpose or because you have excess honey and wax, you can make some extra cash being a beekeeper. This final part of the book outlines what you need to consider when wanting to make a profit. It is time to take your hobby to the next level!

The first thing you need to consider when turning your hobby into a business is whether or not doing so is legal. To find this out, return to your research about your local zoning laws and homeowners association rules. You may already have this information from your research into the laws about keeping bees in the first place, so it could be as simple as a refresher to find this out. If you do not already have the information, use the contact you made before to help find out these specific guidelines. When doing so, make sure also to check out local laws about selling honey and wax to make sure that you have them up to code.

After that, properly plan out your business model before you start selling—this includes figuring out operational costs, deciding where and what you are going to sell, and to whom you are going to sell. Operational costs should not greatly exceed what you already have invested, but make sure that you include any business or operating licenses you will need. Look into whether you need any extra insurance since that could be a bigger financial strain than you anticipate.

During the planning stage, it is important to look back over the records you have kept. The most important of these records are the expense reports since those will be the basis for calculating what price to charge for your services. If you are planning on turning your beekeeping into a business, write down all your expenses right from the start. Hire a professional accountant unless you happen to be one yourself, and ask them to help with the finances, as they will know what deductions you can claim come tax season.

An accountant will also help you maneuver what taxes and fees you will need to pay as a business. They can help you get the proper financial paperwork in place at all stages of your honey business, and that will help you avoid tax-related pitfalls. After all, no one wants unexpectedly to owe more taxes than they thought.

To be best prepared, talk to the members of your club and professional beekeeping associations. They are likely the most up-to-date source of information you have that will help you keep all your bases covered. Many of them are probably also selling their products, so they will know the laws and administrative duties you will need to do and the best places to sell and advertise your products.

They will probably tell you not to jump into business right away. It is best to give yourself time to get used to the duties of a beekeeper before adding the extra stress of trying to turn a profit.

Once you feel confident in your abilities as an apiarist and have made your business plan, make sure that you have planned everything else out as well. Depending on the amount of honey you want to sell, you likely want to buy a honey extractor if you do not already have one. This can be a several hundred dollar cost, or a several thousand dollar one, depending on where you buy it. But the value is well worth it since you will be able to get more honey from the combs much faster than any other method.

Thinking about the honey, you also need to decide how it is going to be packaged. Regular canning jars and lids can work, but if you want to avoid doing the lettering and the look of a typical jar, find a local supplier who has more options. Avoiding the raised lettering is also really good for your labels since they stick better on a smooth surface. Make sure that you check local laws for these labels; most states and provinces have specific laws about what can and can't be on a honey label. These are food items, so health and safety regulations apply and can't be something you skip over.

The last things you need to consider are the more fun specifics of your business. What are you going to sell? Honey is the first obvious choice, but you can also sell beeswax straight or mixed in other products, as well as your bees' service as pollinators. This could be done by having someone, say a farmer, rent the number of your hives they want. They would then be paying you rental fees and the cost of labor and care that you would need to provide in the form of regular inspections. If you live further away, you may even consider charging for travel time.

If you have enough bees and to make your business bigger, you can also consider adding the bees themselves to your for-sale list. You can make your own bee nuc colonies by separating some frames from the rest of the hive. Let them make a new queen and leave them to grow strong over the winter. In the spring, the small colony is ready to be sold to someone new.

There are so many different options for what you can sell. To give yourself the strongest business, diversify your products. Reliance on just one or two items is likely to leave you with less profit than you would like.

After deciding what you will be selling, figure out who you will be selling to and how you will accomplish that. Are you going to sell at local farmers' markets? Rely on word of mouth? Become a vendor at a local artisan store? Have an online store? There are endless possibilities, so make sure to weigh the pros and cons of them all. The great news is that the demand for fresh, locally made products has never been higher, so turning your hobby of beekeeping into some extra cash should be a bee-reeze!

Conclusion

You did it! You finished the book and are well on your way to becoming a successful beekeeper in the next year. Congratulations! Getting the proper knowledge and information is crucial, and it should now be ingrained into your mind.

You may have picked up this book for so many different reasons—you wanted to get a fun but not physically demanding outdoor activity, you are trying to return to the land and away from corporate life, or are wanting to start a new business. No matter what your reasoning, we hope that when you put this book down, you will feel much more confident about achieving your goal.

To be successful in the end, make sure that reading this and other books is not your final step on the knowledge journey. Creating a firm foundation of knowledge and support is crucial to being a beekeeper, and that is why joining a beekeeping club will significantly benefit you. From there, you can draw on the support and knowledge of more experienced apiarists, take courses to help solidify your knowledge, and in time, pass that knowledge on to someone new. Beekeepers of all levels need support and people who share in their passions, and a club is an excellent way to form a community.

As a move to get back to the land, you may be reading this from your home in the city. There is a steady rise in urban beekeepers, so you are not alone if that is something you are planning to do. Make sure that you pick the perfect spot for your hives, be aware of the flight path, have access to food and water, and allow ease of your access to the hives. Optimizing location before buying your bees is the best for ultimate success.

Once your location is chosen, make sure that you know everything you need to set up your hive. This includes choosing the style and material of your hive, giving yourself enough time to get things organized, and how and where to buy your bees. There are numerous options during this stage, so make sure you take your time and have fun with it all.

Getting your bees into your hive is the next important step. This means a proper placing of the queen and knowing how much to feed the bees and when to do so. Once they are housed, make sure that you do regular inspections so that you keep on top of all proper maintenance and care that your bees may need.

With that in mind, there are potential pitfalls that can befall even the most experienced beekeeper. Being aware of these problems and keeping an eye out for them so you can stop them early is much easier than intervening once the issue has taken root. These include making sure that your hive continually has a queen, not harvesting too much honey, using beekeeping equipment properly, and preventing pests from making a mess of your hive. Being aware of these problems can help you stay ahead of the curve and avoid negative consequences.

It is a lot of work and time, but it is worth it in the end when you have that first jar of delicious honey! When you hold up that amber liquid, you should be incredibly proud of yourself. You can then choose to try and sell that honey as well as other products from your bees or keep it all for yourself. Both have merits, and, as we have said, it is a personal choice and entirely up to you. Maybe consider making some honey butter to spread over freshly baked bread? We promise you, the taste is almost addictive, and you will want to do it again and again.

You have the tools—get on out there and do great!

References

Anthony. (n.d.-a). *Essential equipment for beekeeping: 6 things you need to get started.* Beekeeping 101. Retrieved May 31, 2021, from https://www.beekeeping-101.com/essential-equipment-beekeeping-6-things-get-started/

Anthony. (n.d.-b). How to use a bee smoker. Beekeeping Insider. https://beekeepinginsider.com/how-to-use-a-bee-smoker/

Apiguard. (n.d.). Apiguard—Frequently asked questions. Retrieved June 15, 2021, from https://www.vita-europe.com/beehealth/wp-content/uploads/Apiguard.pdf

Arcuri, L. (2020, June 30). Inspecting a honey bee hive. The Spruce. https://www.thespruce.com/inspect-your-honey-bee-hive-3016536

BBC Gardener's World Magazine. (2019, July 8). How to make a bumblebee pot. BBC Gardeners' World Magazine. https://www.gardenersworld.com/how-to/grow-plants/how-to-make-a-bumblebee-pot/

BBC Gardeners' World Magazine. (2019, August 5). How to make a bee-friendly garden. BBC Gardeners' World Magazine. https://www.gardenersworld.com/plants/how-to-make-a-bee-friendly-garden/

Bees & Your HOA: *What Rights do homeowners have to keep bees in their backyards?* (2020, August 1). LeaseHoney. https://leasehoney.com/2020/08/01/bees-your-hoa-what-rights-do-homeowners-have-to-keep-bees-in-their-backyards/

Blackiston, H. (n.d.-a). *11 tips for extending the life of your beehive equipment.* Dummies. https://www.dummies.com/home-garden/hobby-farming/beekeeping/11-tips-for-extending-the-life-of-your-beehive-equipment/

Blackiston, H. (n.d.-b). *Pick the perfect location for your beehive.* Dummies. https://www.dummies.com/home-garden/hobby-farming/beekeeping/pick-the-perfect-location-for-your-beehive/

Blakiston, H. (n.d.-a). *How to control a varroa mite problem in your beehive.* Dummies. https://www.dummies.com/home-garden/hobby-farming/beekeeping/how-to-control-a-varroa-mite-problem-in-your-beehive/

Blakiston, H. (n.d.-b). *How to keep larger animals out of your beehive.* Dummies. https://www.dummies.com/home-garden/hobby-farming/beekeeping/how-to-keep-larger-animals-out-of-your-beehive/

Blakiston, H. (2016). *How to choose lumber for your Beehive.* Dummies. https://www.dummies.com/home-garden/hobby-farming/beekeeping/how-to-choose-lumber-for-your-beehive/

Built, B. (n.d.-a). Buying your first hive. Bee Built. https://beebuilt.com/pages/buying-your-first-hive

Built, B. (n.d.-b). Top bar hives. Bee Built. https://beebuilt.com/pages/top-bar-hives

Built, B. (n.d.-c). Warre hives. Bee Built. https://beebuilt.com/pages/warre-hives

Burlew, A. : R. (2020, September 2). *Sun and shade for bees: What is the right mix?* Backyard Beekeeping. https://backyardbeekeeping.iamcountryside.com/hives-equipment/sun-and-shade for-bees/

Burns, D. (2011, January 17). *How many hives should I start with?* Mother Earth News. https://www.motherearthnews.com/homesteading-and-livestock/how-many-hives-should-i-start-with

Burns, S. (2017, March 19). *How to set up your first beehive.* Runamuk Acres Conservation Farm. https://runamukacres.com/how-to-set-up-your-first-beehive/

Casey, C. (2018, February 12). *Bees need water: Establish water sources in late winter to keep them out of the pool in summer.* ANR Blogs. https://ucanr.edu/blogs/blogcore/postdetail.cfm?postnum=26345

Caughey, M. (2016, January 21). *9 tips when selecting honeybees.* Backyard Bees. https://www.keepingbackyardbees.com/9-tips-when-selecting-honeybees/

Charlotte. (2020, December 31). *How to provide drinking water for bees.* Carolina Honeybees. https://carolinahoneybees.com/beauty-bee-farm/

Charlotte. (2021a, March 17). *Choosing the best types of honey bees.* Carolina Honeybees. https://carolinahoneybees.com/types-of-honey-bees/

Charlotte. (2021b, April 18). *Beekeeping business - starting a bee farm.* Carolina Honeybees. https://carolinahoneybees.com/start-a-beekeeping-business-from-scratch/

Charlotte. (2021c, June 8). *How to clean beeswax the easy way.* Carolina Honeybees. https://carolinahoneybees.com/processing-beeswax-cappings/

Choosing a beehive: Buy or build? (2016, March 19). Paris Farmers Union. http://blog.parisfarmersunion.com/2016/04/choosing-beehive-buy-or-build.html

Cohenour, C. (2008, January 5). Repairing hive bodies. WV Beekeeper - Cass Cohenour. http://wvbeekeeper.blogspot.com/2008/01/repairing-hive-bodies.html

Contributor. (2021, April 11). Bee bucks – The cost of beekeeping. Backyard Beekeeping. https://backyardbeekeeping.iamcountryside.com/hives-equipment/bee-bucks-the-cost-of-beekeeping/

Creating a beekeeping business plan - guide and template. (2010). BuzzAboutBees.net. https://www.buzzaboutbees.net/beekeeping-business-plan.html

David. (2017, November 24). Principles and practice. The Apiarist. https://www.theapiarist.org/principles-and-practice/

Drone uncapping background. (n.d.). Retrieved June 15, 2021, from https://beeaware.org.au/wp-content/uploads/2014/03/Drone-uncapping.pdf

Edmondson, R. (n.d.). *How to harvest honey from a beehive*. Dengarden. https://dengarden.com/gardening/How-to-Extract-Honey-from-a-Beehive

Edmondson, R. (2021, June 3). *How to install a package of bees in a new hive*. Dengarden. https://dengarden.com/gardening/How-to-Install-A-Package-of-Bees-in-a-New-Hive

Feeding honey bees to prevent starvation. (2021, January 21). Agriculture.vic.gov.au. https://agriculture.vic.gov.au/livestock-and-animals/honey-bees/health-and-welfare/feeding-honey-bees-to-prevent-starvation

Forest Farming. (2015, October 23). Hive Placement. Www.youtube.com. https://youtu.be/SEMYPO6ozSk

Foust, S. (2018, August 27). DIY bee fountain. Thebeebox. https://www.thebeebx.com/single-post/2018/08/27/diy-bee-fountain

Fun fact - Why do beekeepers wear white? (2017, September 2). Manuka Vet. https://www.manukavet.com/blog/post/20394/Fun-fact-Why-do-beekeepers-wear-white/

Gardener, A. (2015, May 6). Bee predators in beekeeping. Blain's Farm & Fleet Blog. https://www.farmandfleet.com/blog/bee-predators-beekeeping/

Government of New Brunswick, C. (1996, July 10). *Managing honeybee hives for the pollination of wild blueberries*. Www2.Gnb.ca. https://www2.gnb.ca/content/gnb/en/departments/10/agriculture/content/bees/managing.html#:~:text=The%20number%20of%20hives%20necessary

Hadley, D. (2019, October 10). Why do bees swarm? ThoughtCo. https://www.thoughtco.com/why-do-bees-swarm-1968430#:~:text=Bees%20Swarm%20When%20the%20Colony%20Gets%20too%20Large&text=Just%20as%20individual%20bees%20reproduce

Helpful beekeeping website links. (n.d.). Piedmont Beekeepers Association. Retrieved May 31, 2021, from https://www.piedmontbeekeepers.com/helpful-links

Holly. (2019, August 6). *Is beekeeping legal in my city?* Complete Beehives. http://completebeehives.com/is-beekeeping-legal-in-my-city/

Holly. (2020a, March 17). *How far apart should beehives be placed?* Complete Beehives. http://completebeehives.com/how-far-apart-should-beehives-be-placed/

Holly. (2020b, August 15). *What is the best beehive stand height?* Complete Beehives. http://completebeehives.com/what-is-the-best-beehive-stand-height/

Home and Garden, P. T. (2021). *5 ways bees are important to the environment.* Premier Tech Home and Garden. http://www.pthomeandgarden.com/5-ways-bees-are-important-to-the-environment/#:~:text=As%20pollinators%2C%20bees%20play%20a

How much time does beekeeping require. (2019, July 3). The Bee Store. https://thebeestore.com.au/blogs/bee-blog/how-much-time-does-beekeeping-require

How to create a pollinator-friendly garden. (2017). David Suzuki Foundation. https://davidsuzuki.org/queen-of-green/create-pollinator-friendly-garden-birds-bees-butterflies/

How to get rid of hive beetles – The beginner's guide. (2019, May 22). BeeKeepClub. https://beekeepclub.com/how-to-get-rid-of-hive-beetles-the-beginners-guide/

Kearney, H. (2016, May 31). *How to protect your bees from ants.* Beekeeping like a Girl. https://beekeepinglikeagirl.com/how-to-protect-your-bees-from-ants/

Kearney, H. (2020, August 17). *How to tell if your hive is queenless.* Flow Hive US. https://www.honeyflow.com/blogs/beekeeping-basics/queenless-hive

Lesa. (2014, April 30). *8 honey bee hive inspection tips.* Better Hens & Gardens. https://www.betterhensandgardens.com/honey-bee-hive-inspection-tips/

McElroy, S. C. (2016, December 14). *Ventilation: It's complicated keeping backyard bees.* Keeping Backyard Bees. https://www.keepingbackyardbees.com/ventilation-its-complicated/

Mercedes, K. (2018, December 7). *5 ways joining a bee club makes you a better beekeeper.* Hobby Farms. https://www.hobbyfarms.com/5-ways-a-bee-club-will-make-you-a-better-beekeeper/

Mortimer, F. (n.d.). *Suburban bees: How to keep bees in residential areas.* Pollinator.cals.cornell.edu. https://pollinator.cals.cornell.edu/master-beekeeper-program/meet-our-master-beekeepers/suburban-bees-how-keep-bees-residential-areas/

Nesset, J. (2016, January 18). *Can you keep bees with kids?* Murdoch's Blog: The Dirt. https://blog.murdochs.com/can-you-keep-bees-with-kids/

Nickson, J. (2019a, July 3). *How to winterize a beehive: A beekeeper's guide to preparing bees for the winter.* Honest Beekeeper. https://honestbeekeeper.com/how-to-winterize-a-beehive/

Nickson, J. (2019b, August 11). *How much time does beekeeping take? It's more than you think.* Honest Beekeeper. https://honestbeekeeper.com/how-much-time-does-beekeeping-take-its-more-than-you-think/

PerfectBee. (n.d.). *Finding beekeeping clubs and mentors.* Www.perfectbee.com. https://www.perfectbee.com/learn-about-bees/about-beekeeping/beekeeping-clubs-and-mentors

Plant Health Australia. (n.d.). Sugar shaking BACKGROUND. Retrieved June 15, 2021, from https://beeaware.org.au/wp-content/uploads/2014/03/Sugar-shaking.pdf

Ploetz, K. (2013, May 8). *Dear modern farmer: How do I legally start an urban bee hive?* Modern Farmer. https://modernfarmer.com/2013/05/dear-modern-farmer-how-do-i-legally-start-an-urban-bee-hive/

Poindexter, J. (2016a, June 8). *38 Free DIY bee hive plans that will inspire you to become a beekeeper.* MorningChores. https://morningchores.com/beehive-plans/

Poindexter, J. (2016b, November 20). *15 essential beekeeping equipment every beekeeper can't live without.* MorningChores. https://morningchores.com/beekeeping-equipment/

Queenlessness in Your Hive - PerfectBee. (n.d.). Https://Www.perfectbee.com. https://www.perfectbee.com/a-healthy-beehive/inspecting-your-hive/queenlessness-in-your-hive

Rose, S. (2016, November 1). Build a bug hotel. Garden Therapy. https://gardentherapy.ca/build-a-bug-hotel/

Rusty. (2010a, March 2). Pollen collection by honey bees. Honey Bee Suite. https://www.honeybeesuite.com/pollen-collection/

Rusty. (2010b, May 19). *Reduce varroa mites by culling honey bee drones.* Honey Bee Suite. https://www.honeybeesuite.com/reduce-varroa-mites-by-culling-honey-bee-drones/

Rusty. (2010c, September 20). *Entrance reducers can annoy your honey bees.* Honey Bee Suite. https://www.honeybeesuite.com/entrance-reducers-can-annoy-your-honey-bees/

Rusty. (2011a, February 18). *How long should I feed a new package of bees?* Honey Bee Suite. https://www.honeybeesuite.com/how-long-should-i-feed-a-new-package-of-bees/

Rusty. (2011b, May 19). *Sun or shade: which is best for the bees?* Honey Bee Suite. https://www.honeybeesuite.com/sun-or-shade-which-is-best-for-the-bees/

Rusty. (2014, August 19). *How much honey do bees need for winter?* Honey Bee Suite. https://www.honeybeesuite.com/how-much-honey-should-i-leave-in-my-hive/

Rusty. (2017, June 5). *Sun is for foraging, but bees love shade.* Honey Bee Suite. https://www.honeybeesuite.com/sun-foraging-bees-love-shade/

Schneider, A. (2020, December 9). *The ins and outs of buying bees.* Backyard Beekeeping. https://backyardbeekeeping.iamcountryside.com/beekeeping-101/buying-bees-miller-bee-supply/

Screen bottom boards vs. solid bottom boards: Which is better? (n.d.). Www.perfectbee.com. https://www.perfectbee.com/blog/screen-bottom-boards-vs-solid-bottom-boards-better

7 fast solutions to get rid of ants in a beehive (For GOOD!). (2019, May 22). Backyard Beekeeping 101. https://backyardbeekeeping101.com/ants-in-beehive/

Spinks, S. (2018, November 22). Cleaning beeswax. Norfolkhoneyco. https://www.norfolk-honey.co.uk/post/cleaning-beeswax-part-1

"Start beekeeping" courses. (2020, January 17). The Apiarist. https://www.theapiarist.org/start-beekeeping-courses/

10 free DIY beehive stand plans & ideas you'll fall in love with. (2020, May 19). Backyard Beekeeping 101. https://backyardbeekeeping101.com/bee-hive-stand-plans/

The beekeeper suit: A comprehensive guide. (n.d.). BeeKeepClub. https://beekeepclub.com/beekeeping-equipment/the-beekeeper-suit-a-comprehensive-guide/

The beekeeper's calendar(n.d.). Dadant & Sons 1863. https://www.dadant.com/learn/the-beekeepers-calendar/

The Beekeepers Club Inc - events. (n.d.). Www.beekeepers.org.au. Retrieved May 31, 2021, from https://www.beekeepers.org.au/events

The Editors. (2021a, March 27). *Beekeeping 101: Should you raise honey bees?* Old Farmer's Almanac. https://www.almanac.com/beekeeping-101-why-raise-honeybees

The Editors. (2021b, April 29). *Beekeeping 101: Choosing a type of beehive.* Old Farmer's Almanac. https://www.almanac.com/beekeeping-101-types-of-beehives

The growth and feasibility of urban beekeeping. (n.d.). Www.perfectbee.com. https://www.perfectbee.com/learn-about-bees/about-beekeeping/growth-of-urban-beekeeping

Tips for giving your beehives enough ventilation this summer. (2020, May 15). Beekeeping Resources. https://www.mannlakeltd.com/mann-lake-blog/tips-for-giving-your-beehives-enough-ventilation-this-summer/

Top 10 best beekeeping starter kits (2020). (2016, August 22). BeeKeepClub. https://beekeepclub.com/best-beekeeping-starter-kits/

Top 10 best hive stands for beekeeping (2021) – Why they are necessary. (2018, February 22). BeeKeepClub. https://beekeepclub.com/best-hive-stands/

Trujillo, T. (2019, June 17). *7 essential beekeeping equipment that every beginner needs.* Palm Pike. https://palmpike.com/7-essential-beekeeping-equipment-that-every-beginner-needs/

Varroa mites. (2016). Beeaware.org.au. https://beeaware.org.au/archive-pest/varroa-mites/#ad-image-0

Watson, B. (2019, June 13). *The real cost of beekeeping for the first year (Plus how to save!)*. Backyard Beekeeping 101. https://backyardbeekeeping101.com/beekeeping-cost/

Wildlife Preservation Canada. (2021). Rusty-patched bumble bee. Wildlife Preservation Canada. https://wildlifepreservation.ca/rusty-patched-bumble-bee/#:~:text=One%20of%20the%20most%20common

Williams, S. (n.d.). Managing hive capacity. Www.perfectbee.com. https://www.perfectbee.com/a-healthy-beehive/inspecting-your-hive/managing-hive-capacity

Williams, S. (2021). *The PerfectBee Academy online beekeeping course*. Www.perfectbee.com. https://www.perfectbee.com/academy-beekeeping-course#section-80-203966

Withers, J. (2013, October 21). *How to wrap a bee hive for cold winters*. Honey Bee Suite. https://www.honeybeesuite.com/how-to-wrap-a-hive/

Wyatt, L. J. (2015, June 19). *3 ways to harvest honey*. Hobby Farms. https://www.hobbyfarms.com/3-ways-to-harvest-honey-4/

Woodward, A. (2019, June 21). *Bees and insects dying at record rates are sign of 6th mass extinction*. Business Insider. https://www.businessinsider.com/insects-dying-off-sign-of-6th-mass-extinction-2019-2